Stephen Purvis is a Wimbledon-born architect. In 2000 he moved with his wife and four young children to Havana, where his building projects included factories, luxury hotels and a container port. In his thirteen years in Cuba he became a longstanding director of the international school, enjoyed a spot of boxing and the odd cigar, took up painting and, to the surprise of all, co-produced with Sadler's Wells Theatre the hit dance show *Havana Rakatan*. He returned to Britain in 2013 and now works in Myanmar. In 2017 he won the Crime Writers' Association Award for Non-fiction.

CLOSE BUT NO CIGAR

STEPHEN PURVIS

**A True Story of Prison
Life in Castro's Cuba**

WEIDENFELD & NICOLSON

A W&N Paperback
First published in Great Britain in 2017
by Weidenfeld & Nicolson
This paperback edition published in 2018
by Weidenfeld & Nicolson,
an imprint of Orion Books Ltd

1 3 5 7 9 10 8 6 4 2

A CIP catalogue record for this book
is available from the British Library.

ISBN 978 1 4746 0506 9

Typeset by Input Data Services Ltd, Bridgwater, Somerset

Printed and bound by CPI Group (UK) Ltd, Croydon, CR0 4YY

Weidenfeld & Nicolson

The Orion Publishing Group Ltd
Carmelite House
50 Victoria Embankment
London, EC4Y 0DZ
An Hachette UK Company
www.orionbooks.co.uk

The names of some of the people who feature in this book have been changed to protect their privacy.

'We laugh to win.'

Paul 'Dundee' Clark

It's a shame it ended like this

Yet another bloody endless Sunday afternoon. Christ, and I thought they were boring in Wimbledon during the seventies.

The buffoon Pupi is officer of the day and vindictive retard that he is, he has turned the fans off so that everyone is hot and cranky as well as bored. He keeps grinning at us through the bars and asking if we are feeling good. Most people are asleep but there is a crowd of South Americans draped over chairs watching some godawful Venezuelan music DVD. I am on my top bunk trying to block it all out. I could happily strangle the sod in charge of the entertainment. He is a pockmarked little sneak from Caracas who buys privileges by informing on people. Privileges like manning the central DVD machine that provides the entertainment to the different cellblocks. I am passing the time painting a copy of a photo of Jesus's wife. But she won't like it, I've made her look frumpy. Oh well, I wonder what she will look like when he finally gets out. Perhaps she will age and sag to fit the picture.

Out of the corner of my eye I see Alexei waddling down the cellblock, his face ash grey and waxy. Alexei always walks like he has Soviet-issue haemorrhoids, but the truth is that he was caught smoking crack with one of Fidel Castro's sons. They gave Alexei thirty years and then when nobody was looking the guards at Combinado Matanzas first broke his knees and then his ankles. You won't read about that in the papers. He's definitely out to lunch but probably no more than is to be expected, as he has already done eight years. He is given to violent and strange behaviour, usually triggered by mixing medication that he gets from a nurse who has a business on the side selling drugs. Despite that, I play tennis with him fairly often and we laugh at each other's terrible techniques. He isn't laughing today though, and he walks as if in a dream. He stops at Gadhafi's bunk, the top one next to mine. In grim silence he sweeps the mattress with the snoring Bedouin on to the ground, in the process sending some dozing Ecuadoreans flying. Gadhafi is screaming in Arabic and everyone starts shouting. After savagely stamping on Gadhafi's head a couple of times Alexei pulls a long knife out of his pocket and starts to stab him. It's a 10-inch hacksaw blade filed to a point, with a crude wooden handle. In a split second ten people are on top, restraining him. Fumbling with the padlock, the guards come piling through the door, batons drawn, with Pupi, the coward, at the rear. They drag Alexei and Gadhafi away and the door slams shut with a reverberating bang.

The room is buzzing with conversation as everyone tries to piece together what just happened and why the 150kg Russian giant should try to kill his 70kg friend from Western Sahara on a sleepy Sunday afternoon. As with many things in a Cuban prison, the truth is stranger than fiction.

Yesterday was meant to be the visit of the women prisoners. Once a month the women's prison sends a small busload of very ugly ladies to service some of the male prisoners at La Condesa. The deal is simple. The men arrange, via telephone, for the family of the female prisoner to receive some cash back home. The guards demand a cut, paid in cash or kind. The two rooms officially reserved for conjugal visits from wives are then made available and the amorous couple are locked in for a few hours of rutting. It is an occasion of great importance in the social calendar of La Condesa, more important than the monthly visit from the priest. Many of the guys that make use of this service have some chivalrous leanings. They spend hours getting ready and take small gifts of biscuits, cigarettes and soft drinks. Everyone claps, cheers and makes rude suggestions when the stud is led off to do the business. It's simply the international version of the vegetable ladies of Güines. Güines is the local village and the entire economy of it is based on exploiting the foreign prisoners of La Condesa. For certain prisoners, once they have become trusties they are allowed access to local ladies who sell vegetables, fruit and sex. Would you be totally surprised to hear that the guards take a percentage of this as well? I thought not. But I have ceased to have any moral position on this. This is my new reality. I just have to keep an amused distance and sleep with one eye open.

Yesterday the visit of the female prisoners had been cancelled due to a cholera outbreak in their prison. This being the cholera which does not officially exist despite news of deaths in Havana filtering in from all sides. Alexei had become obsessed with a particular woman and had been looking forward for the past six months to a few hours of musky heaven. His most treasured possessions are his tennis racket and a soiled pair of panties he has purchased from this woman, into which he buries his face from time to time and shouts muffled Russian obscenities. And so this morning, having tossed off a mind-bending mixture of pills washed down with half a bottle of aftershave, he took one long, deep, farewell sniff, put them under his pillow and then waddled off to kill his friend Gadhafi.

The bizarre consensual morality of the prison has judged that although Alexei is a dangerous lunatic he is basically a good guy who should not be punished and that these things happen. There was a small group of people who thought it unfair of him to try and kill his friend, who was two feet shorter and half his weight, but this was merely on the technical grounds of being in different fighting classes. What exactly are friends for?

After the excitement of the act itself and the thrill of the post-mortem, the atmosphere in the cell has become depressed. The realisation of the consequences for all of us is now sinking in. The coronel will use this as an excuse to punish us: it is what he always does. In a few hours the investigation will start and each of us will be quizzed about what we saw, who knew Alexei had a knife and so forth. We will all be found guilty of something and the cellblock will lose some hard-won necessity. Everyone goes back to their bunks and lies down with their thoughts.

My own thoughts turned to the wretched chain of events that had brought me here, and a pessimistic analysis of my situation and my poor family, now a million miles away and wondering if it was going to be fifteen years till I got home. I am trapped in this crazy place called La Condesa. It's a stalag for foreign criminals in Cuba, complete with watchtowers and barbed wire. I live in a large cell holding fifty prisoners from all over the place and we are subject to what the Cubans call a severe penal condition. This is as unpleasant as it sounds. Nobody can remember an Englishman ever being here. My companions are for the most part convicted murderers, drug traffickers, people smugglers, paedophiles and rapists and gangsters, oh, and four other people like me, foreign businessmen held without formal charge pending trial. Having heard many of their stories a thousand times and having got to know some of them like friends, or indeed enemies, I believe probably about 20 per cent are totally innocent. Of the rest I am sure that none of them had a fair trial, certainly as we know it in England. My lawyer tells me that nobody is found innocent at trial after they have been sent to La Condesa and that they will make sure I am guilty of something. He also tells me that the provisional charge against me, which seems to be revelations of state secrets, carries a fifteen- to twenty-year sentence.

But despite all that I am relatively happy, because before I arrived here I spent a terrifying eight months in a dungeon in the State Security interrogation centre of Villa Marista. Eight

months in a tiny, filthy cell being let out for only fifteen minutes a week, in a place where most people lose their mind and
their health is broken. And so I have a freshly forged appreciation for the relativity of human despair. A year ago Alexei's
little drama would have appalled me. I would have thought
that his act of random violence against his little friend was
against nature. But now it makes all the sense in the world.
There is no right and wrong, no centre of gravity: we are all
just hanging on by our fingertips in a place beyond natural law
or society. A place where on a Sunday afternoon your friend
can decide to stamp on your head and stab you, and where the
upholders of the law are rotten to their stinking core.

It's a shame it ended like this. This is like the end of a love
affair, one that ended in the worst possible way where, still
reeling from the blunt trauma of being dumped, you come to
the horrible realisation that you were never loved in the first
place.

Chapter minus one

This is about Cuba, but in a way it isn't. What happened to us could happen to anyone who decides to go off-piste anywhere, it's just that you cannot imagine it could ever happen to yourself. Sadly, stories like ours are being played out all over the world and nobody takes any notice. So not only is this book an attempt to shine a tiny light into the broken heart of Cuba and to honour all the many victims who have suffered at the hands of a paranoid system on both sides of that particular rickety political fence, but it is also a cautionary tale about the price we paid for leaving home.

For thousands of years young people have woken up one morning and decided that instead of dreaming of a life beyond the ordinary they could just go and see what happens. Fortunes have been made and lost, languages sucked up or mangled and cultures loved and loathed. Kids have grown up in a wonderland of smells and sights and have had a lifetime of tales to tell. I read somewhere that the average lifespan of an Englishman in eighteenth-century India was a mere eighteen months. Today we can venture forth, freshly punctured against disease, with the naive assumption that all the safety nets of the modern world travel with us. It isn't so: there are the bird watchers charged with spying in Turkey, businessmen accused of mysterious political murder in China, textile traders disappearing in Iran. Some guilty, maybe, and some not, but the concept and rule of law does not travel with us in our carry-on. I had not considered for one second that what happened was a remote possibility until it was too late.

My parents made their own leap into the void. My father came from generations of miners whose meagre livelihood came from the earth, but he left school in Gateshead at fourteen to become an apprentice millwright in the submarine shipyards a few miles away, and then at eighteen, after pushing himself through art evening class, he won a scholarship from the Workers' Education Association to study theatre design at the Old Vic in London. This was a quantum shift of life on a par with emigration. He used to laugh and say that in pre-Beatles London a Geordie had to learn English to be treated as a human being, let alone work in the theatre. My mother came from farming and army stock, with graveyards of sergeant majors and a house full of exotic memorabilia to prove it. Yet from eight years old she knew she wanted to be a classical ballerina. She swopped a culture of cows and soldiers for ballet and I think the bravery of their personal voyages rubbed off, as in time their three wandering offspring chose to create homes in Italy, Turkey and Cuba.

My wife Sarah and I had been together for ages. She was a nurse, a compassionate and gutsy young woman whose love of life and ever-expanding circle of friends was built on the bedrock of a Catholic upbringing and a student life centred on Camden Palace. I was an architect who loved the great outdoors and urban grime in equal measure, read a lot but went out far too much. We had remained together through all sorts of ups and downs for years and in fact due to the boom-and-bust nature of my profession we married at a time when I was totally skint and starting a new business from scratch. So skint in fact that she had to pay for her own engagement ring.

All the kids had been born at Guy's Hospital, walking distance from our house. In those days, the birthing suite was near the top of the wrench-shaped tower block, with huge vertiginous windows open to the sky and London spread below, a magnificently inappropriate space for something so private and primeval as birth. Four times I had spent cliffhanger hours holding hands with Sarah or, shouting encouragement, having the occasional quick sniff of gas myself and crying with happiness and relief. The whole saga had been repeated in quick succession, in 1994, 1996, 1997 and 1999. Two boys followed by two girls. Nothing quite prepares you for your first one and there is something rather sensible in not doing too much research before the event. The first time, Sarah went into labour after spending a relaxing day laying a carpet in the baby's bedroom. Everything that could go wrong went wrong, but twenty-four hours later we were a family, albeit with Sarah unconscious in a recovery room after an emergency C-section. As the sun spread its warm glow over the city below I was left holding a tiny but perfect ginger boy, humming rusty nursery rhymes and staring into the future that lay way beyond the mossy smudge of the South Downs, wondering what on earth Dad was supposed to do when we got the baby home.

Bermondsey had been our home for a few years before married life. The land that time and London Transport forgot. During the nineties, London's rotten ring of dilapidated sink estates and derelict factories had been swept aside by the flood of city cash 'n' trash; namely the frothy mix of transformative developers, Thatcher's right to buy and an enthusiastic house-buying mixed breed of urban adventurers, hipsters and anyone who wanted something a bit bigger and would rough it for a bit. All except, that is, for Bermondsey, which sat stubbornly in its wheelchair watching the world change with deep suspicion while muttering into a pint. The National Front stalls on Southwark Park Road still sold their poison, the windows rattled to Millwall's roar on a Saturday afternoon and jellied eels were actually eaten by men as young as fifty. But for an architect it was heaven.

The Old Saxon settlement of Beormund's Eyot was a damp, miserable island in the wider, swampy estuary of the Thames. The Romans sensibly decided to burn the grotty settlement to the ground. There is no trace of the medieval enthusiasm for monastery building and fortified houses except in the gnarly street names, and lots of skeletons and plague pits. To the immediate south at the edge of the first hard ground, Chaucer's Old Kent Road led to Canterbury and civilisation. To the north, as the port of London became a powerhouse of the Empire, the banks of the river congealed into a warren of quays, chandlers and warehouses. But every powerhouse needs provisioning and servicing and that is what Bermondsey became. It was the whorehouse, boozer, victualler, brewer and manufacturer for the merchant fleet and trading companies and in time the tanning centre for all of the pink areas of the globe. And so it was that it had one of the highest densities of weird and wonderful eighteenth- and nineteenth-century industrial architecture; left abandoned when the tide went out in the 1970s, ripe for re-imaging in the nineties. For the last few years I had been a design director at a development company, working on regeneration projects all within walking distance. Our home was in a street with an old-fashioned corner shop. A friend went in one day and asked if they had spring onion-flavoured crisps. The owner simply said 'Fuck off yuppie', and went back to reading the *Daily Star* and sipping his Special Brew. It was that kind of street.

After a childish attempt to annoy the priest by insisting our first-born be called Tiberius, after the notorious Christian-slaying emperor, I had eventually agreed to the wholly reasonable suggestion that the name Adam was less damaging all round. We realised when Adam had completed his first year in a city centre primary school that we had reached a crossroads. With the youngest Rosy just born, Sarah would push her and her elder sister Naomi in a double buggy to his school and back, with Oscar number two trotting alongside and Adam, with blue knees, complaining in his school uniform. Their innocent wonder at the world was still intact. A huge old safe, its door blown open, had been left abandoned by some villains under the viaduct and was gradually accumulating a shroud of pigeon droppings. This strange object on the school run was a source of continued questions. Despite the grand storytelling opportunities and despite how cosy and lovely our house was, it was still the land of crunching broken glass, dodging massive dog turds and skirting junkies' needles. And despite being a Roman Catholic primary school the most commonly used words at the school gate began with either F or C. The time had come to move either back to the safer, greener suburbs, to which all our friends seemed to have retreated, or perhaps even further south. We even toyed with the idea of the wilds of Sussex.

We had been viewing little houses near my childhood home when out of the blue a client introduced me to his brother-in-law, who needed an architect/developer for a project in the Caribbean. One thing led to another and after a year spent travelling to Cuba every couple of months, instead of moving to SW19 at the end of 2000 we moved to SW9000. At that time there was a single flight a week on an Ilyushin from Stansted Airport, there was no bread in the shops let alone spring onion-flavoured crisps, there were power cuts, there were only three other British families in the country, none of us could speak Spanish and the job was only certain for a year. The consensus of families and friends was, 'you are totally mad'. But they failed to understand the main point. Sarah and I had come to the realisation that if we did the conventional thing our entire lives would fall into the preordained suburban, middle-class pattern. Not without its challenges and joys of course, but that would be it: a long road to certainty. We knew that if we wanted to do something interesting with our lives and give our kids an adventurous childhood, then here, out of the blue, was a chance. The worst that could happen, we thought, would be scuttling back in a year with not much more than our tails between our legs and some nice photos. So basically, we went to Cuba because we saw an opportunity to escape the smallness of our lives and to have the kind of family experience you cannot buy at Chessington World of Adventures. And one summer's day we left with high hopes and heavy suitcases.

Habana Vieja, where I built my first Cuban project, is a beautiful lozenge-shaped city of mainly eighteenth- and nineteenth-century buildings and is deservedly a UNESCO world heritage site. The third choice for a capital city, Havana came into being as a safe-haven port for consolidating Spanish treasure fleets from South America before they chanced the forbidding Atlantic and in later years for the export of sugar and the trading of slaves. The harbour frontage developed into a myriad of finger quays and warehouses, together with their sinister sisters for warehousing people, the barracoons. At regular intervals stern, star-shaped castles were built to keep marauding pirates and the English at bay and as a place of refuge when the peasants got uppity. The colony was administered by the all-powerful capitán general from an imposing house in the Plaza de Armas, where he would review his soldiers. Spreading out from there a sprinkling of fine churches, public squares, theatres and government buildings sprouted inside the city walls and, like in Bermondsey, a hive of business both official and illicit hummed all day and night off the back of an imperial port that reached across the oceans.

By 2000 the city, now with a population of two million, had seen some momentous events yet, despite flashes of transient glory, for the rest of recorded history it will be remembered as the focus of an insane brinkmanship that brought the world to the eve of annihilation. Actually, not so at all. Humanity has a happy way of forgetting unpleasantness. Ask anyone on this planet what Havana means and they will have forgotten the Missile Crisis. They pluck four things from their foggy long-term memory in the following order: cigars, rum, Fidel and 'say hello to my little friend' Tony Montana in *Scarface*.

For the first five years we lived in the barrio of Nuevo Vedado. Developed in the 1940s, it was perched on the highest hilltop in the city and the wind always blew fresh and strong. To the west, limestone cliffs and escarpments dropped into the river valley of the Almendares River, with its remnants of ancient forest festooned with vines and the special forces base hiding in the bushes. To the north-east was the necropolis of Colon, a vast and monumental walled cemetery. To the east was the ramshackle and depressing zoo. And incredibly, underneath our feet tunnelled the army engineers. The house would be shaken from time to time by subterranean explosions as they burrowed ever deeper hoping to hide from the wrath of America should it ever come. It was rumoured that regiments of armoured vehicles were stored down there; rockets, hospitals, in fact everything to run a war. So in short we lived on a hill surrounded by dead people, special forces and caged animals and with paranoid soldiers digging under our house. We loved it and with little objective consideration we started a new life. Rosy was just six months, Naomiwas two years old, Oscar four and Adam about to turn six.

Our house was Dashiell Hammett style, damp and built for some reason at two-thirds scale. But being perched on the edge of a cliff, the kitchen and bedroom windows opened out into the bird-filled canopy of flame trees. To the boys' amazement, a staircase hewn out of rock went down into a garage that opened up further downhill. Our very own Batcave to park our mafia-style black Volvo. But best of all, we lived on a cul-de-sac perched at a drunken ten degrees, with the road circling around a tatty scrap of woodland and ending in a 20-foot cliff. The children were in heaven. I bought them a rope so they could scramble up and down the cliff, they made camps and bows and arrows and generally ran amuck with the local kids. The place was infested with scorpions which came into the house out of the rain and which Rosy delighted in battering to death with her squeaky hammer. We never had to lock the door until we went to bed, not because it is a crime-free city but because we had inadvertently moved in next door to a senior government official, Chomi. He was a courtly, handsome intellectual in his sixties. He would pootle off six days a week in his ancient Lada, dressed immaculately in dove-grey guayabera and trousers, returning after midnight to nurse his terminally ill wife. He would knock on our door every Sunday wearing only lemon-yellow running shorts, with a bag of greens. His hobby was growing an incredible quantity of vegetables on his roof, and every week he would personally deliver them to all the houses in the neighbourhood.

The contrast with Bermondsey or indeed suburban London could not have been greater for all of us. Adam's class was from every corner of the globe and the language of the playground was Spanish. After a few tearful mornings he took to it like a duck to water. At home the other three revelled in the sunshine, the club pool and the weekends at the beach. Rosy spoke her first word, '*leche*', and the rest picked up Spanish without much difficulty. Sarah and I quickly amassed a network of warm and interesting international friends, the glue to these friendships being children, and although the only foreigners in the neighbourhood we were made very welcome. The years passed and one by one the kids all started school. The days of power cuts, when we had to do homework by candlelight and sleep on the bare cool floor to escape the insufferable heat, went as soon as Chávez fell into a swoon of comradely adoration and sent oil tankers to his chum Fidel. Hurricanes came and went, as did friends, but steadily our business grew into a respected company.

And then, out of the blue, one day the government rules changed and we could no longer rent a private house, and so we moved to the posh suburb of Siboney where all the diplomats and big-cheese foreigners live behind high fences with their *custodios* sat out in front. The house is huge, it has a pool and everything, but despite the comfort and the lovely garden I think we all miss the street life of Nuevo Vedado. The weekends are still special, with a revolving door of hordes of kids staying over, Saturday morning football and parties, but we feel more in the expat bubble now and the children's Cuban friends are no longer from ordinary homes but seem to be the pampered offspring of the elite. And this was where we had ended up in March 2011.

1
....

See you in the morning

This week has been beyond crap, but last Sunday had been a good day. We had a bit of a late night out with some friends, when we'd eaten too much, drunk too much and then flopped into bed around one. It was Sarah's turn for a lie-in, so mine to do the breakfast. There had been a sleepover. Bouncy blonde Rosy, our youngest, now aged twelve, had invited some friends and together with Naomi, a leggy fourteen with flame-red hair and ice-blue eyes, they were already making a colossal, shrieking din at an unearthly seven in the morning. Barefoot and in old gym shorts and holey T-shirt I had made a stack of pancakes and bacon for the horde. I wouldn't have to wake Oscar, a fifteen-year-old pale streak of tight ginger curls; the smell of the bacon would work its magic. And seventeen-year-old Adam would get up in his own sweet time, secure in his delusion that we didn't know he had a hangover, a girlfriend and a smoking habit.

I carted everything to the wooden table on the covered patio that was the centre of family life and called them to come. The skirmishing for seating positions that adolescent girls go in for quickly subsided into general slurping and giggling. I drank deeply from my mug of coffee and stole half the bacon when nobody was looking.

One of the girls piped up, with her mouth ejecting pancake fragments: 'Rosy, there is a pig at the end of your garden.'

As quick as a flash I blurted out, 'That's no pig, that's my wife. Hahahah', which was met with six pairs of pitying eyes and silence.

At which point a loud 'oink' came by way of happy confirmation. Sure enough a huge grubby pig was rummaging through the flowerbeds and bushes beyond the swimming pool.

'Blimey kids, stay here. Don't go near. I will sort this out.'

And I dashed back to the kitchen for the kids' one-hundred-foot stout rope On the way I passed a frenzied, barking blur going in the other direction. Hastily fashioning a lasso, I now had the kids' full attention.

'What are you going to do, sir?' said an overly formal Texan child.

'Why, I am going to lasso the beast, of course.'

I advanced stealthily while the dog went berserk. The kids silently chomped the last of the pancakes, eagerly anticipating disaster. They were not to be disappointed. The pig had been bulldozing the garden at a steady 1mph, pausing only to burp and fertilise, but when the lasso landed over its head it went off like a squealing rocket, launching me after it on the end of the unfortunately stout rope. Thankfully, after a few minutes ploughing the garden with my elbows, the pig took four sharp turns around our huge avocado tree and ground to a bad-tempered, snorting halt.

Spitting out dead leaves, I gave the thumbs up and shouted cheerfully: 'Well that went well, it's safe now kids.'

The boys were now up and ready to join in the fun. We found that the pig had pushed its way under the metal sheet fence from a yard in the rabbit warren of buildings behind. So we went round the block and started knocking on doors. Our cheerful enquiry of 'Good morning. Do you own a pig?' was met with vigorous denial at every door. Meat is scarce and expensive because it is state-controlled: killing a cow gets you more years in prison than killing a man. It is a criminal offence to keep a pig at home or sell meat or eggs on the black market, but people are desperate and so despite the risks there is a large secret population of livestock in urban Havana. So we quickly changed tack and just asked: 'Have you lost a pig?' Four doors later a blowsy forty-year-old in curlers went pale and after a quick check started hysterically whispering: 'My God, my old man will kill me! We will come now.'

An hour later a tightly bound and furious pig was heaved into a wheelbarrow and disappeared out of the front gate. About an hour after that we heard the blood-curdling scream of the wandering hog going to piggy heaven.

Soon afterwards Sarah appeared with a yawn. 'Have I missed anything? There was a lot of noise going on.'

The rest of the day had been a bit of an anticlimax but the whole, silly charade had lifted the mood. Something really bad was breaking into our life, an ominous scratching and digging away at the foundations.

*   *   *

Kerplink. I lay my razor down on the glass shelf, rinse my face with cold water and look at myself. For some reason I always shave at night: I've forgotten why, but I find comfort in the familiarity of the ritual. I like the sounds of the nocturnal house, the distant tinny transistor babble of the custodian sitting on his plastic chair in the carport, the pool gurgling against the rise and fall of insect interference. Felicia, my skinny black street dog, has been cooling her bottom on the bathroom tiles. When I glance down she cocks her head, pricks up her swivelling bat ears, and her yellow eyebrows enquire if everything is alright.

I wish it were.

When they come for you, they mostly come either to your workplace and march you out of the front door in handcuffs for maximum public humiliation, or they grab you off the street like the Gestapo and throw you into the back of a car so nobody knows you have disappeared. But sometimes they appear like phantoms at your house just before dawn, politely dismember your family and dismantle your life forever.

This is what happened to my boss five months ago, leaving a pregnant wife and a confused little boy in a closed-up house. They came and took him away, provisionally charged with revelations of state secrets and corruption. That same morning they came to close the offices and start rummaging through files. I was the only other senior executive in the country at the time. I watched them close the building but they said I was free to go, could keep my computer and phones and go about my life normally.

When I asked if I could leave the country as I had to renew my visa within two weeks, they said: 'Sure, you are not under investigation. You can leave and come back if you want. We are not interested in you. We are closing the office as part of a collateral investigation. The workers can return when we say so.'

I guess if there is one thing that history teaches us it is that vanity, pride and a sense of duty can be a disastrous combination. They blinded me to the risks of the inevitable slow-motion descent. I should have gone to the airport and just left, leaving my family to pack up and follow. And now it's too late. All our visas have expired, they are holding my family's passports and so we are in effect held hostage. I had told myself that as a director of the company it was my duty to not run away at the moment when the company needed me most, that I was the indispensable leader on the ground who would be able to rescue at least part of the group's assets. The vanity of it. Perhaps my greatest stupidity was to argue this passionately to diplomatic friends who to a man all begged me to flee while I could.

I bleated: 'I haven't committed any crimes in Cuba. I'm not a crook so I will not run away. They can't invent a crime. Even they wouldn't do that.'

But they had also arrested a retired company advisor, a garrulous, charming old retired coronel who would tell everyone that in a former life he had been head spook in Poland, had run the Washington desk and had done all sorts of plausibly crazy things. Like all our retired employees we paid him a small monthly pension because if he had to rely on the state pension he would starve to death. Interestingly, Cuba has a very high suicide rate for men of retirement age, as they don't want to burden their families once they cannot bring in money. But like all payments to workers this has until very recently been illegal.

And now I am very worried. My birthday had come and gone but it just tasted like sour wine and borrowed time. I sat on a crumbling sea wall telling the whole story to a visiting Cuban friend and she looked at me in silence, her face immobile. Her sunglasses would not betray her fears but when we hugged goodbye I could tell she thought it was forever. My trainer looks surprised to find me still here every Tuesday morning and then pretends that nothing is wrong. I see pity in the eyes of some of my staff when we talk about my plans for saving the company. Save yourself, they seem to say. The Cubans can smell when the monsters are on the prowl and hungry for fresh victims. And then there was that horrible day about a month ago. I had received a call asking me to present myself at the office of the president of the state logistics company, no reason given. My Cuban number two drove me there through the mid-morning drizzle in silence. I had left my wallet at home and a note under the pillow telling Sarah to contact my lawyer and the embassy.

My colleague shook my hand solemnly and said with downcast eyes: 'My friend, I wait for you. Let us hope for the best.'

The pretty, officious PA, someone I had flirted with a hundred times, told me with an expressionless face: 'A teniente coronel (lieutenant colonel) from MININT (the Ministry of the Interior) would like to see you. Please wait in here.' She showed me into an empty room and closed the door. The hours ticked past. I paced up and down, stared out of the window, sat at the table with my head on my arm trying to sleep. Noon came and went, the showers blew out to sea and the evening traffic started to build up. The swirling, dirty flocks of pigeons began heading to roost and the light started to swell in that gorgeous orange purple prelude to night. The door opened.

'He's busy. He says he can't see you today. Later perhaps.'

Normally I enjoyed following her beautiful, crisp bottom to the entrance but today I could only enjoy the act of leaving. Opening the car door, my hands were shaking. My friend drove me home and we shared a large whisky in the garden. He didn't have to say it but I knew he had been dreading having to tell my family. I tore up the letter.

And then there have been some encouraging signs. For example, having been in a state of purdah for four months our Cuban partner in a prestigious hotel, who is a member of the central committee, agreed to have a board meeting and was friendly to me, confiding after the meeting: 'Well, I had to get clearance to continue the relationship.' But since my boss was transferred to the secure wing of the military hospital the atmosphere has changed. Everyone has noticed it.

The tail has gone from random to constant. When I walk Felicia they follow. I try to work out if their obviousness is part of a game or if indeed they are just simply useless and I get a childish kick about going into the bakery one way and out another, seeing if I can beat them home again. I pop into the most expensive bars, sit down, order a drink and watch the badly dressed Rosa Klebb type dump herself down in the corner, look at the menu in panic and then whisper to the waiter for a glass of water. I down the Red Label in one, throw a ten-spot on the table and rush for a taxi, leaving the flustered operatives wondering if the Stasi had this trouble. The clicks on the phone get on my wife's nerves and she has started shouting insults down the handset, something very out of character. The kids sense the pressure and my eldest, revising for his IB, International Baccalaureate, retreats into the companionship of friends' homes whenever he can. Last Sunday a group of Ladas were parked outside and a bunch of Security guys were standing around stroking their Burt Reynolds moustaches, checking the place out, pointing at things and taking notes. Is this theatre to stress us out? If so it's working. Sarah was in floods of tears, convinced that the axe was about to fall. It didn't. They put their clipboards away and went. But the anxiety remains, building each day and casting a gloom over our sunny home.

Tomorrow is a big day. Another hotel joint venture prospect has agreed to resume board meetings with me, but it will be a tough one. For years we have been fighting a losing battle against the officially sanctioned theft of non-fixed assets, the granting of suspect construction contracts against our express instructions and the siphoning off of cash to other state enterprises. Tomorrow I shall be tabling evidence to support our current complaints, namely that they have signed a $3m refurbishment contract to their own subsidiary without our approval. We should have read the writing on the wall a few years ago when they stopped wanting us on their soil and started the witch-hunts. Fighting these battles is useless: they suck us dry from a thousand directions and when they run out of reasons they will invent new ones. Why did we think we were untouchable? What were we thinking?

I point down the corridor and tell Felicia to go to bed. She scoots off with a downcast face, her nails clicking on the marble. I turn off the lights and walk through the moonlit house wondering if this is my last night on earth.

There is a light coming from under Adam's door. Poking my nose round it I whisper: 'You alright Honky?'

A muffled, 'Uuugghhnn'.

'Okay, goodnight darling, see you in the morning.'

And I do, briefly.

Old string and forlorn duty

The air conditioning hums and the early-hour sounds of Havana reluctantly going to bed are fading away. I cannot sleep despite my tiredness. My mind is beyond restless. I have this rising dread that everything I do is on borrowed time. I am a boat dismasted, blown by a relentless wind and dragged by unseen currents towards the rocks. Every bone in my body is warning me that this will end in disaster, and soon. It will be bad. It's just a question of font size.

My company and my boss, and therefore by extension me, are caught up in events much bigger than ourselves. Insect-like, this country is sloughing its redundant skin. The previous form, no longer relevant to the world environment, had become unsustainable, or worse had shown worrying signs of turning into something uncontrollable. So in an act of self-preservation the Castros have chosen its next incarnation. This one is in military green and has a biblical fury. Those twerps who blather on about Marxism in university canteens would say it is the next phase of revolutionary development as if it was as painless as changing the curtains to improve the house price. In fact the local media describe it pretty much in those terms. But it is now in the final stages of morphing into a new incarnation. The same beast but different habits, and it is methodically eradicating anything that is a threat. Every single high-ranking politician or business leader has been replaced or has vanished in the past few years. Some have been the subject of public purges and denouncements like Carlos Lage and Pérez Roque, but most have simply been edited out.

All have been replaced by military figures. Having allowed foreign capitalism in to rescue the collapsed economy they now want to behead it before it becomes too powerful. They have watched the piggy get fat and now they want to steal the piggy before it goes to market. It's a Stalinist purge for the internet generation and it's all about who controls the economy.

I stop myself pointlessly trying to plan sneaky ways to evade and survive. I have no power over the events that are unfolding. All I can do is think back and curse myself for not taking the warning signs seriously.

Scrolling back to my first visit, 1997, communist Cuba was bankrupt and the people desperate. There was no food. I remember going to a huge supermarket that had just a shelf of 5kg tins of Polish pickled cabbage and an aisle full of bags of sugar. The whole country felt and smelt like a pair of tramp's trousers held up by nothing more than old string and forlorn duty. Coming from flabby London, the entire population were startlingly thin, superficially like a teeming horde of extras from a Calvin Klein advert, but once you looked past the young and sexy you saw prematurely aged and crushed people standing exhausted in line for their meagre rations. Yet instead of forcing the people to act out the State Department's *coup de main* by proxy, the cruel embargo seemed to achieve nothing except hand Fidel the moral high ground and give him every reason to blame the US for all his nation's woes. His position was strengthened by the sanctions because he could claim with some justification that Cuba was in a state of eternal war against the Yankees. To save his wonky world Fidel gambled on opening his country to the Pandora's box of tourism and allowing direct foreign investment. Which is where we came in with two left feet, an engaging smile and lots of cash to invest.

Between then and now the early triumphs have slowly given way to disappointments or illusions. And so, many years later, at last month's management meeting of this huge resort hotel we co-own, I listened dumbfounded to a speech made by the president of a Cuban tourism company to all the senior workforce of our joint venture. At a personal level, I really liked the man with his sixty-a-day cough and co-ordinated teeth, but this just made his world view even stranger. After listening to a brief and wholly fictitious summary of the last quarter's financial performance he congratulated all workers for meeting the ministry plan for occupancy, room rate, profitability and grams of meat per tourist per day consumed. Then to the mystification of everyone he explained that to run a tourist resort efficiently the staff had to think like Gadhafi planning his counter-attack against the counter-revolutionaries. They should not let setbacks deflect them from their true purpose and they had to fight every second of the day against the enemy. It wasn't clear whether he was saying that the enemy was me, his foreign joint-venture partner or the fat Canadians crisping up on our sun loungers. It clearly wasn't meant to be the policemen I regularly see loading their patrol cars up with frozen meat in our service yard, or the state officials that can make a few hundred grand of inventory magically disappear before the audit each year. The staff gave him the obligatory ovation and trooped out of the door to continue pilfering under the table and writing fantasy reports on top of it.

That was a month ago and today I have a shareholders' meeting. My damning evidence lies on my desk upstairs, printed and ready for a good punch-up. I guess I am the enemy now. And with that I drift off.

Time to get up. The patio is cool and I have a cup of tea and listen to the wonderful dawn chorus of birds, bugs and insanely barking dogs. The buses are labouring up the hill, air brakes gasping, taking the patient millions to their work or classrooms. It is still dark but the horse in the house behind is asking for his breakfast. Sarah appears and starts laying the table on drowsy automatic pilot.

There is some banging of car doors outside and then without

announcement the front door opens and a secret policeman with a red moustache walks in and introduces himself as Teniente Coronel Ivan of the State Security. This is my boss's interrogator. It has happened.

A horde of officers swarm past us and head for the safe, the home office and my bedroom. My wife dashes out of the kitchen saying 'What's going on, what's going on?' and a female officer closes in on her. I stand there in distracted silence looking at the flower arrangement on the living-room table and thinking: 'Thank God I wasn't still wandering about in just my underpants.'

While the officers quietly move to the prearranged positions the teniente coronel looks at all the books in the bookcase, his hands behind his back. He pulls out *Jane's Fighting Ships*, a book on the world's navy list which I had bought at a Havana book fair for my lads. We regularly spot the Cubans' clapped-out missile boats chugging about. He holds it up and looks over his right shoulder at me and raises an eyebrow. I see he is missing the tip of his right index finger and can't help thinking of the evil agent in *The Thirty-Nine Steps*. He puts the book back without comment and continues browsing. He pulls out *Wild Swans*, an uplifting but rather harrowing account of life under Mao's dictatorship that is banned here. He waggles it at me and puts it back. Then he pulls out *The Pursuit of Freedom*, an excellent history book on Cuba, also banned. It has rather illuminating sections on the Castros' early years, covering Fidel's criminal activities at university which included murder of a rival, Raúl's recruitment to the KGB and all sorts of exciting skulduggery. Sighing loudly to underline his disappointment at my choice of reading matter he puts it back and then turns.

'You have heard of me?'

'Yes, the ambassador described the person who arrested my boss. You are a chief interrogator for the State Security.'

'Good. Then you understand.' A predatory smile under

emotionless eyes that warn me that this is not a game.

I'm not sure I do understand or want to. But clearly he is the enforcer of the preordained. His own officers walk like they are in a room with an unpredictable tiger. He exudes a power that makes my gut shrivel under his gaze and yet I am strangely calm even though I can sense that an abyss is opening beneath my feet.

A self-satisfied man with a Filofax in one hand, car keys hanging off his belt and a silly mobile phone holster saunters in and sits on a sofa.

Pointing to him, the coronel continues. 'This is the representative of the Comités de Defensa de la Revolución. He is here to ensure that everything is done in accordance with the law. He will sign for any evidence removed from the house.'

'Please, before you do anything can you please wait for the kids to go to school?'

He stares at me for a few seconds, long enough for him to let me know I am begging, and nods. Up to now the kids had all been in bed, oblivious to the silent invasion of the house. Sarah is now going from room to room to wake them and give them some kind of sensible explanation of who our mysterious guests are.

'Oh, it's nothing. Just some people come to ask Dad some questions about work. Come on, have your shower and get dressed and then let's have breakfast. I need you to be very good today.'

They emerge from their various rooms, give me a cautious hello as they pass the living room and troop to the kitchen for breakfast, their eyes alive with questions and a child's foreboding they cannot articulate as they take in the stern-looking men.

The coronel and I stand without further talk, listening to the muffled kitchen noises. He is absorbing the rhythm of the house, feeling its beating heart. Making a hunter's appreciation of the vulnerability of his victim.

'Who arranges the flowers?' he suddenly asks,

'Ummm, I do.' He nods his head.

I let this sink in. He must have known and he thinks I'm a wimp. Real guys don't do flowers in Cuba. And he thought I would lie.

It's 7.45, time for school. The kitchen door creaks open. Must get round to oiling the hinge. And there is my wife shooing them out: 'Go say goodbye to your Dad.'

One by one they hurry to me, struggling to get their packs on, bits of homework and sports bags clutched in one hand. To each of them I give my normal morning kiss and hug. Nothing special, it's just another day.

With Adam my eldest, I hug him close and say in his ear: 'Come home early today, son. Mum will need a hand.'

And then they are gone.

3

....

Instruction

The ancient, unmarked Lada has long ago left my part of town, and with its oversized engine it is hurtling in the rough direction of the airport. The handcuffs are digging into my wrists and despite the sagging back seat my head is rubbing and banging against the roof. The hot, dusty lunchtime air is blasting through the driver's quarter light. And each time we take a left turn I tip over against the door, which has no lining, and the primitive system of exposed wire that works the door lock jabs me in the kidney. They don't say anything, but the officer beside me keeps telling me to look straight ahead and not to the side. They drive like they have watched too many movies. Maybe they think somebody will drop out of the sky to rescue me from their clutches. Finally we are back on the 5km stretch of airport dual carriageway, built initially to impress Pope John Paul and subsequently two million tourists a year.

Part of me is hoping that this is just an express deportation and that they will bundle me on to a plane bound for anywhere just to get rid of me. A bad result in one sense, as it means the end of my professional life in Havana and the family will have a rotten time organising their exit mid-term, but it could be a lot worse. Then all of a sudden, a few kilometres short of the airport, we turn a shuddering hard right and I realise it really is going to be a lot worse. We rattle along roads that get progressively dustier and bouncier. Smallholdings flash past and people stop what they are doing and stare as the unmarked Lada with a worried white face in the back

roars past. They know what this car means. They must have
seen it a thousand times before. I carefully keep mental track
of the route. Part of me is curious to know exactly where it is
that I shall leave my daily extistence behind but in reality I
am sucking in the bright sights of this wonderful world. Who
knows when I will see it again?

Random thoughts flash through my head. Batista owned a
lot of land around the airport, which was consequently confiscated after the revolution. I wonder if one of his villas has
been converted to some sinister house of pain. I have heard
rumours of foreigners being kept incommunicado in remote
and secure houses for long periods of time. A hand roughly
pushes my head between my knees and I am told not to look
up. Staring at my feet I concentrate on the movement of the
car and the sounds outside. I can tell when we weave through
a small village then slow down, turn right and start bouncing
down an unmade road. The car stops. The driver gets out and
I can hear him talking quietly to someone. All the sounds
of the Cuban countryside fill my ears. The buzzing of horseflies,
the humming of the hot soil, far-off cow bells and chickens,
the faint pop pop pop of an ancient moped, but mainly a
dread stillness after the crashing gear changes and road roar of
the drive here. The engine ticks itself to sleep and the guard
keeps his hand on my head. I imagine it as the hand of an old
campesino calmly controlling a New Year pig, steadying the
neck ready for the knife. A burst of walkie-talkie garble, then
swift footsteps crunching across stones and the Lada groans as
the driver slides from behind the wheel. I can hear a big metal
gate being swung open on a rusty hinge. We shoot forward
for ten yards and finally come to a stop. In a flash the doors are
open and I'm helped out. I have a few seconds to glance about
me. It's a badly maintained art deco villa that is obviously
missing its original owner. It must have been the country
house of someone from the prosperous middle classes, a doctor
perhaps, before coming under new management in fifty-nine.

Noting the blacked-out windows and the tough-looking guys with sidearms closing the gate, I am led through a door and swallowed by the darkness.

It's a plain front room with a table, a chair and a small terracotta vase with a tiny bunch of yellow plastic roses. In the corner are two black armchairs in cracked black vinyl. Rather grubby antimacassars are draped over their backs in an attempt to create an ambience of unthreatening, gentle home-liness. The air conditioning drones on and a few chinks of light spear into the room, which for the most part is under-lit by a single, two-foot fluorescent strip. A taciturn plain-clothes guard tells me to sit in one armchair and he sits in the other. He stares at me for what seems like hours and I stare back. Nothing is said. He has the body and demeanour of a simple mountain man: the sun, wind and endless toil have boiled out any mercy he may have had as a child. His eyes show no emotion at all. No hate, no liking for this business. Certainly no liking for me. Nothing. Just a reptilian, unblinking gaze. It is really rather unnerving. Finally a side door swings open and a cheerful, prune-faced older lady bustles in with a plate, knife and fork and a jug of water. After bidding me good afternoon she asks me to sit at the table. She serves me a black bean soup then roast chicken, rice and tomato salad. I scarf it down and then a second helping. The cheerful prune pops in again to take away the dirties and plonks a pudding down with an encouraging smile. If it wasn't for the eyes of the guard boring into me, I would fool myself into thinking that perhaps everything will be alright.

As soon as the pudding is removed the guard tells me to follow him down a short corridor. There is a beefy-looking youth guarding the door. He says good afternoon, unlocks it and ushers me in, then turns the key. It's a plain room with a single bed, a shuttered window with a toilet and a sink off to one side. Nothing else.

I put my eye to a crack in the shutter and can see through

a chain-link fence to open, dusty fields that wander off towards dense forest. Far away a young woman in a pink top is
walking, holding the hand of a small child. I can tell by the
way she holds her head that she is singing a pretty song to
the child. Maybe '*Arroz con leche*'. The sky is bright blue and
I can just see on the periphery of the garden some red flowers growing together with a few heads of lettuce. Suddenly
there are loud footsteps; the sandy scrunch of military boots
on a cement path. I instinctively pull back and a green uniform flits past as the steps recede down the garden. If this tiny
crack is to be the only connection I have to the outside world
then I must treasure it. God knows how long this is going to
take. The door opens and the young guy walks up to the shut-
ters, fiddles with them to make sure they are really closed,
then leaves. A short while later and he is outside, hammering
the slats shut with his fist. Somehow they knew I had been
peeking. So the watcher is watched. I surreptitiously scan the
room trying to find out where the camera is but cannot work
it out. Obviously their technology is better than their interior
design.

Blimey, it's hot in here. That must mean above me is only
a flat roof. My armpits stink and I have no change of clothes.
I take my shirt and shoes off and lie on the bed trying to
rationalise things and come up with a positive scenario. I decide, surely against reason, that after a few days of questions
they will realise I am innocent and take me home. I will have
missed Oscar's birthday but no real harm will have been done
and we can just continue with our lives. I am just getting
comfortable with this, working out my magnanimous little speech to the teniente for when he salutes me farewell on
my doorstep and apologises for the inconvenience, when the
tough guy opens the door and tells me to get ready as interrogation is about to begin.

Before I have time to process this information and panic I am ushered into a small room with four armchairs in a

circle. The room is brightly lit and badly decorated in pink and orange. A smelly, swirly carpet crackles with static. The teniente, who is in a well-pressed uniform, says hello and asks me to sit. Before I do, I make a point of going up to the others to say good afternoon and shake hands. I am pretending to myself that this is just another tedious business meeting to discuss the threadbare investment strategy for a Cuban business. An elderly black man with a face like a tired grouper is obviously an interrogator. He considers me over his half-moon glasses with a disappointed air, as if I have already started lying to him. I suppose in a way I have. The fat lady with a bun explains that she is the translator. She exudes apology and is clearly not looking forward to this. Just doing her job. Everyone has their role it seems, including me, and then the fun begins.

The teniente gives me a big smile. 'Pubis, we have brought you here so that we can have a conversation. You are provisionally charged with revelations of state security and illegal activities. These are serious crimes. We need to know many things and it is easier for you to concentrate here. You will find there are no distractions. But we have plenty of time. I will visit your wife later today and tell her you are fine and collect a few things for you. Toothbrush, underclothes, that kind of thing. You understand?'

The unstated implication being that this will take as long as they feel like. He continues.

'You can have a lawyer, it is in the law. But it is very difficult and takes a long time to get one. It always takes a long time, you know Cuba, you understand. My advice is that it is better if you start to co-operate immediately.' He smiles and nods to himself in agreement.

'So let us begin. First of all we want you to tell us all about yourself. Your family, your upbringing, your education, your hobbies, that sort of thing. Talk.'

And so I told them about my life, my parents and my family,

talking earnestly and throwing in detail that I thought would put me in a better light. I wanted to burn up all the inter-rogation time in waffle, hoping they would get bored with a boring account of a boring life. They nodded politely, making no notes, waiting for me to peter out, which I duly did. In silence they willed me to keep talking, so after getting my second wind I was off again, babbling on about my mediocre education. They let me rabbit for some time and then put me out of my misery by asking the first question in what seemed like hours, but was probably only thirty minutes.

'You are a director of the international school. Correct?'

'Yes, I have been for eight years. In fact, I am the vice chairman.'

'We know. So who are the other directors then? When do you meet them?' the coronel grins.

Oh shit. I walked into this one. There has always been at least one director from the USINT (United States Interests Section) plus half the board are always foreign diplomats and some have been very active in assisting the dissidents. Every month I have therefore been meeting people they consider their enemies in semi-private situations. At these meetings I made a point of only ever discussing school business with these people, and certainly kept well clear of the Americans, but that is going to sound pretty feeble to these cynical bastards.

I rattled off the list of current and former school directors, emphasising the majority of African, friendly or neutral dip-lomats and casually seeding it with the Americans and the handful of aggressive European ones. I took them through the hierarchy of committees and the meeting calendar, chart-ing my slow progress up through the pecking order. I started to think that perhaps this close connection with the wider diplomatic community would act as a protective cloak. That because I was a trusted member of that circle of people, State Security would treat me with kid gloves. But the grouper just sat there, eyes closed in concentration, with his hands clasped together as if in prayer, tutting from time to time and shaking his head as if his worst fears had been confirmed and that the meeting of the school's health and safety sub-committee was nothing more than a front for handing over secrets of coconut production to the ambassador of Ghana. You see, for the Cuban state all foreign diplomats are spies and there is no such thing as an innocent conversation with a diplomat.

My throat was getting dry and the room was chilly, so I asked for a glass of water and a pee break.

On my return, the grouper asked about my Saturday mornings. I explained that years ago, when both my lads were in junior school, I started a Saturday morning football session at the local park because there was nothing organised by anyone else. Over time it became more serious and more popular. So much so that for the past couple of years I arranged for a proper coach to take the session while I acted as goalkeeper for the losing side. It was very popular with other parents because it meant that they didn't have to do anything to entertain their boys on a Saturday morning and could lie in bed hung-over. When the dads came to collect them at lunchtime I would often chat with one or two of them while the boys squabbled over plans for the rest of the day and threw football boots at each other.

The coronel showed me a photo. It was of me talking to a German diplomat in the car park at Eduardo Saborit, the playing field at the end of my road. Fritzy looked as fresh as a daisy and rather pleased with himself and I looked like a rather sweaty and puffed out fat bloke in a muddy T-shirt.

'So what was this about?'

'Well, he is the father of some boys who are friends of my children and he is picking them up from football.'

'What were you talking about?'

'I have no idea. It happened every week.'

'Don't underestimate us, Pubis. Perhaps you were planning one of your trips?'

'We used to go away for holidays once in a while that's true. To Cayo Coco, and Pico Turquino.'

'Yes, I know. So you had plenty of opportunities to talk.'

'Sure.'

Raising his voice suddenly and leaning his face forward, red with threat, he jabbed his finger at me. 'You are in serious trouble. We know you are giving information to our enemies. This is not a joke.'

This particular friend had been a thorn in their side until the day he left. He had been very busy cataloguing the attacks of the Security henchmen – the Contingente Blas Roca – against the famous Damas de Blanco and other dissidents. But he had never discussed any of this with me and never asked me about my work. He was wise enough not to complicate a casual friendship by straying into complicated areas. So having tangentially established that as far as they were concerned I was guilty by association for hanging out with the enemy, they changed topic.

'So where have you visited in the last ten years?'

'Lots of places. Let's see . . . France, Italy, Spain, Germany, USA, Mexico, Jamaica, Bahamas, Dubai. Oh yes, Canada. I think that's it. No, Holland and Austria. Oh, and Belgium and the Cayman Islands. And Ireland. Switzerland?'

'Which ones did you visit for business, who did you go with, who did you meet and what did you discuss?'

And so an hour must have passed as I tried to recall every trip, and who with and why. In describing pretty much every trip I could see how these paranoid sociopaths could sniff out all manner of evil intentions. He would raise rhetorical questions about each place. Italy of course just deserved a derisory snort.

'Mexico. You say you visited for meetings on the port project and for meetings with hotel operators and for the golf project. But Mexico is in the hands of the *narcotraficantes*, isn't it?'

And so on. Even Belgium it seems is suspect to the Cubans. Strange. I thought it was famous only for chocolate and pae- dophiles, but apparently that barely scratches the surface of its depravity.

I was crapping myself as I got closer to having to talk about Dubai. I had spent a week in Dubai with the son-in-law of Raúl Castro, Luis Rodriguez Lopez Callejas This man is presi- dent of GAESA, the holding company of the military which, since Raúl assumed the presidency, has forcibly taken control of tourism, oil exploration, telecoms, logistics, retail, part of non-banking finance, a big chunk of shipping, the remittance business and credit card transactions. The current thinking in the foreign community is that this one man controls over 60 per cent of the real economy. One man. The son-in-law of the president. Join up your own dots. We had been in Dubai to sign the heads of terms agreement for the port and the economic zone of Mariel and I spent all day and most of the evening with the man for a week. That week had impressed and terrified me in equal measure and in the subsequent months during the predevelopment work leading up to the binding agreement he had regularly requested my presence in his of- fice. A huge room with a commanding view of Jesus across the bay, the marble arms outstretched giving benediction to the undeserving. A table as long as a cricket pitch, a room for res- pectful listening and not debate. Photos of the anointed one in military fatigues cradling an AK. 'It was an honour to fight in Angola,' he once told me, yet the rumours circulate that he was gun shy and always far from danger. A massive, stern desk was built like a veneered tank behind which was a map of the world that must have been four metres wide. Cuba was dead centre with this desk at point zero. Ernst Blofeld would have felt totally at home in this fantasy of domination.

So sitting here in this run-down house being interrogated by State Security, the one and only thing that made me feel vulnerable was the story of this man and the port project. For eight years, at the request of a succession of Cuban organisations, I had developed the proposals for the new container terminal and economic zone of Mariel. Mariel is a lightning road for Miami exile anger. It was the filthy mouth which vomited the scrapings from the Cuban prisons and mental hospitals during the boat lift. Among them, of course, good, ordinary people who had simply had enough, people who understood that it was always going to be a life of crumbs from the master's table and were brave enough to act upon it. And so they went, a slick of humanity that changed Miami forever. So as a project Mariel was a hot potato from the get-go. And for us, or rather me, there was a rather more worrying story hidden inside the potato. We had a joint venture with Dubai Ports World, the third largest port operator on earth. With DPW I had commissioned the navigation study, the dredging analysis, the engineering design and the marketing study. From this we had built the business plan and done the feasibility study. And with this we had negotiated an export guarantee from a Belgian dredging company for $80m. In the end a deal was negotiated with the Cuban side, led by the anointed one, in which a twenty-five-year joint venture was to be signed. It was a 51:40 equity and the Cuban side would only have to put up 20 per cent of the total capital required, which was $350m for the entire port: dredging, construction, equipment and working capital. Everyone was happy and the Minister of Foreign Investment officiated at the signing. Then six months later Luis Gallejas called me in and simply said, his piercing blue eyes belying a sardonic smile: 'Well, in Cuba we don't like to see the word binding in contracts and we have to cancel the project for reasons of sovereignty. I hope you understand. Please explain to Dubai.' And that was that. Eight years of work and a few million dollars of shareholders' money down the toilet.

I did what any rational man would do in the circumstances. With my team I took the entire set of paper files of the project down to Jibacoa beach, built a bonfire and barbecued a few dozen sausages and drank beer. And that was the end of that. Except it wasn't. About three months later it was announced that my erstwhile Cuban partners had signed an agreement with a Brazilian construction group backed with a Brazilian state loan and that they would borrow $850m to do the project. Now there's a thing. It did raise the obvious question: what is the extra half a billion for? It seemed I wasn't the only person to think about it. Military intelligence officials quizzed various people in my office about why this had happened. But as always in Cuba, a blanket of silence soon descended. I forgot about it and got on with developing a golf-course project. I had never talked about my misgivings to anyone and it always amazed me that the foreign journalists were so lazy that they had not picked up the huge discrepancy of cost.

And that is why I suddenly had a sinking feeling.

We had started on the thorny subject of visits to the US when the coronel interrupted me and said that we would break for dinner and resume in about an hour. I spent a gloomy half-hour pushing food round a plate, my appetite gone. I was getting very concerned about where this could all end up. I just had time for a pensive crap and to splash cold water on my face when I was called back to continue.

They made me recall every trip I had made to the US in my life. Where I had stayed, who I had seen, why I had gone. They just looked at me while I spoke. The grouper got up and went out for a few minutes, then came back with a file and sat flicking through it while I talked. A bit of theatre I surmised. At the end he asked only one question.

'Do you ever have any trouble with US immigration when you enter America?'

'No.'

'There, you see. You live and work in Cuba and they say nothing. You must be working with them.'

There was not much to say about that. So I sat in silence

waiting for them to get to Dubai. But they didn't. He changed tack completely.

'When were you last in Las Terrazas and who were you with?'

This is a popular mountain nature reserve and eco-village about forty-five minutes' drive to the east of Havana. I regularly go there with my family for a walk and a slap-up meal at the weekends.

'Oh, about a month ago with my family.'

'What did you see?' interjected the grouper.

'Eh, trees?'

The teniente exploded. 'This is not a joke. We are the Cuban State Security not the Pink Panther!' he screamed.

He calmed down a bit, sat down and then gave me my instructions. 'Now you have to work. Here is paper and a pen. I want you to write down everything you have told us today.'

About two hours later, with a throbbing head and itchy eyes, I was finally allowed to go back to my bed. If they can read my handwriting then they probably are more professional than the Pink Panther I thought. The light was kept on and the guard periodically checked up on me. I ignored him but I couldn't ignore my conclusions. They didn't want to talk about Mariel, at least not now. That was a relief. So far, they haven't actually accused me of anything specific. All they have done is use my own words to show that I have had plenty of opportunities to pass on these mysterious revelations. And they have got me worried by showing me photos of me doing something totally innocent but implying that I had been up to no good with confirmed enemies of the state. The only good news was that they hadn't beaten me up.

After a sleepless night and a bucket shower followed by a very welcome fried egg and coffee I was led back to the interrogation room. I put on a brave face, and walked in.

4

Small

The focus of the questions abruptly shifts. Now it's all about my boss. They want to know all about his family and friends and his history. To this day he remains something of an enigma to me. He is one of those people with a glittering surface that distracts and beguiles people. But the real person underneath? A total mystery. I can't really tell them much despite knowing him for years. Frustrated by my lack of information, the instructors start an aggressive new approach. Laughable, but frightening in the insanity of their conviction.

'He was a Maronite terrorist who participated in the Shatila camp massacre. Did you know that?'

That stunned me. 'He can't be, he was a student in London. He is just interested in his family, making money and women. He's not interested in politics. He couldn't kill anyone. He's a Buddhist. Besides, he can't stand the sight of blood.'

'We have information he was working for the CIA or Mossad.'

'That's crazy, he's always moaning about Israel and he hates the CIA.'

And so it went on for the rest of the session. They would get angry and start banging things around if they thought my answer was disrespectful but it was difficult to answer dumb questions without sounding dumber. Then they turned their attention to a couple of shareholders with similarly bizarre and vague accusations. After I had dutifully written up what I could recall I went to bed tired and with a thumping headache.

That night I had a bad dream, one that I was to have again and again for months. A moonlit barren desert landscape is rushing past the windows, the shattered land empty with not a scrap of humanity. Outside it is cold, clear and unforgiving. Inside, the hot smell of stale cigarettes and fear. A stony, armed man sits beside me and we race along the endless tarmac. The bouncing headlights occasionally pick out a tiny tortoise, frozen with fright, and then there's a sharp pop as another little life is extinguished. After an eternity the brooding passenger in the front suddenly turns round, his remorseless coal-black eyes glistening over a captain's moustache. All he says is, 'Justice is like an arrow', then he turns round again to direct the driver to our lonely destiny. And I sit in the back with an overwhelming feeling that I have lost all that I love most dear.

The next day, Oscar's sixteenth birthday, it began all over again. Now they were asking for details of various transactions that my boss had negotiated and various high-level Cuban officials, none of whom I had heard of. Luckily for me I knew nothing about them, so the day ended with them being very frustrated and probably having a headache. I went to bed thinking about what was going on at home, and whether the party had distracted them all for a few hours.

Then they started on a more slippery and sinister line of questioning. With stern faces, they demanded: 'Tell us about the reports you had to write. The reports to shareholders.'

'Well, it was my task to write an annual report that looked at the macro position of the country and relate it to the various business lines of the company.'

Leaning forward now, with colour rising, they snarled: 'Where did you get the information from? Did you pay officials for information?'

'No, of course not. I would get it from things like the EIU report on Cuba, CEPAL, the news agencies on many different public platforms. And then of course all my foreign friends in business here talked about what was going on in their businesses. Everything I wrote was public information. I would just analyse it and then at the end do a short forecast on the next year. It's the kind of report that any responsible company does.'

But they really didn't like it. In retrospect it was obvious really. I remember reading in the United Nations Human Development Index that Cuba comes joint bottom in the whole world with North Korea for freedom of information.

Why did you make comments about the health of Fidel? Where did you get the information? Who is the doctor you know? I told them the whole world was interested in the health of Fidel and that every Cuban had a theory or gossip about it. That made them mad again.

Then questions about a farcical episode. The minister of the interior had shot and wounded his sixteen-year-old girlfriend. The whole of Havana knew about it and laughed about the scandal.

With grave faces, they enquired: 'What about our minister? What do you know about recent events?'

'Well I heard about the shooting. But I never write about gossip, just published facts.'

'What else?'

'Well I know he keeps a chimpanzee at the end of his garden and it masturbates in front of the neighbours every morning. My friend lives next door and it frightens his wife.'

The translator burst out laughing and my instructor couldn't help smiling as he waved for the guard to take me away for lunch. My food tasted like ashes. I was putting on a brave face with these officers but I was really worried now. People do disappear for knowing the wrong thing. There are just too many stories out there for them all to be bullshit. Jesus, this is out of control.

Dawn breaks on the fifth day in this spooky house. So much for the maximum of forty-eight hours before they have to charge you. Yesterday, there had been just a final couple of hours of interrogation in the afternoon. Specific details about the work tasks assigned to various specialists in the company. There was nothing in the questions that made me nervous: it was simply a matter of confirming specifics. It wasn't problematic because everything I had done at work had been done with complete transparency when it came to our local partners, I didn't have any secrets from them. Ivan's manner is no longer aggressive. He's now an insurance broker going through a list of boxes that needed ticking. A task which bores him more than it bores me, trying to assay the risk of something nasty happening to me.

It definitely felt like they were running out of things to ask. It just sort of fizzled out.

All this time from the silence of my room I could hear the sound of footsteps hurrying back and forth down the cement path and the 'ratatat-zip-ting' of typewriters at the end of the garden. Strange that they use typewriters. They would bash away for an hour or so after an interrogation session. Then muffled voices, a single pair of boots marching, a bang of a car door and the unmistakable sound of a Lada achieving lift-off. Putting two and two together it seems that they were hand-delivering transcripts to some mightier brain in town and probably quite sensibly didn't trust the security of electronic media. If anyone in Cuba could afford computers it was State Security.

All day yesterday, the ratatatting had gone on for hours and hours. They must be doing some kind of a report. Off went the Lada and then nothing. I was just let out to eat once in a while.

Today after lunch the instructor pops his head around my door.

'I will allow you to go in the garden for a few hours.'

And the young guard fetches me and lets me out into the back garden. As I suspected there is a cement path running past my bedroom to the end of the garden. Beside a derelict swimming pool full of algae and leaves is a large outhouse. The windows are open and I can see an official at a desk reading. The garden is wide and enclosed with an out-of-control hibiscus hedge preventing anyone seeing in or out. Strange that it should be that plant. In most Asian cultures it is the symbol of death and it is considered very bad luck to have it in your garden. There are one or two very big mango trees giving shade, and a few spindly lemon and guava trees suffering from sooty blight as they don't have enough sun. The sparse grass has been machete-cropped close to the grey dirt and erratic lines of ants go about their eternal business. Along the borders are a few more fruit trees and in the one sunny patch a few lines of lettuce and herbs with a beautiful strip of vibrant red velvet flowers that I had glimpsed on my first day. I used to buy those for the house. The guard says I can go no further than halfway down to the pool and he settles on to a rusty stool in the shade to observe me.

I walk up and down and round and round, inspecting the trees, trying to spot the birds hidden in the branches and enjoying the bright flash of the first butterflies of the year. The mangoes are about half-formed and still pale. It will be a few months yet before they are ready. The guava and lemon trees are on their last legs, but the chirimoya has a number of perfectly ripe fruit ready to eat.

The guard has an open face and the neck of a wrestler. He was not picked for his razor-sharp intellect but for his ability to subdue and crush on command, it would seem. I make a guess.

'So do you do judo?'

Visibly puffing up, he replies: 'Yes, I was champion in my school and in my province. I enjoy it.'

I can't place his accent. They always move police away from home, so they won't suffer the embarrassment of having to beat up a relative.

'So where are you from, Oriente?' They are all from the east in Havana.

'Yes, Bayamo,' he replied, his nice but dim face amazed that I could have guessed that. 'Have you been?'

'Yes, it's a beautiful place. I've climbed The Yunque, been down the Yuma. Been to the Magellan National Park. It's a great place. Are you from the town or a village?'

'A village close to Magellan Park.'

'Wow, I loved the horsetail ferns. They are the oldest plants in the world. Really interesting. I saw a pygmy owl and lots of tocororos. There's that tree the yao that is so poisonous the sawdust or sap will kill you. I also saw loads of the *Polymita* snails.'

'Did you see any boas? There are lots up there.'

And so we spent a couple of hours, him on his stool and me with my back against a tree trunk, exchanging stories about the most mystical place in the country.

Bayamo is where Columbus landed, where he established the first town and where the genocidal tendencies of the Spanish first took root. It was from here that they started to weed out the Indians from the mountains and jungles. This is the spot where year zero of the colonisation of Cuba started. There is so little remaining of the pre-invasion culture. No temples, no abandoned cities, certainly no pure-blood Indians. All that is left is a certain look, a swiftness of foot and an affinity with the natural and spirit world beyond most modern, mini-conquistadors. By some quirk of geography and fate, the single place in Cuba where the scent of the pre-Columbian era is still strong is Bayamo. The weird mountains and rivers and the roiling dark forests have been resisting the modern world for 600 years, trying to push the fragile town back into the sea from where it came. For centuries the scattered, mixed-seed remnants have been culled or converted. The Spanish tried to own these people for centuries, the French tried to lure them away to pick coffee in plantations, the Cornish and

Welsh rounded them up to toil away down the dark, copper mines of Santiago. No doubt the Americans did something nasty, but I can't remember what exactly, maybe fatty Roosevelt and his rump riders had some fun, and then of course the crackpot communists found it a good place to find sturdy young chaps bored from staring at trees all day and eager to join a marching band of happy thugs. There are strange foods and customs, pre-dating the second genetic earthquake that African and then Chinese slavery engendered. If there is one thing that symbolises all this haunting heartache it is the anvil-shaped mountain that looms over the town, The Yunque.

I climbed it once. An act of thanksgiving and recuperation. I had been stabbed in the back of the neck one night in Havana, a '*mata vaca*', the abattoir stroke used to kill a cow and adopted by the filthy bandits that lurk outside the official statistics. A bloody and surreal experience that had ended in my first brush with Cuban justice. I had to attend the trial, a shocking farce; not that I wished for anything but painful punishment on my would-be killers. I had also a couple of interviews with the investigators.

After they got the guys, one said to me: 'You wonder how we got them so quickly? Well, we beat the confessions out of them!'

They were perhaps implying that if our police wanted to fairy about with things like due process and human rights that was our lookout. The entire experience had made me feel dirty, beaten and sick. So, covered in bruises and with the stitches still in, I decided that The Yunque was just the ticket. There was something about swimming in the crystalline river water after the descent that made everything better in the world and the memory of that part of Cuba is something I shall treasure for the rest of my days.

It was therefore a real pleasure to chat away the hours with this oaf about his other world a thousand miles and a thousand years away.

A Lada arrived out front and a few minutes later Ivan came into the garden. He picked a chirimoya from the tree and walked across and gave it to me. I thanked him politely. From his chest pocket he produced a cigar and handed it over.

'Is it a fake?' I asked.

He smiled an inscrutable smile and walked off to his little bunker at the end of the garden. The oaf gave me a light and I puffed slowly and contentedly in silence as cicadas droned on in the lowering sun.

It must have been about midnight. Banging on the door.

'Quick, get dressed!'

Blinking in the fluorescent light, I am led back into the interrogation room. Ivan is there. He has some sheets of paper in front of him.

'Under the power given to me by the laws of the Republic of Cuba I am detaining you in preventative custody. You are provisionally charged with revelations of state security and illegal activities. Sign here.'

I was shocked silent for a few seconds. 'What if I don't sign?'

'It doesn't make any difference.'

I read through the badly typed two sheets. Lots of bla bla and the meat and potatoes of it was just what he had said, but with reference to some statutes in the penal code.

I asked him quietly: 'What now?'

'You will be taken to another place, Villa Marista, and we will continue the process of instruction there. I will inform your wife this evening.'

'What is it like?' I stammered, knowing full well as I had been trying to find out for the past few months.

He smiled thinly. 'Small.'

VM

The gorilla politely knocks on the door before unlocking it and then brings in a bucket of hot water for my shower. They seem to work twenty-four-hour shifts and he looks as drained as I feel. I thank him. My clothes are pretty smelly by now, not just that sweaty bloke smell but something more animal as well. It must be the fight-or-flight pheromones. I wonder why human biologists decided on just the two options. What's wrong with three: fight, flight or panic? Isn't that the real human default mode, to faff about in terror between two terrible alternatives?

Being March, there is a slight chill in the air – it's probably around twelve degrees – and so the bucket gives off faint wisps of steam. I strip and carry it to the bathroom, stand in the defunct stall and ladle it using the old yoghurt pot left for the purpose. There is a foxed and badly scratched mirror over the sink. I can see my fuzzy reflection, a vague white arse with brown sleeves and legs. The morning sun catches the water splashing off my shoulders and it feels like I am already fading out of the real world. When will I wash in hot water again? When will I dress in my own clothes again? The day has started as it will finish, in a weird, dream-like trance. I feel strangely calm, a passive acceptance of what will happen. There is nothing I can do to change the process of State Security. They will do things their way and I will just be carried along. I need to save my strength for the interrogation and not waste energy fighting the mechanics of the system. I wonder what Felicia is doing. She's probably hunting all over the house for me, opening doors with her nose, having a quick sniff to check and then click, click, click, off down the hall.

Breakfast is a rushed affair ending in a quick pee and then handcuffs. I am led by silent, hard men to another beaten-up old Lada under the porch and pushed into the back. They lean against the car smoking and chatting, their radios squawking and jabbering. The temperature is starting to build up. The sun is boiling by 8 a.m. and hot dusty air gusts in. I can feel the sweat running down my shoulder blades and the cuffs are cutting into my wrists. They look like kids' toys but I can't break them. Another plain-clothes guy comes around the side and all of a sudden everyone is jumping into the car. An armed guard opens the gate and with crashing gears we are off. The thug beside me has roughly pushed my head between my knees without warning but he jerks me up after five minutes and the fields and villages flash past, gradually giving way to the outskirts of Havana. It's just another day on the street: hopeful shoppers scurrying to the Bodega ration stores to see if the black bean ration is available, kids kicking cans to school, workers pushing to get on the overloaded buses, everyone wrapped up in the daily grind. But in my house about ten kilometres from here they must be in a state of gut-churning worry. No doubt the kids will gamely be going to school, hoping that I will be there when they get home. Sarah will be trying to organise a lawyer, talking to the embassy and trying to stay calm.

The journey lasts a lifetime and yet it is over in seconds. A kaleidoscope of noise and smell sucked down a drain. I am now in a dimly lit room. The ceiling is made of broken fibre tiles with a great section missing, collapsed and never replaced. There are some random fluorescent strip lights. The capacitor of one is on the blink, so it clicks on and off. The walls are entirely covered in a dark timber-effect panelling that is coming off in places. A few derelict brown vinyl sofas are pushed against one wall and a timber bench screwed to the other. The air seems to be full of plaster or cement dust. It looks like a ransacked government building in post-invasion Baghdad.

I am sat on the bench and the guards slouch on the sofas. There is a high desk, also in dark timber. Behind it is a big dirty glass window into some kind of control room. Banks of CCTV screens flicker in the gloom. A fat old uniform with a row of decorations waddles out from the back, chewing a cigar. He looks at me briefly and waves me over. Then he sticks his one hand out in the direction of the guys that brought me here. No love lost between them, they heave themselves upright and slap the transfer documents into his hand. He signs various bits of paper, gives them a receipt and they unlock me. They leave saying nothing. Fatty coughs a bit, picks his nose and then asks me to empty my pockets and hand over my watch and shoelaces. I sign a chit for them but he keeps both copies so maybe it's the last I shall ever see of my watch.

Then two very young guards in MININT olive fatigues take me off to a side room. Another boy, earnest yet nervous, is waiting at a desk. Stumbling over the words he explains that I have to fill in a form. I can feel his fear of me. They must tell them we are dangerous monsters. Another man enters and what little confidence the boy has now evaporates. About my age, he is a handsome man who introduces himself in perfect American English. He is a major. He asks me about my family.

'How do you think they are coping with the situation?'

Is this a genuine question or some kind of threat? His face gives nothing away. Then he explains the rules. They are pretty simple.

'From now on you have no name. You are prisoner two one seven.'

My lucky number.

'When you are out of the cell you walk on the left-hand side with your head facing down and hands behind your back.

You never look at anyone. At each door or staircase you face
the wall until told to proceed. You will obey the officials. If
you do not you will be punished. If you are ill then call for
the nurse. You will be fed in your cell three times a day. Any
questions?'

'Can I call my wife?'

'No, we will arrange for her to visit.'

'When will the embassy visit?'

'These things take time.'

I can feel a desperate lump forming in my throat. I concentrate hard not to tear up. 'Can I have something to read?'

'That depends on your instructor. Your instructor decides
on your conditions and safety. This depends on your conduct.'

'Do I have a lawyer?'

He laughs. 'This also takes a long time. Take my advice,
don't wait.'

I am then led off to a succession of dingy rooms where I am
fingerprinted, photographed and have blood taken to test for
hepatitis, Aids and TB. Then I am pushed into a musty laundry and told to strip while they issue me with a second-hand
uniform. It's a washed-out slate-blue number in scratchy nylon. Very me. I get shorts, long trousers and two shirts with a
stinky towel thrown in, plus two sheets and a pillow case. In
a bit of a daze, all sounds scrambled and muffled, I am prod-
ded along a tiny corridor that feels subterranean. There is the
unmistakable smell of mouldy earth and damp concrete in the
air. My shoulders feel like they are brushing the sides and my
head skims the ceiling. It's *Alice in Wonderland* by sociopathic
commies.

This place was originally meant to have been a seminary
but there is no sign of any heavenly inspiration now. God
has deserted the place and it is in the hands of the dark side.
The pretty Catholic bit must be at the front, on the public street. This section at the rear was obviously designed by
the KGB but then pimped and crimped Cuban style. This

means that the basic structure is built of precast concrete panels, beams and slabs, like a giant's Lego set, but all the finishes and alterations are half-sized and use a bizarre range of domestic materials. This is where captured suspected CIA guys are brought, where purged officials repent and where all Cubans fear to tread. This is where American pensioner Alan Gross was interrogated for months on end to try to prove that he was a spy and not some deluded Jewish activist. This is their Lubyanka, their Gestapo headquarters. These crude, hulking green blocks are designed to extract confessions, real or fantasy, and then mentally cripple the enemies of state. It has a fearsome reputation for psychological torture. 'Everyone sings,' they say, and nobody leaves without being changed for ever.

We pop out into a broad corridor. It's the cell block. No time to look as the rules now kick in, so head down I shuffle along as instructed. I am pushed into a side room and told to put all my things on top of a disgustingly filthy, shit-stained, one-inch foam mattress. A pillow mottled with bloodstains is chucked on the top. I stare at the blood in disbelief, a wave of despair building inside me. They cannot be serious. I am told to pick up the entire load and walk down through the first set of gates. It's a long corridor with dirty chipped tiles underfoot, lots of pipes slung from the ceiling and the occasional pool of dirty water where rusty taps drip. It is brightly lit and the walls had once been painted a dirty yellow grey. A wall-mounted, cartoon-sized fan is humming, sending a faint draught towards me. It smells strongly of sadness and faintly of shit. I shuffle along, now almost catatonic. The guard in front has a long chain looping around him and a huge wobbly rubber baton that bangs against the wall as he marches. All is silent except for the dripping of water, the squeaking of the guards' boots and a man sobbing in a cell. I count thirty-two doors. I am told to stop and face the wall while Mr Rubber Baton fumbles with his key chain.

My nose is six inches from the wall. I read the guards' obscene graffiti, scrawled in childish pencil. And then the true significance of what has happened hits me. It isn't going to go away and it isn't going to get better for a long time. The gate and then the door clang open with a foul rush of stale air, revealing a tiny cave with three pale faces blinking like moles in the light. I step into my new life. My dungeon.

Castro's zoo

A US king-size mattress measures 72 inches by 80 inches. That is about 1.8 metres by 2 metres square.

Introductions are brief and conversation is halting and sparse. The burned-out Cuban wrecks are silent for hours at a time, just faint mutterings as they succumb to imaginary conversations. The despairing air slows my metabolism to a crawl and I lie panting for oxygen and leaking sweat. I can feel my tongue turn to aluminium.

The universe has shrunk to the size of a five-star mattress. A perverse professional reference point that comes to me in a moment of bleak, black humour. But no cool Egyptian cotton sheets, no pillows smelling of my wife's hair, no lazy Sunday morning with the kids all snuggled up reading books and squabbling over who gets to lie with their head on my chest.

No. This is a standard cell in Villa Marista. A dungeon I will have to share with three other people for months, even years. My God, four people in a tiny concrete box in a country where the summer temperature is 40 degrees with 80 per cent humidity. I make an inventory of the grim cell.

The concrete walls were painted many years ago but are now encrusted with what you would expect: a splattered dank canvas crawling with spidery, hopeless scrapings of graffiti and cancerous blooms of efflorescence from the reaction of decades of human effluent on ancient cement.

Man-sized metal folding shelves hang from the wall on rusty chains. The lower ones are dank and fetid, the upper ones brighter and hotter, an inch of rotten foam mattress the only relief from the hip-shattering hardness. With the bed shelves folded down the space between them is about twelve inches. Just enough for a man to move crab-wise up and down.

I can touch the ceiling. Flakes of powdery paint come off on my fingertips. The floor tiles have lost their glaze, the central strip rubbed down by the eternal shuffling of the damned. Cockroaches scuttle in under the door. There are three narrow, angled slots to the outside which allow a little air to circulate but no view of the sky. Ancient underpants are drying slowly.

There is a strip light on permanently. It casts a sickly fluorescent pallor that makes my hands look jaundiced and my cellmates resemble the living dead. I will find in time that it is so weak it damages your eyesight and yet perversely so harsh that after a few weeks it burns like a desert sun.

The washing and toilet facilities are a three-foot-square sunken trough by the cell door. A revolting scupper in the middle is for shit, piss and washing water. I am told I am to get four one-and-a-half litre bottles of water a day. In time I will discover there are two luxury cells that have bunks instead of shelves and the space between them is about four feet, big enough for a chair and some limited exercise. They have slightly less primitive bathroom arrangements but apart from that they are the same.

These dungeons were built to KGB technical specifications. We are reduced to animals in a zoo for enemies of the state. The real Havana zoo is a profoundly depressing place. Crumbling concrete pits with sheer walls entombing deranged and lonely bears, tiny concrete and steel-barred pens where big cats pace back and forth hissing in mangy fury, and saddest of all a catatonic Andean condor sat on a perch in a bell-shaped rusting cage with a diameter less than its majestic wingspan. Beneath it the half-eaten leg of a street dog, covered in a living carpet of maggots and flies. Standing in front of these sad creatures, licking ice creams, the whole family, even the tiniest child, is affected by the cruelty of it all.

'Can we go Dad, it's scary.'

And now here I am in Raúl's private zoo. No visitors here. Just us, alone with our thoughts.

At random times the Judas hole bangs open and a disembodied voice shouts: 'Two one seven, prepare yourself!' They never say why. The interrogation rooms are off the tiny corridor that leads back to the entrance. They are brightly lit, a plastic chair bolted to the floor set back from a simple table. There are two chairs on the other side. A ceiling-mounted camera blinks at me, recording everything. Compared to everywhere else the room is clean, but it is freezing cold. The air conditioning is on full blast and the contrast with the cell is horrible. Within thirty minutes the sweat has chilled and I am trying to control my shivering. It also makes me want to urinate. At times the interrogations are very formally structured, with a translator faithfully repeating each sentence. Ivan's moods vary. Sometimes he is really aggressive, shouting and banging the table while making all sorts of threats. Other times he makes jokes and gives the appearance of being friendly. But it is not his mood that changes: it's all part of the game. I see this clearly now. He wants me to be scared of his aggressive unreasonable persona and thus to create a need in me to please his nice persona. Some days he is alone. He asks me a question that requires a long explanation and then just sits there looking at me in silence. Not saying a word. Then he calls for a guard to take me back to the dungeon.

During one session they show me a handful of photos of people taken at immigration, asking if I know any of them. They were pale, bug-eyed and guilty-looking as they shuffled in front of the immigration counter. Two of them I did recognise, both ex-British embassy in Havana: one had been the consul, now retired, the other a number two, now an ambassador elsewhere. Ivan is testing me; he knows I knew both of them socially.

Ivan's mood darkens. 'Are these the people you pass information to?'

I try to reply calmly. 'What information? I don't have any.'

'Don't lie to me. You have no idea how serious this is.'

Oh, but I do. And so it goes on and on, day in, day out.

In time the subject changes to the financial transactions of the company. He tells me that three workers in my office are undertaking unlicensed activities, namely processing bills of exchange. I argue that this has been going on for ten years, that we are inspected and audited three times a year and that every transaction has to be approved by both the central bank and the relevant ministry, so how can it not be authorised? But he isn't listening, he is just adding it to the list of crimes.

The interrogations pluck me out of the never-ending routine of jail at random intervals. I am carried off down twisting and tortuous corridors and past padlocked doors with whimpering inmates to another parallel world, a world that is brighter, harder and more dangerous. The reasonableness of the clean laminate table and the cheerful photo of Raúl smiling like a reluctant headmaster invite me to confess or, better still, denounce.

The hours creep along in a slow routine. At 6.30 a.m. the Judas hole bangs open and the nurse passes through pills. My cellmates are all afflicted with a variety of illnesses real and imagined. Two are on heavy tranquillisers, the other is ill with hypertension and diabetes. At 7 a.m. a 50-gram roll spread with some kind of meat paste or margarine is passed in. Sometimes with a powdered soft drink that we all think has bromide in it. At 11.30 there is a metal tray with some rice or beans, a tinned sardine or a tiny bit of gristly pork with some shredded cabbage or pickled vegetable. We take it in turns to sit with a sheet of newspaper on our laps to stop our clothes getting dirty. At 5.30 p.m. the same again. The nurse returns at 7.30 p.m. and then sometimes another bread roll at about 9 p.m. Then from 10 p.m. drifting in and out of consciousness to wake exhausted at 6 a.m. to the tannoy blasting out the national anthem. Despite the rigid regime of mealtimes and medication, I lose track of time.

Unusually, now I get called after supper.

Ivan ignores my 'good evening' when I enter the interrogation room. He looks up, his eyes dark with anger. 'Sit. Tell me about X. What was the business you did with him?'

Taken aback, I struggle to even remember the man. 'Hmm. About five or six years ago he was introduced to us. I think he was a business development guy from the Basic Industry Ministry. He was trying to get us to invest in some projects. It's a long time ago.'

'What projects exactly?' he interrupts impatiently.

'Hmm. A salt pan evaporation project, a zeolite mine and a gypsum mine. Zeolite was for a material to use on stable floors to soak up horse piss and the gypsum was for plasterboard.'

'What information did he give you?'

'Urr. Business plans and that sort of thing. I studied them, did some research, we had a few meetings and we declined. Not cost-effective in Cuba. Low market price, no off-takers, high investment. Useless really. The salt could have worked. After all, the sun is free, the salt in the sea is free. But the labour cost here is high. More expensive than Jamaica. We found out that for the gypsum business you had already signed up with somebody else. You were using us to simply get a dummy price to use in your negotiations. And as for zeolite, well, it was just useless. So we didn't do any business.'

'You capitalists make me sick,' he sneered. 'All you think of is profit. We are poor but we have dignity. Why did he come to you?'

'We invest in projects in Cuba, you know that. Minvec send people to us all the time. The guy was just doing his job. Until you closed us down we were funding all sorts of projects for Cuba. But we probably invested in only one project for every fifty we looked at.'

Checking his notes he started closing in. 'Who did you share the business plans with?'

'Well obviously we talked to various international mining companies to see if they were interested. We would need a technical partner. We would supply Cuba know-how and capital and debt.'

'When did you last see him?'

'He turned up at the office a few years later. He had been fired and had a broken arm. I think he had some complicated story about his apartment and his wife. I can't remember the details but she had kicked him out.'

He leaned back and looked over steepled fingers. 'Did you give him money?'

'Sure, we gave him a few hundred bucks, wished him good luck and never saw him again. It was years ago. Why? What's wrong with that?'

'Why did you give him money?'

I sensed danger was approaching now. 'We felt sorry for the guy. No job, broken arm, wife left him and kicked him out. It was just a gift.'

Leaning forward he banged the table. 'You're lying. You capitalists don't give anything for nothing do you? It is your religion. You gave him money for information. And he has been arrested for giving information to our enemies so far unrelated to your case. So now you have a new problem.'

And with that he stood up and called the guard, with a final, 'Get out.'

Words in my head on the way back to the dungeon. Fuck. Fuck. Fuck. This is madness. We are all getting arrested as spies just for doing our jobs. This is really scary. I'm in here forever.

The cell door slams, a voice in the gloom asks: 'How did it go? You look shit.'

'Not good I think,' I mutter and crawl on to my dark shelf and face the wall. The line of tiny, orange ants passes through the wall that entombs me and I lie for hours thinking about the hopelessness of it all and wishing I could do the same.

I succumb to a Cuban fear. Every day I wake to find I am still buried alive. A hundred years ago a wealthy socialite requested that a working telephone be installed in the family catacomb in a Havana necropolis, as she had an abiding fear of being buried alive. It was disconnected by the revolution, the same revolution that has buried so many of its people and guests, also without telephones. Beneath the Marxist–Leninist voodoo is a stranger and stronger force, Santeria. And the same necropolis that disconnected the wealthy still has to post nocturnal guards to stop the theft of human bones. In this country a small pile of black, burned bone dust left for you will guarantee calamity, and from the time of the slaves people protect their home with a steel chain cast in the concrete step. One night, a cellmate snaps out of his week-long stupor, opens his mouth in a hyena gape and curls his tongue in my face. His rotten breath smells of death. It is tattooed underneath with the secret symbols of the Abakua. These are a dangerous offshoot of Santeria, one that has been implicated in ritual death murders and has blossomed into a criminalised secret society that revels in violence. With a grin he licks his lips and slips back on to his shelf and back to sleep.

This place is really freaking me out.

I lie hugging my knees and with my face to the cell wall, thoughts flitting like a paranoid bee, trying to make sense of everything. Well, anything actually. What are these secrets I have given to their enemies?

A Cuban saying goes round and round in my head, 'For every solution we have a problem', and as lunch is approaching in a few, or is it a million, hours one of my favourites bubbles to the top: 'The three great successes of the revolution are sport, health and education and the three failures are breakfast, lunch and dinner.' But these bitter sweet truths, dear to all Cubans, are elbowed aside by a darker, official phrase,

'Patriotism or death', a statement brutal in both simplicity and implicit menace.

*   *   *

Oh Cuba, what a mad, bad history. What did you do to deserve it and what did I do to deserve this? A mountain of words have been written trying to document, sieve and sort and then attempt to interpret the secret, impossible dreams of Fidel. But what of his brother? The charisma-free enigma that weaselled his way to dictatorship. I haven't met a single Cuban that has a good word to say about him.

It seems these wispy threads, strong as steel and longer than a monk's memory, have bound me to my destiny. A nebulous web across time and space connects me to characters that shone from the front page of every newspaper on the planet on 1 January 1959, two years before I was born.

Fidel, Che, Camilo and Ochoa smiled incredulous grins. A bunch of handsome guys riding a tank who had pulled off the impossible by bringing a fat rotter to his knees in a short, Homeric campaign which saw a band of fifty-three dreamers morph into a popular army of peasants and intellectuals. Chomping cigars, cracking jokes and blowing kisses to the ecstatic crowds, these were the four commanders of the revolution that swept the squalid US puppet Batista from his palace. Two of them, Che and Fidel, became the poster gods for generations of deluded students and their names continue to inspire hope for millions of the dispossessed on the world stage. But for the other two, Camilo Cienfuegos and Ochoa, obscurity and damnation were waiting in the wings.

Camilo was adored by all. Being a brave and successful combat leader he had earned the respect of his revolutionary movement. And with his silver-screen good looks and his humble, amiable demeanour he was the natural housewife's choice, a friendly open face who promised reconciliation to a broken country. Ochoa had proven himself to be the most gifted military leader and, in the brutal meritocracy of war, while Fidel had the innate gift for political strategy it was Ochoa who had won the battle. Every single soldier knew it and they saluted the man, not the uniform. And so it was that afterwards, while Fidel orchestrated his bid for immortality and Che stalked the underground chambers of Morro Castle, conducting executions, Ochoa retained command of the largest army, the Second Front, in Oriente and Camilo toured the country pressing the flesh, sweeping rocks from the road and giving absolution to the vanquished.

History isn't absolving me, it's eating me alive. This filthy dark dungeon is consuming me. I can't even work out if I am awake or asleep half the time. It's turning into one endless nightmare. History has squirmed and turned so many times in Cuba. The party's editorial nib has scratched out and rewritten so much newsprint and the persecuted, secretive theories of the people have created an insane layer cake of parallel realities over which Fidel and now Raúl reign absolute.

Camilo's little Cessna just vanished one day. A tragic accident with no evidence. Any lingering chances of a happy ending for Cuba died that day. The facts invite conspiracy. The entire country called Raúl 'Chinita' behind his back, the little Chinese girl, an insult that reflected the people's perception of his character and their lack of respect for his achievements. Fidel had just announced that Raúl was to be made supreme military commander. Ochoa, with the army behind him, refused to accept a subordinate position, probably smelling nepotism and worse. Camilo was asked to try and patch things up. On his way back he just disappeared. Exiled former bodyguards spread different endings to the story. Camilo came back with no deal and during the ensuing argument challenged Raúl 'to shoot me in the balls if you have any, you pussy!' and Raúl did exactly that.

A few years later a disillusioned Che discovered that there was no room for him in Cuba and after a series of doomed attempts at fomenting world revolution he was betrayed to the CIA and murdered in Bolivia. Who knew his location on that mountain path? Well, the people of Cuba had their private suspicions about who told the CIA.

And then in 1989 came the trial of Ochoa. More popular with the army than ever, having just returned from a distinguished campaign in Angola, he was charged with treason and trafficking of diamonds, ivory and drugs. After a brief show trial he was executed and the great purge of the army and the police commenced.

Fast-forward to last year. An elderly Fidel has been ill for months and the country waits for news. Media rules the mind these days and so instead of a flat-footed trial, meetings are called at every party branch office, every union and youth party office, every ministry, university or institution and they are all shown a video that condemns the two most senior politicians in the land: Carlos Lage, the prime minister who engineered the engagement of international investment that rescued the country, and Felipe Pérez Roque, the foreign minister who has led the recent changes in foreign policy. The video was a masterpiece of political assassination. It mixed taped conversations, surveillance footage and solemn denunciations of treason and corruption. Not only Lage and Roque but an entire political class is doomed in the first five seconds and with that Raúl starts his slow-motion *coup d'état* that gifts him the seat he has dreamed of all these long years in the shade.

Rather more worryingly for us, the central scene was secretly filmed on the rooftop pool deck of the lovely hotel which Lage had hired for his nephew's wedding and which we had built and part owned. What a ghastly coincidence. Surely anyone can see that.

Visitors

I've been here seven days and still no visit from my wife, no news about a diplomatic visit and no lawyer. The initial shock has given way to numb, dumb disbelief.

The Judas hole bangs open and a guard shouts: 'Two one seven you have visitor, get ready for shaving!'

My cellmates explain that I will be led off to a room to be shaved. I grab a towel and soap and put on my flip-flops, just in time for the door to open. The guard asks to see my identification. This is a little scrap of cardboard torn from a carton with 217 written on it in biro. If I lose it I am in trouble. I am taken through a locked gate and past the landing of an echoing staircase, all the while with my head down and keeping to the left. The room has a dirty window high up and I get a glimpse of the sky, the first since I got here. My God, it's bright and sunny outside. There are two guards, one absent-mindedly squeezing his blackheads in a spattered mirror, the other lying back in an ancient barber's chair, humming to himself. Weirdly, a broken contraption for drying Soviet beehives stands in the corner. The kind of thing they must have had in Iron Curtain salons in the fifties but now are perhaps used for some sinister kind of electrical torture. The guard who isn't busy picking spots gives me a broad grin, the first kind face I have seen for some time. He tells me to soap my face and sit down. We exchange places and I lie back, zoning into the sky while he scrapes my stubble off. Clouds drift past, thousands of feet above and indifferent to all this sordid mess below. It's over in a few minutes and I catch sight of myself in the mirror while I rinse. My face is drawn and haunted.

'Quick, quick,' he says, not wanting me to dawdle. I rub my face dry and then it's back to the cell. I have mere minutes to flap about and take the letters I have written from under the mattress before: 'Two one seven prepare yourself.'

The door bangs open and I am led off through some gates back to the echoing staircase. In a tiny side room I am searched. Then it's down a level and I am pushed to the left of an office door, my nose pressed to the wall. A woman official comes along, checks my cardboard ID and curtly orders: 'Two one seven, come.' She glides in front to double-check the visiting room.

The urbane major is sitting in there. In perfect English, he tells me that my wife has come to visit. While we wait he wants to chat about literature. He is a great fan of Dickens apparently. So am I, but I wonder what Charles would make of *Great Expectations* being considered a seminal critique of capitalism and preferred reading for the Cuban state thought police. The room is painted pale yellow and overcrowded with tatty lounge furniture. Our knees almost touch. I sit there nodding in agreement, hardly paying any attention, my heart bursting with longing and dread. Then he changes gear and tells me bluntly that I am not allowed to discuss details of my case with her.

A side door opens and there is Sarah, preceded by a grinning Ivan. Uncertain about protocol, about whether we can touch or not, we hold back for a second and then Sarah and I hug and sit side by side on the sofa, cautiously holding hands. She is wearing a big brave smile, white trousers and, rather touchingly, a favourite team polo shirt I had for last year's marlin fishing tournament. Her hair is freshly cut and I breathe in the comforting scent of my darling wife.

She wants to know how I am. My mouth says 'I'm fine' but my eyes must tell a different story and she bites her lip and gives my hand a damp squeeze. Neither of us wish to gift them the pleasure of our tears. I ask her about how the family is holding up and how Oscar's birthday party went. She says they are all being terribly brave and that all our friends are being very supportive. Oscar's party was a bit subdued, poor boy. He was already having a difficult year and now this.

'Well the good news is that your mum took the first flight out, so she is taking charge of the kids while I concentrate on the lawyer and the embassy. She's being her usual no-nonsense self. Thank God she turned up. Your sister will arrive in a week or so and then your brother will turn up when she has gone, so we have lots of support. Now, I have lots of questions for you.'

She has brought in a little notebook and runs down a checklist. It has been very difficult to actually get a lawyer appointed. She wants to double-check I am happy with the selection. He is one of the most senior lawyers in the land, a former chief prosecutor of Cuba with a rather formidable reputation. The lawyers and the police are all working for the Castros so my family decided we might as well have one with good contacts and who has batted for both sides.

I turn to Ivan. 'When can I see him?' He shrugs his shoulders.

Sarah tells me the ambassador has personally dropped by most days and is taking a very active interest. That is heartening news. I always felt that she was a dependable professional and, above all, a friend.

I again turn to Ivan. 'When is the diplomatic visit?' Again he shrugs his shoulders.

Then Sarah starts to crumble. Her face buckles and with a wobbling voice she blurts out: 'Ivan tells me you are held for something called revelations of state secrets. Spying. He says we have to prepare ourselves that you could be away for fifteen to twenty years. Oh, darling.'

And tears start to well up in her eyes. Getting control of herself she continues: 'Don't worry, we will get you out of here. Don't give up, it's only a matter of time.'

Ivan snorts derisively while the major smirks, twiddling his thumbs. We drag our conversation back to safer, more practical ground. In a voice gradually rediscovering its strength, she tells me she has brought some books, underwear, a flannel and towel, a pen and some paper and, most preciously, some letters plus of course the undying love of all the family. And then Ivan wraps it up.

'I will check the letters and books and you should get them in a day or so. It's time to finish. The family visit is once a week for twenty minutes. I will agree which day with Sarah. You are allowed a maximum of three visitors but all must be family.'

So with a final hug I am led out and I dare not look back. Twenty minutes snatched from a softer, brighter world after all these days of lonely despair and sucker-punch interrogations. During the search on my way back to the dungeon, I pluck out the lining of my pockets to show no contraband while warm tears of despair well up from my belly.

A few days later, my things are delivered to me. I treasure the letters from the kids. Naively articulate, with styles as distinctive as each of them is in the flesh, the carefully printed sentences briefly transport me back to my home. The flannel is immediately put to use as a sleeping aid. It becomes a most valuable possession. I place it over my eyes and nose when I lie down to sleep. It blocks out some of the light and masks a little of the smell. For a day or two it carries an elusive faint whiff of sunshine from the clothes line, and it reminds me of bees buzzing and the brilliant dragonflies that hunt between the stirring sheets. This is the first tiny, tiny way to have some control over my life. I need to discover more.

Then another mid-morning shave. The same jolly guy does the honours. They are not allowed to make conversation so it is a companiable silence, ending with orders to dry and go. On the way out he winks and mouths, 'diplomatic visit'. My heart does a somersault and on the march back to my cell I quickly rehearse all the things I need to say, the things I need to hear and my plan of action.

In the time it takes to change from uniform shorts to trousers and vest to short sleeves I am called out. It's back down to the visiting room and there are the ambassador and Ivan exchanging pleasantries, a tray set with the Bulgarian china coffee service between them and a plastic bag overflowing with magazines and stuff sat on the sofa. Ivan leaps up and shakes my hand vigorously, smiling like a crocodile on its best behaviour.

'Ah Purvis, how are you?'

He had clearly forgotten that two hours earlier he had been grilling me in the freezing blast of his chamber. Diana, the ambassador, stands up and gives me a proper bear hug, then holds me at arm's length, looks intently into my eyes and says brightly: 'How are they treating you?'

'Okay, I guess.'

'I'm sorry it's taken so long to see you, you can imagine. MININT are pretty slow at access and they blame MINREX. It's very frustrating. We had to write four diplomatic notes.' Looking imperiously at Ivan, she continues: 'I've brought you a few things and Ivan promises that you will get them. Magazines, a few books. I apologise for them, they look a bit chicklit to me but it was all I had on the shelf. Oh, and some biscuits.'

We sit down. The ambassador asks if I would like some coffee. There isn't a third cup.

'I would love some.'

'I think we are missing a cup,' she says to the room. Ivan shifts his bottom as if an ant was beginning to annoy him, jumps up and shouts out of the door for a cup and then explains the situation in a ruffled sort of way. The caffeine kicks in like a mule.

'Well Purvis, you know we have detained you for revelations

of state security. This is difficult and the sentence is severe. We will need you to co-operate so that we can clear it up. I have explained to the ambassador that your case is a closed file, it is secret, therefore special rules apply. Your lawyer will be able to advise you.'

'But I haven't seen a lawyer. When can I see a lawyer?'

Opening his hands in benign innocence, he replies: 'Your wife has been very slow in appointing one. This is not our fault.'

The ambassador and I exchange a look. 'So tell me about the interrogation.'

'It's not interrogation, it is the process of instruction,' he interrupts.

'You were saying, Stephen.'

'Well, it has been pretty much constant now ever since they arrested me. Sometimes once a day, sometimes three times. That's about two weeks now. No lawyer and I have no idea what my rights are. The cell is filthy, dark and very small.'

'And the food? You look a bit skinny. Are they starving you?'

'It's horrible, but I eat it. I need vitamins and calcium and there are hardly any vegetables and no fruit. I need water as well.'

'Your cellmates?'

'All Cuban, they seem okay.'

'Don't discuss your case with them if you know what I mean.'

Ivan looks insulted at this. She continues. 'And how about exercise?'

'They say I will get fifteen minutes of sun a week but so far nothing.'

'Time to finish, ambassador.' Ivan taps his watch, a wistful smile suggesting that it pains him to bring this jolly gathering to a close. She lets go of my hand, which she has been holding for the last five minutes, and puts it on my knee. Is it compassion or is it a gesture of solidarity? Whatever her reason, it gives me more comfort than her words.

'Ivan, I want you to promise me that he gets proper drinking water and vitamins. His family can bring them. Is that clear? I insist that he gets his exercise. Can you promise me that as well, please? I don't need to remind you of the great friendship that exists between our countries and also that Cuba has signed international conventions regarding the treatment of prisoners, access to lawyers and diplomatic visits and the legal process. I will be writing to Minrex and starting the process for the next visit.'

'Of course ambassador, of course. So Purvis, time to go.' We stand and he shakes my hand with an oily smile. 'See you soon.'

The ambassador gives me a big hug and whispers: 'Be brave, see you in a month.'

Going to see Fidel and Raúl

A week passes. Interrogations come at random intervals. Some days three sessions, some days nothing. Apart from a trip to the medical room for weighing I never leave the dungeon and the walls begin to sing to me. With a heavy heart I write a resignation letter to the board of the international school. I know that the chair and the principal will be happy for me to keep my position as vice chair until I am either charged or released, partly because they will have faith and partly because that is what should happen in a normal country. But it is crystal clear to me now that I am caught in the grip of something terrible and it isn't going to let go of my ankles soon. So I write what I hope comes across as a brave farewell. I was quietly proud of what we had managed to do in the school over the past eight years and there were a few times when I had actually done something half decent. Originally I had led a sort of peasants' revolt at a hike in school fees that would have meant that many of the poorer kids would have to leave. The board at that time were so irritated by me that they suggested that instead of moaning I join and do something productive. So I did and I have to say it was the first time in my life when I felt I was actually contributing something concrete to my community. I felt part of something bigger. Now I would never get that plaque. Then I write to the kids, a letter to each in turn. I spend hours on draft after draft, trying to get the balance of honesty and cheerful calm just right. Each time I get to the last sentence I have to start swallowing while I screw it up and start again.

A 5-litre bottle of clean water arrives for me one afternoon and the next morning the nurse has a multivitamin tablet for me. Thank you ambassador.

It's Tuesday. I know because I have made a tiny calendar so I can keep track of time. Ivan has told me that I have the family visit organised for Tuesdays, so I wake today beside myself at the prospect of seeing Sarah and two of the kids and getting some news.

The shave, search and staircase pass in a blur and all of a sudden I am in the visiting room waiting for the second door to open. Sarah walks in without the kids, looking terribly tired and careworn. She has taken care with her clothes and hair but something is not right. Her smile is brittle, about to shatter into a thousand pieces. As we sit she is wringing her hands. Her skin is as grey as mine feels. We rush through the 'how is everyone' questions and then she fusses over a list of things to do. She is talking abstractedly as if she were outside her body looking in.

'I think I am doing very well,' she tells Ivan. 'I have been making lists.'

Ivan looks at me and in an instant I can see that he senses something is wrong as well. For a millisecond he looks almost concerned, but then his bluff, secret police interrogator moustache takes over and he is acting the part again.

Her list is totally random. She ranges from the irrational 'I think we should sell the dog' to the panicky 'I want the kids to go to England now' to the matter-of-fact, 'The lawyer will only accept a cash payment of five thousand dollars but it's almost impossible to get a bank to give me that much. Do you think I should tell them it is for lawyers' fees?' I try to calm her down and she pretends that she is fine. 'I'm just a little tired, that's all. I think I will take the phone off the hook. It never stops ringing.'

After the visit I return to my cell very worried. She is not coping with this. I read the kids' letters. They don't mention her odd behaviour and neither does my mum in hers. Instead she focuses on news from London and the practical things in play. I take small comfort from that but have a nagging feeling that things are not right. I will have to wait until next week to see how things develop, but I am sick with worry now and not just for myself. While I fretted in the gloom, things at home were starting to reach a crisis. I had a bad feeling and, as I was to find out later, things unravelled very quickly.

Friends, both true and false-flagged, dropped by at all hours motivated by compassion or curiosity, or both. The phone never stopped ringing and the emails pinged twenty-four hours a day. Sarah, already worried sick, never had a minute to be calm and quiet in order to rationalise the situation. People were anxious for news and because there was none of substance, gossip ballooned to fill the vacuum. The only concrete facts given out by the family were that I had been taken by State Security, that I had disappeared off the face of the earth and that after five days of interrogation I had been taken to the notorious Villa Marista, where dissidents, spies and enemies of the state simply vanish, that I hadn't seen a lawyer or a diplomat and finally that this sinister teniente coronel had come to the house to tell Sarah that I could be away for up to twenty years. Revelations of state secrets is such an incendiary topic that the family decided to never mention it, instead just saying that it was for 'illicit activities', a rather vague crime that covers anything from selling potatoes to running a back-street café. But the word was out, leaking from the company. So in the absence of anything more toothsome, and like a fire fuelled by speculation, the stories swirled around the bars, cocktail parties and coffee mornings that I was a spy, that I was involved in dark things, that they had always suspected me of being a bad one and so on. Supposed friends repeated the most outrageous nonsense, which like all gossip in a sensation-starved environment took on a life of its own, morphed over kitchen tables then mutated through drivers'

windows at traffic lights before finally coming full circle in
the school playground. The children, already very concerned,
were now confused and frightened by this crazy gossip and
Sarah and my mum tried patiently to explain the facts and to
play down the likely future scenarios. The ambassador continued to be supportive, checking up on the family daily, which
helped to calm the situation. But it was simply prolonging
the inevitable calamity, and the situation appeared to be
getting bleaker by the day.

The lawyer prevaricated and shuffled paper, explaining that
the procedure for appointing a lawyer was slow and formulaic.
In reality it was part of the script, the lawyer having to keep
well out of it until the initial interrogation is over. It was to
be twenty-eight days before I finally saw him, by which time
the lemon had been properly squeezed and I could enjoy hearing my rights retrospectively. Apparently I had always had
the right to remain silent.

Sarah developed a hypersensitivity to sounds and smells.
Her suspicion about the extent of State Security surveillance
of the family tipped in slow motion into a full-blown paranoia. My mum started to screen all calls and emails, diverting
all except those she felt would not overstimulate Sarah. She
had convinced herself that they were coming for her next. Exhausted, she would weep uncontrollably, the kids taking it in
turns to lie with her during the night, stroking her hair and
trying to take her mind off it. Even the previously feral cat,
Misou II, pitched in to help, moving in to take permanent
residence in our bedroom.

Sarah started to talk about herself as if she were an observer
of her own body, repeating a heart-breaking mantra: 'I think
I'm doing rather well considering. I've been making lots
of lists.' Finally, after two weeks, in an exhaustion-induced
panic, she called our friends Frans and Lotte at 3 a.m. and
begged them to come straight away. When they got there
a terrified guard rushed them through, all his bluff military

pretence blown away by the appalling scene inside. Sarah was standing wild-eyed in the kitchen screaming hysterically, the kids with their arms wound around her trying to calm her down. My mum was on the phone trying to summon help while Felicia the dog cowered in the corner, terrified. Frans and Lotte bundled her into their four-by-four and immediately set off for the foreigners' hospital. And so started my family's parallel nightmare.

Frans drove fast through the dark streets, Sarah being comforted in a tight embrace in the back by Lotte. Dozing orderlies jumped up to help drag Sarah into the treatment area. The smart, ordered calm of Cira Garcia at midnight, where Naomi had been on an intravenous drip after a terrible throat infection, where I had been stitched up numerous times and where we all get our teeth done, was fractured by incoherent shouting. The doctor gives her a huge injection of tranquilliser and then confers with the bosses. They cannot treat her here, they simply don't have the facilities or the expertise.

The drugs take their effect and Sarah is calmed. Frans and Lotte are summoned into the room to take her away and the hospital administrator makes his excuses.

Sarah, though calm, is clearly not well. 'I know why they have injected me. It's because they are taking me to see Fidel and Raúl and they want me to forget the route. But I will stay awake,' she confides, nodding firstly in agreement with herself and secondly to sleep. After she had been carried unconscious to a bed in their silent house, Frans and Lotte drink tea in the kitchen and confer on the telephone with my mum. Together they try to decide what to do tomorrow.

My mum gets the kids up at dawn, sits them down for breakfast and gives them a simple, factual account of what has just happened. It is received with a mixture of concern about their mother and relief that she will get medical treatment, but hanging over the subdued kitchen table is a menacing cloud of uncertainty. My mum calls a conference of Sarah's closest friends, who all want to help. Between them they create a simple rota. They will take it in turns to shop, cook and deliver an evening meal and the children's packed lunches so Mum can concentrate on dealing with the embassy and the lawyer. And so started a support network that lasted the entire ordeal.

A couple of well-connected friends lead the charge on finding a hospital that will accept her. They are able to find a sympathetic doctor at the best psychiatric hospital, who says he is willing to help. So Frans and Lotte take Sarah there. But it's a horrific-looking place, with all the patients dressed in Belsen-style striped pyjamas wandering around dusty wards in various stages of dementia. After one day, some well-meaning friends storm the ward and demand that she gets better conditions. The doctor, who was going out on a limb letting in a foreigner, takes fright and tells Frans and Lotte that Sarah will have to leave with nothing but another injection, and makes a recommendation that she is to be kept secluded and should avoid all emotional stimulation. So after just one night of care it's back to square one.

More bad news. The airlines have confirmed that they will not take her in that condition, so the family is stuck with no way to get her home for treatment and no treatment in Cuba. My mum has to start the process of getting custody of the kids, which the ambassador then solves with great speed. The next day another hospital is found that might take Sarah. So again Frans and Lotte take her to a new hospital. On the way, Sarah in her drugged delusions tells them that she is on her way to see God. She thinks she is going to be killed. After a consultation, they also turn her away. They cannot treat a non-native speaker, as part of the therapy is cognitive and relies on the patient having perfect Spanish.

As the options run out the mood darkens. And it then dawns on Frans and Lotte that they have become de facto carers of a seriously ill person. Finally on the fourth day after the storm broke some good news. Our friends have found a sympathetic psychiatrist. He will accept the language issue and has a good reputation. The only problem is that the hospital is meant to be in bad shape. In the absence of any other alternatives a decision is taken and off they go.

This doctor immediately takes control of the situation and Sarah is admitted. Dear old Delice, a rather undomesticated domestic help, has volunteered to stay with her. This is a beautiful act of selfless charity from someone who the world has often judged badly. Cuban hospitals are so under-resourced that somebody always has to stay with the patient to wash them, change them, feed them and attend to their toilet. The carer has to sleep in the chair and some even bring a mattress on which they sleep under the patient's bed. So Delice's offer is incredibly generous. But she quickly found it too upsetting and so a new hired help was found to work in two shifts with her.

But there is a problem. Not only do the lavatories have no doors, so that the entire ward can enjoy the humiliation of their fellow patients, but there is no running water. Frans, being the kind of guy who gets things done, then goes off to find the hospital engineer to ask him what the problem is. In ten minutes he is in the bowels of the hospital deep in conversation. It seems the water pumps have broken because they don't have the spare parts and there hasn't been any maintenance. Frans calls an engineer who arrives in half an hour. They quickly determine which items are needed and Frans gives the guy the cash to go and buy the bits. The hospital engineer tells him that he needs permission from administration to accept a donation and he is duly summoned. The administrator comes on the scene and tells him that it is not permitted and that he needs approval from his ministry. But by this time there is quite a crowd of interested passers-by and word is spreading that there is an unconventional solution to the water problem. Staff and patients alike are at the end of their tether. Frans and the administrator are still arguing when the parts arrive with a couple of technicians. Reluctantly the administrator caves in to public opinion and retreats to his office, turning a blind eye to the proceedings. An hour later the water is turned on. As Frans and his engineers leave they are cheered and clapped by the whole hospital. They had been without running water for ten days.

But I knew none of this. I just had a horrible premonition.

One day my lawyer finally appears. It is a brief meeting. We know each other from before and he simply explains the rudiments of the process. But I cannot concentrate, I am too worried about what is going on at home. All I can hear is the chilling phrase: 'Be patient, it is a complicated case and this will take at least six months before the trial.'

I ask him about Sarah and he gives a lawyer's weasel answer: 'I am dealing with your mother.' As he goes to leave, he pulls me to him and with sour, old man's breath wheezes: 'There are microphones in the cell, don't discuss your case with the other prisoners.'

Tuesday comes. It is my mother, looking cheerful and determined. We hug and she explains Sarah's absence. 'She's totally exhausted and it's all too much for her. She had gone to Frans and Lotte for a few days' rest and the doctor had given her some tranquillisers. But we decided she would be better off in hospital where she could be treated properly. Don't worry, they're all looking after her. She is okay, you really mustn't worry about her. You need to concentrate on yourself.'

I must have been staring at her in blank incomprehension, so she continued. 'It's been non-stop, with people calling all hours of the day and night. She just burned herself out, that's all. She will be back to see you as soon as the doctor says it's okay.'

I sit mute. Running through the permutations of what Mum is really telling me with her omissions, I realise things must be pretty bad but that to protect me she is not giving me the full picture. Knowing I have to play the game I ask lamely: 'How are the kids ?' And Mum tells me that they are all doing as well as can be expected.

Then we turn to practical things. Small steps that we can plan and get done. Not that I can get anything done at my end but at least I can be involved in the decisions. I lay out a plan for dealing with household financial matters and we schedule out the various handwritten instructions I need to prepare for the next visit. I give her some names of friends and specific messages, plus of course the means to contact them. She tells me the company is being very supportive so far and that they have paid for flights and things but that nobody wants to set foot in the country. They are all too afraid. Ivan studies us in immobile silence.

We have settled into a familiar rhythm, a pattern that's been there all my adult life. Chopping the insurmountable into bite-sized chunks that can be dealt with little by little: each day will have to be a tiny victory and each week a minor yet concrete achievement. The way we have always done it.

The visit is almost over. 'I need to cut my nails,' is met with silence.

'He needs to cut his nails.'

'Yes, yes, I heard.' Then grumpily clarifying. 'Bring something in to cut them next week and you better bring some hair clippers as well. Okay. That's it.'

Ivan calls a lanky oaf in smudged green to take me away. And it's back to the dungeon, my head ringing with concern about the home situation and desperate to get the letters which may shed some more light on things.

* * *

We are all just dozing off, alone with our thoughts. I am trying without much success to keep positive. Bang. The Judas hole slams open and a disembodied voice shouts: 'Two one seven, get your things!'

I swallow my panic as the obvious questions surface. Where am I going? Can it be worse?

With a mumbled and hurried goodbye I take my leave. Everything is rolled up in my rotten foam mattress and I change cells. I enter another gloomy dungeon at the end of the corridor. To get there I had to circle round a guard sat on a high stool peering through a Judas hole. I guess it is suicide watch. Thirty-three is pencilled on the door in a childish hand. The cell is slightly better in so far as there are bunk beds and the occupants seem to have accumulated a few books. There is also a definite whiff of semi-permanence mixed in with the stale cigarette smell. The other three occupants swing out of their beds and introduce themselves. But their first question is to ask my number, from which they all update the throughput.

A pleasant open-faced character of around forty-five with a firm handshake says: 'Hi, I'm Alfredo. I've been here six months.'

Then a shaky shadow offers his hand. 'Good evening, I'm Francisco and I'm four months.'

Finally a very fat, sweaty man, clearly not well, wheezes: 'You can call me the President. I've been in the cell for twenty-three months. We can talk more tomorrow.'

I chuck my things on the lowest bunk furthest from the ventilation grille and console myself with the thought that at least they seem to be clean cellmates.

Next morning, there is constant noise from the corridor. Cell doors opening, squeaking boots and whispers. A pattern is discernible. Then mid-afternoon a disembodied Judas hole voice shouts out: 'Prepare yourself, sun!'

The door opens and we troop out with heads hung down. In front and beside us guards swing truncheons in careless time to our steps. We move in fits and starts, stopping at corners and stairs, bunching up on command. Up and up we go past dim corridors of silent cells, padding through pools of leaked waste that have left a rusty rime on ancient tiles. Cobwebs thread between spindly pipes that once brought water to thirsty inmates. Up and up we traipse until with one last corkscrew a heavy steel door crashes open and the intense magnesium flare of a Cuban afternoon blinds us. We stagger out, hands over our eyes, cursing the light. We lean against the wall, panting, battered by the smells of early summer. Gasoline and jasmine, frying chicken and ashtrays, dogs' beds and nappies, spilt rum and women. It is a good couple of minutes before we can move or speak. We pull off our shirts in slow motion, arms outstretched to the sky, worshipping the flaming rays, bathing in the light. Our bodies are consumed with heat and heavenly joy. The intensity of pleasure in *sol* after endless days of gloom is shocking. We turn to baste our backs and study the yard. It's a cell without a ceiling, open to the sky except for a tight grille of heavy r-bar. Just the beautiful blue bowl overhead and some lazy honey buzzards circling a mile high.

Bangs and a shout. It's time to go. Back down to the grey, stinking hell. We pull on our shirts, skin on fire and troop off in silence.

That night the dripping, groaning and wheezing of the silent corridor was broken by a horrible scream and then banging on a door and shouting.

'Help, help, he's killed himself! Help!'

We sit up, look at each other and listen to the theatre of running boots, a body being quickly dragged to the infirmary and then silence again. The President crosses himself. We all lie down and offer a silent prayer for the poor sod. We never find out if he was successful or not.

During the last visit my mum told me that Sarah is showing improvement and will probably be discharged from hospital soon. To be honest I am still reeling from the news that she was ill in the first place and have been trying very hard not to panic about the impact on the children. Their father dragged off as a spy by State Security and their mother tormented in a Cuban psychiatric ward. I sense I am being told half-truths to protect me, I can see it in my mother's eyes, and I have a horrible feeling that the situation has been a lot more serious than anyone is telling me. So many things just don't add up: Sarah can leave hospital but for some reason they say she is still too fragile to return to the house, and will instead go and stay at the house of some close friends. What the hell does that mean?

The kids are so brave during the visit and of course I try to be brave for them. Huddled patiently on the cracked vinyl sofa, the afternoon rain slowly chilling on their shoulders, they have been waiting a long time. I enter with hands behind me and head down and give them my most reassuring smile. They try to hold back the tears until after I have gone, and generally they make a better job of it than their Dad does. I think part of it is because they don't want to give the instructor, who sits in the corner chipping in with stupid comments and enjoying his power over us, the pleasure of seeing the family in such distress. And they treat him with a fierce and cold politeness. How wise kids can be without even knowing it.

We sit holding sweaty hands and talking about practical things. I have made the decision that when school breaks up they will all return home to London and start a new life without me. I have explained to them that it could be two weeks, two months, two years or twenty years until I am free and that they need to be strong and be positive about a new life and that one day I will join them. My youngest daughter, only twelve, doesn't say much but just squashes up close while we talk about what to sell and what to keep, what to give away and who to give it to and most importantly whether to take my darling, daft dog Felicia back to dreary London. The thought of them leaving fills me with dread: not for the children, because once back in school their lives will fill up with new friends, noise and distraction, and not because Sarah will be returning home a fragile shadow of her former self, but because of the selfish fear of being totally and completely alone in my dungeon with no family to visit and the days and nights blurring into an eternity.

Then the visit is quickly over and now all of us have moist eyes and make brave British chit-chat, as if making plans to meet at the club after school. Oscar has gone as white as a sheet and is rigid like a somnambulist. I think he feels an appalling weight of family duty on his shoulders.

The instructor promises faithfully to hand me my letters the same day, a cynical smile lurking under his moustache. A promise we all know he may or may not keep, depending on how he wants to play my mental state and what he has planned for his interrogation. One last hug and then the guard comes for me and I am taken away, head down, hands behind, shuffling down the gloomy tunnel to the first of the many gates. This guard, a tall soulful mulatto with bony wrists sticking out of his cuffs, has a silently compassionate nature. He can sense that I have a tear dripping down my nose and so when he takes me into the side room for a pat-down search before returning to the accommodation area he gives me time to compose myself. He isn't allowed to chat and I am only supposed to talk when spoken to. But every hour of every day he takes people back to their cells from the visitors' room and has absorbed so much of the choking sadness that hangs in the air that he can't stand to look me in the eye.

Wiping some snot off on a scrunched-up piece of toilet paper from my pocket I take a big gulp, hold my head up and go through the process of returning to the cell. Stand to the left of the door, nose just an inch from the wall. On command pass through the door and stop immediately on the other side to wait for the command to proceed. Stop in front of the cell door to wait for the officer with the keys. And read the uplifting graffiti left by the guards: 'your ass is mine you fucker', 'this princess will die in here', 'your wife is a bitch and I fuck her while you rot'. Then when the swaggering imbecile with the keys and the two-foot baton finally starts fumbling for the keys I take strength from staring the bastard down, willing a confrontation with my defiance. For this they can restrict privileges, though the only privilege I have left is that I have air to breathe. But they don't have the stomach for it. Their bosses would castrate them for damaging a precious prize like me before the trial. There are few limits to the physiological violence they can dish out, but they don't want any physical marks before the trial. They can come after.

Out of an instinct for self-preservation I don't want to articulate my fears and hurt. I sense that once you let your emotions breach the dam, the waters of grief just keep pouring out until you have nothing left and no strength to fight. Very rarely do I allow myself the indulgence of self-pity and never with the family. A few weeks ago I wrote to someone, someone who I thought was a very special friend, 'I was waiting for you to launch the lifeboat and rescue me with kind words', but then found that the weightlessness of the reply was a cruel, cruel disappointment. It was stupid of me. In rational moments I know that it's impossible for anyone to do anything apart from distract me with news of home and make comforting noises. I have to learn to control my impossible expectations if I am going to survive this.

Going places

I have to find something to calm me down and fill these limit-less hours. If not, my fear and frustration will end in savagery and any blood spilled on the floor will turn into my time on a piece of paper in a drawer at the Ministry of the Interior.

With four people in this cell taking rotating turns on the two-metres-long strip of free space, I spend an extraordinary amount of time lying on my bed staring at the rotten chip-board of the bunk above and breathing in its mustiness. Being the last one in I am naturally last in the pecking order for exercise and I'm made to feel that if it were not for my pres-ence the air would be less fetid, the water would go further and everyone would have more time standing up and moving around. It's too cramped to sit up on my bed, so the choices are limited to either lying on my back or lying on my side. Variety is the spice of life and the views in either case have neither interest nor beauty, but to ease the sore places I can play around with my knee positions. I cannot lie face down because the smell of the pillow and the mattress is so rancid it makes me gag and I have a nagging worry about developing asthma in this filthy dungeon, plus of course the view truly sucks.

I resolve never to think about my case, write about it or discuss it with my cellmates after midday. To do so is to turn panic into a guarantee of insomnia, and from observing my fellow inmates, insomnia is a demon to be feared. Insomnia exhausts the body then the soul and then, hard on its heavy heels, comes the MININT doctor with his Cuban brain-fuck pills. Francisco dropped himself down that particular hole. Younger than me by ten years, he's been here for four months and yet looks about sixty. Imagine a person with all their electricity turned off. He chats from time to time but periodically he is off in some dark place, rocking back and forth, moaning and muttering. I know that humans are preprogrammed to be finely attuned to the suffering of their fellows and I feel sorry for the guy, but being shut in this tiny trap with somebody in mental anguish is incredibly unsettling. When he starts on one of his whimpering sessions I have this irrational desire to beat his face to a pulp. I have always thought I was a considerate sort of a man, kind even, but there is something about this man's weakness that brings out violence in me. Turning it over in my mind while I lie on bunched fists, I try to rationalise my behaviour. I guess my brain is automatically going into self-preservation mode. Basically we are four rats in a hole, four highly stressed and disorientated rats who are slowly losing our grip on social norms. Fear and panic are infectious and so it follows that this guy is now the enemy. Maybe he is to be pitied but now he is just as much the enemy as my smiling interrogator with all his henchmen and apparatus of cruelty. He is now the enemy because his weakness is slowly eating away at my foundations. A turning point comes one afternoon when the sound of heavy rain through the ventilation slot preludes a night when the damp air will lie like a suffocating blanket on our chests. He suffers from a disgusting fungal infection of the toenails, and they are rotten like yellow cheese. Every time he climbs off and on his bunk he has to stand on my mattress and his bare toes curl and grip my bed sheet. Revulsion and anger have been building in me for weeks. And so this afternoon, when he is picking his toes and casually flicking the bits off, letting them drop down on to my bunk, I explode in the batting of an eye. The President quickly calms things down and then defuses the guard's interest when the Judas hole flicks open.

'No nothing, we were just moving the furniture, ha ha ha. Give us a light.'

The slow-burning taper is passed. The President lights his millionth cigarette and considerately blows a huge cloud of smoke in the general direction of his bunk. He says nothing, sighs the sigh of someone who knows the way of the world and gives me the benefit of a cautionary glance. I can now see how murder happens. This is a truly dangerous place. If I cannot control myself I will gift them a charge that actually justifies my detention.

To my shame I rejoice when Francisco's health finally cracks and he is removed to the military hospital with serious diabetes-related problems. Now it's just the President, vice minister Alfredo and me. We have more air, more water and more time walking the slot. No more moaning. And most important for me, I move up to the top bunk and I am no longer the last man in. Another sucker will turn up in a day or so.

I kept a record while I was in Villa Marista: the simple maths of misery. I was in a cellblock row with thirty-two cells. There were on average three people per cell. That's ninety-odd prisoners. There was on average one proper suicide attempt a month. And more often than not, when walking down the corridor keeping to the regulation left-hand side with face down, I had to divert around a guard sat on a high stool in front of an open Judas hole keeping a disinterested eye on some miserable occupant The mechanics of suicide are simple: a strip torn from a sheet to make a short noose and then tied off from the bed chain or top bunk frame. I shared cells with a total of nine prisoners. Of these only I and three others didn't end up in the military hospital. So two out of three go mad. Regularly I would hear someone start screaming and raving, followed by the guards' boots clattering past and then the sounds of some poor soul being dragged to the doctor for sedation. This always seemed to happen at night, when the human spirit is at its lowest and home seems so very far away.

I have to discipline myself not to think about loved ones when I feel vulnerable. That luxury has to be rationed for times when I really need it, or when I feel confident that I can master my emotions. There is no way to describe the sense of loss that overwhelms you when those you love are taken from you in this way. All I can say is that part of you wants to curl up and die. And so to save myself I go into protective hibernation: like some hairy-arsed Sleeping Beauty in my forest of thorns. The back-chat of my cellmates indicates that this incarceration could last for weeks, months or even years. There is no logical way of estimating because logic does not enter the Cuban legal process. I have now lost control over almost every aspect of my destiny and face the long haul. When I think about the poor bloody President, I can sense the waves of panic rising in my belly. I have already missed my middle son's sixteenth birthday, and even the most optimistic calculation shows that I will miss my eldest son's graduation and eighteenth birthday, plus the birthdays of my wife, brother, mother and two daughters. And that's just the next few months. How much more will I miss? Not so much the diary dates but the intimacy and struggle of daily life. I feel so guilty I despair some days. Not guilty because I have committed any crime. No way. I will go to my grave protesting my innocence. No, I feel guilty because I feel I have failed as a father, a son and a husband by being the cause of so much suffering to them all.

I know I need a strategy for keeping sane and thank God that one night I hit upon something by pure chance. I learn quickly that faces and feelings are initially soothing but quickly turn melancholic: they simply reinforce the sense of loss and estrangement. I need to focus on something neutral but vibrant, something interesting but not dangerously emotional. Randomly I cast my mind back to one of my earliest adventures. Something about the sea is calling.

* * *

An entire summer spent camping illegally on a bird reserve
off the North Norfolk coast instead of mooching around
South London waiting for the O-level results to plop through
the letterbox. Penniless and with nothing but a couple of
second-hand tents, some threadbare sleeping bags and
a few bits of army surplus kit, we scavenged and stole our
food for four glorious, piratical weeks. Potatoes, corn, carrots and greens pinched from distant farmers' fields formed
the bulk of our diet. We made shrimp nets from washed-
up woven potato sacks and spent hours wading across the
treacherous flats, turning up the occasional baby turbot
or sand eel. The nets were spectacularly inefficient, more
hole than net and constantly needing repair and adjust-
ment, but slowly over slack water one could gather enough
for our supper. We weathered tremendous storms where we
had to flee to high land and we burned our backs stupid ex-
ploring the tidal creeks on rafts made from washed-up oil
drums.

But burrowing my way back through time I discover that
in my Cuban rewind version the weather is always an opal-
escent, overcast grey. Not the flat oppressive grey of London
but a crystalline, salty wash that brings out all the greens,
greys and yellows of that desolate landscape. The steep sand-
banks, lapped with banks of heaped cockle shells like dead
men's fingernails, their crazy wigs of marram grass dancing
about in the North Sea blast. The slate-grey horizon merging
into the muddy middle distance and bright white froth on
the yellow sediment spattered with all the weird and wonderful things the sea throws out when it gets tired of drowning
them. The flicking, hysterical shrimps in the blackened billy-
can: sand-given spiky life turning a nutty pink in their death
spasms.

The soundtrack of this daydream is the unceasing wind:
the thwack, thwack, thwack of guy ropes hitting canvas,
the sand-blasting howl of the gathering storm, the insane,

bad-tempered shrieking of gulls and the menopausal twittering of the plovers.

Using a twenty-yard cord, tossed over an arm, with about six number 2 paternoster hooks baited with cockles and lugworms and a flint with a hole in it as a weight, we caught the occasional bass or plaice: the golden iris and flame orange of the spots of their back dull and the green-tinged cream of their stomachs drips red under the gutting knife. We would take it in turns to cross the marshes on ancient dykes for the six-mile round trip to get the water ration while the rest played the game of finding enough food to survive. The water came from a standpipe in the graveyard of a solitary Norman church, its curious round tower the only sign of civilisation visible from our camp. The church was a reminder that certain ideas can have a lasting benefit.

We hadn't yet developed our adult tastes for smoking, drinking or sex, and so life boiled down to the absolute essentials of hot tea, food cooked on a driftwood fire and keeping our shelters dry and safe. We had our limits which never even needed debating. We happily killed and ate rabbits, but would not have raided the seal colony that basked and honked on a remote strand a mile away. We ate any cockles, mussels, crabs, shrimps or fish we could get our hands on, but would never harm the millions of birds or their pretty eggs. We scrumped crops but would rather starve than shoplift.

Our parents were mystified on our return; we were filthy, smoked by a thousand camp-fires, incredibly thin and with nothing much to say to adults about the entire adventure. Since then, part of me has never been happier than when I am just simply surviving.

Since that revelatory trip back in time and space I take a mental vacation whenever I feel down. I retrace my steps in all corners of the world. Hiking in the awesome quiet of the Great Western Desert with its extraterrestrial slit canyons and abandoned peyote cliff caves. Desiccated blue corn grains spilt

on hearths that had been cold for three hundred years. Dozing
under the shade of twisted screw pines waiting for the bread
to rise and the rocks to stop broiling. A week-long, freezing
struggle across the snowbound Pyrenees. Waking up in snow
holes shrouded by ice-encrusted bivi-bags and then walking
some warmth back into crab-stiff legs. Months of marching
to supposed safety out of the civil war in Uganda and over
the Ruwenzori mountains into the darkness of Zaire. All the
beauty and primeval freedom of wild Africa. Almond blossom
and the tinkle of meltwater streams outside stone shelters in
the mountains of Corsica. I remember details I have forgotten
and see things I have no conscious memory of at all. As I retrace old paths, tiny doors open up on to other tiny doors and
a kaleidoscope of vignettes flashes before me. A beaded lizard
sitting on a rust-stained rock, its blue-black tongue flicking in
the arid air. The drip, drip of summer rain from alder boughs
and a brown trout eyeing my Black Gnat with disdain from
the bottom of the pool. Hiding behind the blackened stumps
of a ruined banana plantation watching the militia approach a
rebel roadblock with evil in their hearts. Skulls, rotten scraps
of cloth and excrement strewn about me . . .

Countless sound- and smell-filled journeys, some joyful
and some terrifying but all ending with the knowledge of
coming home in one piece. Significantly, they feature only
the sketchiest of outlines of the friends or lovers that were in
the original adventure, now mere shadows or silhouettes. I
don't try to analyse this; I don't want to break the spell. I am
nervous that one day it just won't work any more, but I think
it is keeping alive a connection with the natural world, one
unpolluted with my waking nightmare. It reaffirms that I am
part of something more wonderful than this crazy old miser's
meat grinder, something that will exist when this foolishness
is just a dusty chapter in a history book that nobody even
cares to read. It gives me the strength to see how pathetic
this prison and these guards really are. To convert a seminary

into a torture chamber in a land Christopher Columbus called paradise; what were they thinking? The delusion of it all is laughable.

They may have the key, the truncheon and the sentence already typed up but I am going places whether they like it or not. So fuck them, I'm off to enjoy the scenery.

*   *   *

And so the days pass, waiting for the next family visit and the next interrogation. The President and the vice minister show no interest in my offer to make a chess set out of paper. The President continues with his weekly superficial clean of the cell and accepts no interference or help with this routine. His wife sends in a hearty Cuban meal once a week, which he shares out with admirable fairness. For a former glutton it must be difficult to part with even a mouthful. He doesn't read much, just seeks solace in a cigarette every twenty minutes. I don't begrudge the man this, even though the smoke has permeated every cell of my body. I wonder if I can remain this superficially sane after nearly two years in here. The vice minister is never allowed food. It is a curious feature of the process but every tiny detail of a prisoner's life is decided upon by his instructor. They fine-tune the abuse, the access to privilege and the conditions depending on where they want to take things with their victims. We are reduced to laboratory specimens. And so one man gets allowed a home-cooked meal once a week while the other man doesn't. Yesterday the President gave me his only piece of direct advice, although I have already learned a lot from observation.

'Listen, the only important thing is your instructor. The facts don't matter. He decides how many years you will get. All he is interested in is getting an extra star and petrol allowance and of course doing as little work as possible. And he has to get a convincing conviction. Dropping a case or losing is impossible for him. So don't lie to him and don't insult him. If he wants to screw you he will and smile while he does it.'

His back story is interesting. He was the third most senior person in a famous Cuban–Chilean joint venture that made fruit juice. It was the first to be hit in the purge. Immediately after State Security swooped, the top foreigner and the top Cuban both died of mysterious heart attacks within a short time of each other. So despite having had his trial and sentence they weren't about to let the President out on the streets as he had too much to tell.

The vice minister is more of a mystery. While I know about the sinister corpse-strewn series of events leading up to the President's detention, I know nothing about this guy. He never talks about his case and with sign language he has told me that the cell is bugged. He reads sci-fi and technical books on sugar production. He has a calm kind face with a New-Age hippy style shoulder tattoo. I instinctively like and respect him for his dignity. A closet hippy in a communist cadre's ministerial Lada. He is still being dragged off for interrogation every day or so even after six months. I guess they still haven't found anything they can nail him with and he is keeping his mouth shut.

My interrogations abruptly come to an end. Sitting for the last time in the freezing interrogation room, the camera winking at me, my instructor laughs.

'Well, you haven' t been a very bad boy, have you?'

'No, I haven't.'

'There's something you haven't told me.'

'I have answered all your questions. I never lied to you.'

'Yes, but you haven't told me everything.'

'I'm sorry. I don't understand you.'

'Listen, you are an intelligent guy. You want to get out of this place, don't you? You know the kind of things that interest me. You must know things about people that we haven't talked about. Think about it. The sooner you tell

me something interesting about somebody, the sooner I will
transfer you to a better place.'

So that's it. They want me to rat on somebody, they want
to start the next wave of arrests. He puts his unused pen back
in his pocket and buttons up his tunic. He rarely makes any
kind of notes as the interrogations are extensively filmed and
taped anyway. I guess they spend hours trying to spot incon-
sistencies or interpreting body language. Sniffing around for
weakness to exploit in their mind games. Little threads to
pull that will unwind my reasons to exist.

He calls for the guard to take me back to the cell. Wagging
a finger at me he gives me his advice. 'When you think of
something nice to tell me just let the guard know and we can
talk. Then you can go to a better place.'

I nod. And with that we shake hands and he pats me on the
back. As I'm shuffling out he shouts, 'Are you sure you can't
remember that elegant man in your office?', and laughs as the
door shuts. Bloody comedian.

So he made that crystal clear. I rat somebody out and things
will get better. Bastards. Of course this is why I am here and
why the next sucker will end up here. What a decision to
make.

That night I think it over. It would be so nice if I could say
that I decided to do the honourable thing, that being a man
of principle I refused to even consider such an ignoble act.
But that isn't the truth. There are instead two more practical
considerations. Firstly, I don't know of anyone actively doing
anything against the state or committing any crime more serious than drink driving and adultery. And that seems to be a
revolutionary duty here. Of course every single Cuban official
in every single enterprise we have in the blasted country is
stealing something from the business, either for themselves
or for the government. But that's not what he's after. The
Keystone Kops could solve the mystery of theft from every
business in Cuba if they wanted to. No, what he wants is some

foreigner's head on a plate, preferably a fat head from a nice valuable or high-profile business. But to invent something against somebody really would be the pits; only a complete scumbag would do that. Secondly, and even more importantly, I don't trust my instructor further than I can throw him. About the only thing I have learned so far in this mess is that the instructors are consummate liars, the most duplicitous, double-crossing twisted little shits one can imagine. It is totally possible that if I say anything at all it will simply justify prolonging their investigation into me. So, it is a relatively easy decision to make. I will not denounce because I cannot denounce and if I could it will inevitably backfire. Not a terribly noble analysis of the situation, but practical and I can look myself in the mirror. If I had one, that is.

This decision was to cost me a further six months in the dungeons of state interrogation but I never once revisited the issue. In fact I never even gave it a second thought. I had to concentrate on just surviving.

With a mighty clang

The end of interrogation signalled a slow improvement in conditions. I was to be allowed more books, some food, access to more letters, a small electric fan and best of all a small TV. It goes without saying that books would form the bedrock of my life going forward and that letters would become an increasingly vital link with normality. The fan would stir the air up a bit and alleviate some of the discomfort of the nights. God knows what the temperature is in here but it isn't even summer yet. I can now empathise with steamed vegetables, I feel their pain. The TV will be an incredible improvement to my life when it finally arrives: news, albeit the rather warped Cuban state version of it, bonkers Brazilian soap operas, a few old films, but best of all the London Olympics is coming up so I can look forward to seeing glimpses of familiar places and the proud but cheeky butts in beach volleyball. I feel a wave of relief. Conditions will improve and thus each day will be marginally better.

My mother, who had dropped everything to rush to the aid of the family, was now being helped by rotating visits from my sister, brother, cousins, sisters-in-law and various friends from England. I get to see close family members briefly during family visits. It is surreal but supremely comforting talking to them and hugging them, but I can see the concealed horror in their faces. I have lost 20kg in a few months, that's 18 per cent of my normal body mass. Can you imagine 20kg of pork sat on the kitchen table? It's a huge amount of meat to lose, carrier bags full of the stuff. I did a back-of-the-fag-packet calculation and came to the amusing conclusion that this diet had cost me personally about $100,000 a kilo. I bet even Oprah paid less than that. Surely the most expensive diet ever. But it isn't just me being thin. It is the ancient scratchy blue prison uniform that could tell a tale or two, my greasy transparent skin, the shaggy hair and long nails; and, of course, I must smell awful. It is the artificially jolly banter, partly for the benefit of the microphone hidden in the tatty wall hanging, and the looming presence of the surly official, his legs spread out absent-mindedly while he examines the contents of his nostrils. It is the humiliating waiting and questions in the gloomy room where visitors gather to patiently waste hours for the chance of twenty minutes with a loved one. I think the entire experience must be fairly shocking for them, flying fresh-faced from comfortable suburban lives in London or Europe. Visiting the family for a week must be like dropping out of the sky to join the lives of a band of shipwreck survivors, marooned in a slowly sinking lifeboat. Everyone trying to be strong and not wanting to accept that the situation is dire, the outlook is bleak and no end is in sight. They must feel terrible waving goodbye, leaving them to wallow in this ocean of sorrow and dread.

During this unravelling crisis my mum is an absolute marvel. Keeping the kids together and the house running despite not one word of Spanish. Ensuring Sarah is fed and cared for in hospital and afterwards, itself no easy feat. It's a far cry from the glorious health service that sycophantic journalists love to scribble about. My mum is making sure all this happens. She is also orchestrating what passes for a defence in Cuba with my lawyer and most importantly she is also making my instructor curse the day he ever decided to arrest me on these ridiculous charges.

To my dying day I shall treasure her iron fist in the velvet glove approach with him. Incredibly, and even though he is a teniente coronel in State Security and thus someone used to abusing his unlimited powers, he is becoming more cowed and exasperated by her at each hand-bagging he receives.

'Now listen here Ivana, it just isn't good enough,' she would say, blithely ignoring that she has not only corrupted his name but feminised it, a serious insult in a macho culture, basically calling him gay. 'My son needs proper food. I insist that he has a home-cooked meal once a week and that you let him have dried fruit and the basics to keep his health.'

Ivan's junior officer in the corner is squirming with embarrassment, stifled laughter and horror.

'We have our regulations but I will see what can be done. We all eat from the same kitchen you know,' Ivan replies stiffly.

'I don't care about that nonsense. And you don't seem to be losing weight,' she retorts, pointedly looking at the food stains on his taut tunic.

Subconsciously sucking in his gut, his ginger moustache bristles with affronted dignity. 'I said I will see what can be done.'

'I have brought him pasta, salad, some fresh fruit and sufficient dried food to last him a week. Please see that he gets it. If he doesn't then next week I shall want to know why. Is that clear?'

The translator looks to the ceiling for guidance from some higher being and tries to get the message across to his boss in a way that doesn't make it very clear that a seventy-five-year-old English grandmother can publicly castrate a top interrogator of the headquarters of Cuban State Security without breaking sweat.

I just love my mum.

It's a useful illustration of a certain aspect of how the system works. There is a game in Cuban society in which everyone is complicit. State Security are simply untouchable and thus only dissidents or the insane stand up to them. Everyone else will just lower their head and offer their neck for sacrifice. And that is how it is sold and swallowed. Sacrifice for the common good. It is so engrained in society that it is inconceivable that a normal citizen would just stand up for their rights in front of MININT. The thugs just don't expect it. So when my gloriously indomitable mum gives them a withering broadside they don't know what to do. Of course if she were Cuban they would just beat her up and throw away the key, but protected by her passport and knowing that our hordes of diplomatic friends are keeping a close watch on what happens, they can see where that would get them in the international press and so just have to take it on the chin. As it is, they just dread her visits and count the seconds till she will go away. I've come to the conclusion that she is one of the key people that will get me out of here. I can imagine Ivan muttering in his sleep. 'Who will rid me of this meddlesome dragon?' Maybe they will deny her visa. I'm sure they are thinking about it.

She is such a contrast to the Foreign and Commonwealth Office. What a bunch of supine, wishy-washy paper tigers they are turning out to be. Despite my being arrested on the totally spurious grounds of working for the British government or one of its allies, they don't want to do anything to rock the fragile boat of diplomacy. Various friends and family have tried all sorts of ruses to get junior ministers or anybody to champion my cause. And all we are asking for is a quick and fair trial. It's not as if we are asking for anyone to use up any valuable bilateral favours. All they got back was a handful of brief letters pointing out that hands were tied, that assistance in some vaguely defined form would be forthcoming, that due process has to be observed and a handful of leaflets about a charity that visits people banged up abroad. A totally and unequivocally pathetic performance. The Cubans just laugh at it. Literally laugh, and to my face. They tell me that our government is naive and boast that the Cubans are experts at manipulating the various international agreements they have signed up to. They joke about it. The only person to show spine, integrity and ability is the actual British ambassador. Despite being told by London not to visit me 'as it is against protocol' she bullies her way in using a barrage of diplomatic notes fired off every two weeks. She has consistently fought my corner with Ivan during the visits. She has even brought me a plate of filet mignon from her own kitchen, the sight of which had Ivan drooling. And she has trimmed my Gandalf eyebrows and given me one or two much-needed hugs. I bet that was against bloody protocol. But what she has been doing is not just compassionate but actually very intelligent, show-ing the Cubans that even though Whitehall isn't making a fuss I am not forgotten and that she is watching like a hawk. The physical theatre of the visits is full of significance for the Cubans, who take great care of the stage management of of-ficial encounters. The ambassador sitting beside me, holding hands from time to time like friends, and the eyebrow cutting and hugs is making it very clear that there will be diplomatic problems if I am harmed. She is playing them at their own game of subverting the rules, keeping them off balance. She and I both know that HM Government won't lift a soggy fin-ger, but now Ivan isn't so sure. This isn't cricket.

Without these two wonderful women I would be truly sunk.

*   *   *

A million years later I was asked to go for a debriefing at the Foreign Office. Some swivel-eyed schoolboy said he was pleased to see me come home, though the big pansy clear-ly could not have cared less. An earnest woman with podgy paws, pretentious spectacles and the firm convictions that can only be held by someone who had never peed their pants in some hellhole a long way from their suburban world told me that conditions in Cuban prisons were much better than those in Peru. A bustling lady, proud holder of the title Political Officer Caribbean, or some such thing, wanted to know what

I thought of the political situation in Cuba at the moment and then had to leave halfway through my brief answer. Nobody thought to ask whether the Cubans had named the diplomatic people they suspected were spies, the people I was meant to have passed information to. Nobody asked specifics about La Condesa, where no Englishman had been held in eight years. Nobody asked about what went on in Villa Marista, the most secure installation of Cuban State Security, where my boss and I were the only Englishmen in living memory to have been detained. It seemed to me that these were questions that were entirely relevant because what goes on in these information black holes must be unknown to HM Government and in fact throws a searching light on to the current thinking of the Cuban hierarchy. If the people of Britain realised that some of the people defending British travellers' interests in foreign territories were of this calibre they would never set foot in an aeroplane again. Thank God for the handful of gifted and dedicated people that do exist in the organisation, people such as the wonderful ambassador. Sadly she was in turn superseded by a different type of ambassador, one who wanted no direct involvement with me or the family and cited Foreign Office protocol to my family as the reason for lukewarm support. In seemed to me that unlike other ambassadors who I had seen prioritising the rights and safety of citizens in jeopardy, he was more interested in forging political and commercial links.

*   *   *

Another tedious morning. Shouts to get up. A snatch of the national anthem blaring out of the tannoy. One of my favourite guards is handing out breakfast though the hatch: bread roll and margarine, an extra one with a wink, and then a ladle of national liquid in my battered beaker, but with a genuine smile. The national liquid is a drink of probably lethal properties, a bit like the nation itself. He's almost at the end of his twenty-four-hour shift and his three-year conscription, his Miami T-shirt peeking out and his good nature lighting up my morning for a few minutes. We can never talk but I can tell that all he believes in is beer, women and roast pork: a sensible philosophy in the circumstances. Then comes the rubbish guy; and as it is a country that believes in equality but recognises the historical significance of being the last country in the Caribbean to abolish slavery, the rubbish guy is always black. All black conscripts are given an equal opportunity to be the rubbish guy. Anyone who knows Cuba understands the significance of the finger on the right hand rubbing the left forearm. The person doing the rubbing is making the sign of a black person and it seems everyone uses it irrespective of the social context or the extent of the offence caused. So one eighteen-year-old conscripted official will cheerfully make it about his barely darker colleague to me, a white prisoner, and expect me to chuckle as if we are all happily complicit in his casual racism. It's one of the few things about Cuba that I really hate. This rubbish guy is always so sad, maybe because he's condemned to work in this evil place. Surely it must eat away at your decency. More likely it is deeper than that. He knows that whatever he can achieve in this uniform everyone – his superiors, lower ranks and even his prisoners – will collude behind his back to remind him every minute of the day that he is inferior because he is black. I always thank him politely when I hand him the stinking basket, but when he looks at me he is trying to work out if it's some kind of sneaky English insult on top of all the usual Cuban ones. He expects nothing less. If I were in his shoes I would definitely take my chances on a raft, or more probably burn this place down and then take the raft.

Today it is the worst of the nurses handing out her sweeties to keep the President's failing systems ticking over. She hands me the vitamins that my family have supplied and then cheekily asks if she can have the spare bottle. I hate that bitch. She is everything that a nurse should not be, the anti-nurse of Villa Marista.

We are just about to settle down for a morning that stretches before us as always for light years when a shout comes. My two cellmates are to collect everything. They are going; the President to house arrest and the vice minister to a work camp, pending trial. They scrape together their pitiful belongings, roll up their damp overnight washing and give me a hug and a handshake. I have grown to like them. Then a quick pee and wrestle the mattress, towel and pillow out of the door and with a mighty clang I am alone. The space seems so wildly and extravagantly huge. I can stand up when I want, fart freely if the mood takes me and hang my wet pants up wherever I want. I can do 4,000 turns of the cell if I feel like it and not the 400 maximum that was the agreed limit for any one turn (400 turns equates to 1km). But instead I feel horribly alone, almost scarily alone. It's just my breathing and the prison noises echoing around the bare walls. The faint dusty tweeting of sparrows and the tinny parps of car horns are the only indication that I am still on earth and that there are other humans out there. I'm not sure I like this version of freedom.

But before an hour has passed, enough for me to realise that only the very tough can survive solitary undamaged in these circumstances, the door opens and a rather dishevelled little white worm of a man is thrown in and his mattress, towel, sheet and belongings in a great tangle after him. Introducing himself as Osvaldo, he gave a brief summary of the catalogue of justifiable stupidity on his part and certifiable greed on the part of his boss that had led inexorably to this smelly dungeon. Within a few hours we identify a mutual desire for chess and so we set about making a board and a set of pieces. The board is simply marked out with toothpaste on the base of the vacant bottom bunk and the set from scraps of paper. From that moment on, never a day went by in which I didn't play at least three games. And so another small part of my ad hoc strategy for mental strength was born.

One of the things I like about Osvaldo is that he is honest

about his feelings, a rare thing in Cuban men. He also cries freely for all the right reasons: not because he is broken but because he is sad about his wife and children. He cries after visits, not just because he is missing them. He is crying because he can see with great clarity how this will end. His wife is twenty years younger than him; pretty, frightened and now poor. He admitted readily that he is guilty and that as a result he will have to do a minimum of three but more probably four years of labour in a work camp before he goes home. Oh dear, life is not a love song and he knows that the home will not be his when he gets there.

On our infrequent trips to *sol* on the roof, we try to orientate ourselves by attempting to guess the directions and distances of meaningful parts of Havana with nothing but the sun overhead and the prevailing wind to base our guesses on. So six and a half kilometres in that direction my daft Felicia will be snoozing under a chair on the patio dreaming of the massive Sunday walks we used to take to the public beach at Santa Fe: seaweed, bones and all the lovely stinky mess of God's creation, sore paws and a bowl of water and then the sleep of the righteous bitch. Without fail, Osvaldo would stand facing the direction of his home, soaking up the sun, eyes shut and willing that everything would be alright in the end. Without fail he would say, 'Do you know my wife is just over there?', and then go back to musing about what she was up to on this glorious afternoon when the lazy sun shines down on the sunburned back of a city that chooses between family or fun on a Sunday afternoon.

And then one day, when I got back from being weighed, he was gone. Just disappeared. After half a day his replacement turns up, a very self-assured, supremely fit man of about thirty who I have to assume is a MININT plant. He spends all day devising new and sneaky ways of trying to get me to talk about business and politics, both of which are no-go areas. When not asleep or outside on one of his mysterious absences he is rather ostentatiously wandering up and down in his scarlet budgie smugglers. It really is a bit too much. The only good thing about him is that unlike Osvaldo he is very enthusiastic about cleaning the cell and really gets stuck into the washing and scrubbing.

Gone

Thank God the time for *sol* has been called. It has been weeks again. The plant declines. I guess he manages to top his tan up on his frequent sessions out of the cell. I get to see the sky for a blissful few minutes, feel the wind on my face and then trudge back in a trance. The cell door bangs shut, the humming white noise fills my ears and I know that there is just a long wait of another seven days and nights to the next visit and hopefully some good news about Sarah.

My cellmate is exercising in his tiny red briefs and his sweat adds another layer to the rancid fug. We exchange pleasantries and I decide that to kick myself out of the path of lurking depression it's time to write to some friends.

Dear Cate and Dundee
I am short on both paper and pen, and so as you are consenting adults I have decided to kill 2 birds with a single letter. Thank you for your letters and books. Dundee, did you realise that Lucifer Fox is a sodomite? A worrying choice of book for someone in my situation. What on earth will the censor think? I've had a rather rotten day but I won't bore you with that. But something happened a few days ago that I think you will enjoy hearing about. . .

Custard yellow and rhubarb pink. What a treat! At last a colour other than filthy cadmium blue. More importantly it is freshly painted and despite there being no water in the bog it's a delightful change from the scabrous walls I've had to stare at for the past eighty days. My usual address was painted a long time ago. Whoever commissioned the original paintwork was obviously a traditionalist with simple views on the appropriate colour scheme for a boy's room. Sadly, his successor seems to have been influenced by Jackson Pollock but with little sense of hygiene. So, overlaying the blue we have swathes of black mould, grey particles of filth, broad splotches of Vandyke brown that for sanity's sake I assume is simply bean soup residue and worst of all random greasy handprints straight out of CSI.

So despite the bed, the regulation model ie 1 ft shorter than the average human and sprung with weak knicker elastic, which would provide perfect conditions to rest a 4ft long banana, I was happy to wake up in a cell on the ladies' floor. We had been moved at short notice the night before.

I disturbed a cockroach breakfasting in the dry toilet bowl and ignoring his desperate attempts to surrender, unleashed a torrent of piss and laughed at the memory of yesterday's events.

At 5 in the evening my current cellmate and I were as usual guessing what war crime the prison cook would deliver us in the evening. This game is fairly tedious as there are only two possible options: something grey and greasy with black bean soup or something brown and greasy with chickpea soup. So it was with great interest that we noticed murky water pouring out from the bathroom.

Before going any further and to avoid confusion I shall describe no 33. We call it the presidential suite, as by all accounts it is the best room in the establishment. It is a concrete cube 8ft on each side, equipped for four gentlemen of leisure and boldly decorated as previously described. The only notable features apart from 2 bunk beds are a 2ft strip light left conveniently on all day and night and a 6 ft by 1 ft concrete ventilation grille that is basically there to dangle your trollies out of after a brisk scrub. Oh yes, of course there is a door, easy to forget as it is so infrequently used. This door has a hatch through which random commands, drinking water and pills pass. It is filthy and bolted and padlocked theatrically *by the officials as jealously as a chastity belt. What we call the bathroom is in reality an en-suite trench, a lavish 3 ft wide. The fittings are somewhat unconventional/distressed: a WC that is white on the outside yet beige on the inside with a purely decorative cistern, a sink attached to the wall with old shopping bags, a battered old milk churn of water with a bucket and a shower stall with a rusty pipe sticking out of the wall. The main function of the shower is to provide convenient facilities for hanging oneself. I hear the previous occupant took advantage of these facilities so the door has been removed and instead we have a sheet. Neither gas tight nor soundproof, with my bowels and this diet it spends a lot of time flapping and bulging like a spinnaker in the America's Cup. And it was from under this sheet that the tide of filth came.*

There had been random, yet alarming, banging and crashing noises coming from adjacent rooms for weeks. All the jolly sounds of the honest Cuban craftsmen at work, so I had immediately assumed the worst. They were attempting to solve a problem with the drainage. If there is one thing I hate it is shit. I don't like the smell of shite and even the sight of shite leaves me gagging. So the prospect of being in a small room rapidly filling with other people's ancient floaters almost had me in a panic.

We hurriedly moved our possessions to the safety of the top bunk, drew our feet up and shouted for help. The Judas hole flew open, but because the official on duty was shorter than the opening, it was a green forage cap that enquired with a detached voice what we wanted.

'Silence, what do you want?'

'We are sinking! There is water pouring in!' A short silence while this information was digested and then, 'Open the door if you don't believe us.'

He must have been standing on tip toe because a nose appeared, the flap slammed shut and we heard boots running down the passageway. Green lonely fibrous blobs were swirling

and I concentrated on breathing through my mouth and not
looking. After a while another official came back and with
a lot of muttering opened the door. The water cascaded over
his boots and swooshed down the hall while he looked down,
mournfully nodding his head. Confirming the situation he
asked us 'Why have you broken the toilet?' then slammed the
door and stomped off.

Up came the water again, but thankfully he returned many
handed. It was a scene straight out of the Titanic, except
with an all black crew and no orchestra, about eight of them
squeezed into number 33. The head engineer carried the tools;
a 6 ft length of pvc tube and a plastic bottle cut in half. It was
going to be very interesting to see how they were going to un-
block a main drain buried in the cement floor. I had a horrible
thought that they would simply tear the crapper out leaving us
to dump in a rough hole for the rest of the voyage. The chief engineer handed his bottle to an officer and bare-chested reached
down to pull the grating out of the shower stall floor. Standing
legs astride, arms bulging he started rhythmically pounding
his huge pole in and out of the u bend. All the while shouting
'fuck your mothers cunt, fuck your mothers cunt.' It was clear
to me that this man needed some lessons in plumbing, a few
tools and probably a psychiatrist. Obviously the foul water just
kept pouring out.

While they were all standing around scratching their heads
with the putrid effluent still rising, dinner arrived. I declined
as I feel strongly that one should never eat in front of the staff,
and instead decided to encourage them by whistling 'I will
always love you . . .'

Admitting defeat they unlocked the door, unleashing another
torrent down the passageway and told us that we would have
to temporarily move to an empty (sadly) cell on the ladies' floor
above. Hooray! This just shows the benefits of travelling 1st
class. The other passengers in 3rd class had to remain in their
cabins poor things. So with our mattresses on our backs, we

*paddled away from the tragedy like huge beetles with pockets
full of toothbrushes and soap. All in all a most memorable
evening.*

*This is probably the most interesting thing that has hap-
pened to me for some while so I thought it was worth relaying
in detail.*

*Dundee, I strongly advise you not to attempt anything on
wee Johnny's new skateboard. Physics will not forgive you. I
was very happy to hear that your wife has had some success at
work, it was long overdue. Please send her my best wishes and
if you can steel yourself maybe even a big kiss.*

*Cate, big hug to you and your tribe. Is it true that Fred has
a girlfriend?*

Lots of love prisoner 217

Am I a secret bipolar? Rereading my letter the morning after
I realise how easy it would be to end up with a permanently
split personality in this situation. In my letters home and to
friends I can't bring myself to tell them truthfully how bad
I feel and how ghastly the situation really is. My kids and
family in particular are suffering enough, it's better that they
don't know, but I have to tell them enough so that they can
get a picture of what my life is like. So I try to paint a vivid
picture but one that turns the cruelty on its head and tries to
disarm my demons by ridicule.

Tomorrow is visiting day. Last week Mum and the lads told
me that Sarah was coming home and may be well enough to
visit. It's been two months since I saw her. Having insisted
right at the start that they all go back to England and start
a new life, the main topic of conversation in visits since has
been about the practicalities of getting out of the country.
They will go in two weeks from now. It is finally all sorted
out.

MININT had taken the whole family's passports when I

was arrested as part of their cruel hostage strategy. This of course was totally against all international law. Our embassy very efficiently immediately procured new ones but still nobody had a visa. So technically they were in Cuba illegally. This meant they couldn't legally rent our state-owned house, pay for the electricity, drive, get cash out of the bank, go to school, have a mobile phone or an internet account; the list was endless. So it criminalised all of them, the whole lot, down to twelve-year-old Rosy. They could be stopped in the street at any time, kicked out of the house or have the phone cut off. All during the interrogation Ivan tried to use this as part of his nasty game. So there was a never-ending battle between my mum and Ivan, with the ambassador chipping in when needed. Everything needed him to sign it off. He really had us by the short and curlies.

Trying to get the family out was hugely problematic. Not only did they have to close down our home for the last twelve years but they had to deal with customs agents and shippers. There was to be a massive garage sale just to get rid of the non-essential stuff. We would have just given it away but we were haemorrhaging money, plus $8,000 disappeared from the safe when the cops raided the house and it has not surfaced again despite our repeated questions, so we are counting every cent. Then at the other end they have to get the kids into new schools at short notice and Adam to university. It is a nightmare.

They all want to get Felicia out but I insist that it was not fair on them or the dog. She hates the cold and the rain and they have enough problems without a depressed dog. A nice young *custodio* agreed to take her. The cats were too wild to ever leave their familiar surroundings.

So visits were taken up with agreeing lists of furniture to sell and checking high school résumés. And playing out alongside this were all the dashed hopes and rampaging hormones of a bunch of kids. They had had their innocent childhood terminated in a brutal way and had missed out on a lot of joy that was rightfully theirs. Just when they should have been enjoying the flush of adolescence they were traumatised. And so I have been thankful that we never have the time to get emotional about what this all really means. They are going and I am not.

The interview room door is opened by the lady captain and there is Sarah with Mum and the girls. They have made an exception and allowed four today. It must be raining as they all have wet trouser legs and there are small pools forming around their shoes. We hug and kiss and then sit. Sarah looks older, drugged, and has lost a lot of weight. But then I probably look older and drugged as well and I've certainly lost weight. An officer had shaved my head last night. A brutal number two. Last vision of Dad, a tropical Magwitch.

'Who cut your hair? It's terrible, it makes your nose look big,' were her first words after 'hello'. That's the kind of thing she always says, so perhaps it isn't so bad.

Sarah makes a huge effort but is drowsy and rambles. She manages to explain a little about her recent recuperation and tells me that she is now on half medication but it will be six months before she will be 100 per cent and can drive and do normal things. I'm overjoyed to see her, but it's still a terrible shock. A physical injury would be somehow easier to cope with, but being confronted with half a person is very unsettling. To my eternal shame, selfishly I think: 'My God, what if this is forever?' When she falters in her train of thought Rosy or Naomi finish the sentence for her and affectionately tease her for being such a twit. They are wonderfully matter-of-fact about it.

'Oh, you all know I'm mad. Just get used to it,' Sarah laughs.

With mixed emotions I kiss them goodbye, but they leave having got two important concessions agreed with Ivan. He will allow them three visits in the last week before they leave

Havana forever, and he has agreed to the three Cuban visitors that I have nominated to replace them and who will be my lifeline for a long time.

Getting the three Cubans approved was not easy. One of the first people I asked flatly refused. I guess they were too scared but I was disappointed as I thought our friendship was stronger than that. I had to think practically. They needed to be dependable and one at least should have internet access to communicate to London, and have excellent English for any legal stuff that came up, plus they needed to be able to visit in the afternoon. Being cheerful was going to be important and of course it wasn't worth nominating anyone who would fail a MININT security clearance. But most of all they have to be brave. So it was an easy choice in the end. Dear old Gilberto, whom I have known for twelve years through thick and thin and is retired now. Niara, whom I have known for around ten years and is my partner in a dance show that I helped produce. She's in and out of the country all the time but is as brave as a lion and never gives up. And Daniela, an old work colleague and all-round good person who is always cheerful no matter what and totally dependable.

The annoying plant cheerfully bids me farewell one morning, which relieves me no end. He is immediately replaced with a real victim. This is an old man who introduces himself as Rafael and despite his not wanting to play chess I take an instant liking to him. He appears totally undaunted by his circumstances, likes to make jokes about our miserable existence and initially has no interest in poking his nose into my case.

The last week for the family comes round all too quickly. The initial visits are so bitter-sweet I die a thousand deaths when I get back to the dungeon. And Rafael does his best to cheer me up. The final one is pure torture.

There is no weeping and wailing, just a gentle banter as we skirt around the awful finality of it all. As the clock nears the appointed hour I sit with each of them in turn moving round the room. Adam, despite being the eldest, has always had his heart on his sleeve and just can't stop the tears. He struggles to say a few words but throws his arms round my neck. I can feel him shaking. Oscar, so reserved yet so loving, gives me his wooden hug and kisses me tenderly. Poppy, her face blank with grief, says goodbye, her mouth crumpling and tears blurring her beautiful blue eyes and leaving wet stains on my shoulder. Rosy just buries her head in my chest and heaves, never wanting to let go. Mum, the strain of the past months showing clearly now, gives me the mother's brave farewell as she has the job of getting them all home in one piece and Sarah, trying hard to swallow her demons and not scream, whispers goodbye as we hug for the last time.

I can't remember getting back to the cell or what happened over the next few days. All I remember is lying staring at the filthy ceiling. My cellmate Rafael kindly makes me get up and eat when food is delivered and makes sure I drink water. But I have no appetite. The nurse from hell asks me if I want a tranquilliser and I tell her to fuck off. I wake up hungry and eat something.

Today I receive the first letter from Mum after their return to England. She explains that they are all fine but that there was a last-minute drama at the airport when one immigration official didn't want to let three of the kids out because they didn't have a visa. Thank God they were accompanied by Spanish and Dutch diplomatic friends who bullied immigration into letting them through. Unbelievably, after all that had taken place in the previous months, nobody from the British consular staff went to supervise an expulsion orchestrated by State Security. My mum was livid. As she puts it rather eloquently in her letter:

'Bunch of bloody hypocrites. They used to wheel you to every single diplomatic event and expect you to boost UK business but when the **** hits the fan they forget all about you and don't even make sure your family gets out safely. I hate them all. Well, not Lisa. She's wonderful.'

She goes on to say something rather extraordinary.

'I know you think Ivan is an utter swine, but those last few weeks he was very kind, especially to the kids. He says that Naomi reminds him of his sister. Whenever we left after the visit he would hold my arm to the car and if it was raining would always hold an umbrella. I think he has tried to make it as painless as possible for us under the circumstances.'

Well there's a turn-up for the book. The sneaky sod. If you ask me he just doesn't want any unnecessary dramas and is hoping we don't resort to publicity as he knows that they have done something really stupid.

Finally they have agreed to have my eyes tested. Tomorrow I shall leave Villa Marista to visit the military hospital. Thank God for that.

Endless

The excitement of that short trip to the outside world to have my eyes tested has worn off. Now it's the pathetic waiting game to have the specs actually in my hand, or better still on my nose. As with everything here there is total confusion. Depending on who I ask the glasses are either (a) free and will be delivered here, (b) free but my friends have to collect them and bring them to Marista, or (c) not free and somebody has pay and collect them and then bring them here, (d) not free and somebody has to pay somewhere but the Security will collect them and hand them over. That covers about every conceivable permutation I can think of, so I wait fully expecting to never hear anything about it ever again. And while I wait the killer headaches come and go, the regular episodes of blurred vision and shooting stars frighten me and the godawful tinnitus just keeps on sawing away, a hacksaw in my head.

The visit this time is from Gilberto and Niara. She tells me she has cooked some nice food for me and Gilberto has letters from home that he hands over to Ivan's handsome young assistant, who sits observing us. But I can't concentrate: my mind is all over the place and I can't really follow their chatter. It's been over three weeks now without leaving the cell for sun and I feel lower than I have ever felt. Tears keep brimming up and I struggle to stop breaking down. I have this terrible sensation now that I keep drifting away from my body. My friends sense my distress and beg the guard to let me have some sun.

'Maybe, I will ask,' is all they get.

Rafael and I try to cheer each other up. The endless tales of the totally inappropriate sexual adventures of a sixty-eight-year-old wizened monkey with spina bifida never fail to astound me. He is either a gifted fantasist or he has magic powers. It's extraordinary that a chap who hasn't the vitality to lift a finger except to root around in his nostrils, and has a lower back in permanent agonised spasm when it comes to cleaning the cell, can get up to all these things. Perhaps he's still worn out and the six months' rest he has enjoyed so far hasn't been enough to get his energy reserves back. Suspiciously, when meals are served he is up and out of his bunk like a whippet out of the trap, inspecting each tray with great care before without fail handing me the smallest helping.

That night, in the hell of the sleep that gives no rest, I dream a few seconds of simple joy. I hear the distant drunken shouting of young people, 'Stephen! Stephen, we love you', followed by some aggressive yelling telling them to shut their mouths. I sit suddenly awake, but it's nothing. I turn and face the wall and try to think of happy places.

Occasionally our conversation strays into areas relating to Rafael's case. Because of the microphones we have to be oblique and whisper and because his English is non-existent and my Spanish verbs are notoriously existential I am sure it confuses the hell out of the listeners. He has been charged with the serious crime of economic damage to the country. It sounds rather dramatic and thus it carries a heavy sentence, being considered worse than corruption. Unless there is some miracle he will physically have to complete at least five years inside. That's a lot for a sixty-eight-year-old man with a high libido. He was in charge of projects in the nickel sector in the mining town of Moa. He cheerfully admits that every month he spent a fortune on lavish parties for all the local officials, party people and bigwigs visiting from Havana. When the merry-go-round stopped in Moa, all the party-going party people were pointing the finger at the man who paid for the pork.

He wants to understand what is considered normal in the outside world. It appears that they have nailed him for being overgenerous with his entertainment budget, but what they really want to get him for is to show that he signed contracts that were not favourable to the country. Specifically that he favoured foreigners to the detriment of the Cuban economy. The nub of their accusation is that he agreed contracts in which foreign suppliers charged interest on money lent to the Cuban entity and obtained a profit on the underlying buy/sell transaction. Rafael explains that the deals in question were all approved by his ministry and minister, the central bank, the ministry of finance and prices and anyone else who had to stick their oar in. On top of that the deals were all within the accepted financial parameters of 3 per cent over LIBOR, for a minimum of eighteen months with no security given. In international banking terms, a Christmas present to a borrower who has consistently demonstrated that he is terminally flaky. In the current parlance a NINJA borrower, in so far as the country has no income, no jobs and no assets. Rafael, God bless him, actually believes that perhaps he has done something dreadful and got the country into some giant pickle.

Today is Wednesday and we are suddenly told that the random excursion to the roof is in a few minutes. Rafael is too depressed to go and just lies on his bunk staring into space. So I will enjoy it solo today. Maybe it is so he can help them search my possessions for secret messages or whatever it is they search for. I swear their desire to put me on the roof is not motivated by humanity or respect for my rights or my friends' begging, but because they just want to copy my notes regarding my case. This long-awaited fifteen minutes of sunshine does little to alleviate my health problems: it is too short to do more than lift the spirits for only an hour or so. In fact, the brightness of the outside world is excruciatingly painful. The step back into the mouldy fug and gloom of the cell will, as always, be a kick in the gut.

The rap on the steel door alerts me to the start of the long shuffle home. One last deep breath and one final glance up through the rusty grille to the intense blue bowl of the heavens. When I first came here I could do pull-ups from the bars. Not any more. Then down the wormhole staircase, stooped over to avoid the low beams, with guards in front and behind. Pass across the passageway to the women's cells. They are in there, I can sense their presence, but no physical sign or sound, just the tell-tale pools of leaking water from the standpipes where they enter the cells and a suicide watch stool further down. Wait at the head of the next stairs, face towards the wall. Then, on command, down the stairs again to wait face to the wall at the bottom. Then down another corridor towards the watch commander's office. I always slow down for this bit because I get a reflection of myself in the glass of his office. A pale ghost gradually coming into focus, with an ape on my shoulder. Then turn to the right for another nose to the wall. This part of the journey is where one can pick up little scraps of information. At this confluence of passageways and doors there is a desk on uncertain legs and a curious guard keeping paper notes of this and that. The dirty laundry basket sits becalmed on its smelly voyage. The dinner trolley stands with lunch trays set out for the benefit of the flies. A quick mental calculation and the block population can be estimated at a glance. There is a huge clock hung from the ceiling. Sometimes the face is swivelled away in spite, so one cannot see the face. Other days it has stopped. Maybe they just change the time to screw us around. Whatever, it is nice to see what passes for time in the outside world.

I have never seen another prisoner, not even a hand, on this short, unvarying journey. Then the final leg past every single cell, as ours is the very last in the line. I always stare hard at the faces of the guards in the walkway. The few I like are blessed with the hint of a cynical smile; the rest get a stone-cold glare. Almost to a man they are mere boys, without the

balls to confront me. They are impotent in the face of my in-
solence and it gives me a tiny crumb of satisfaction. But these
are conscripts, and standing back lurking in the shadows are
the hardened non-comms. You cannot mess with them. Their
hard horny hands and rheumy eyes have had every last drop
of humanity screwed out of them. Unfit for anything in the
outside world, too stupid to rise up the ladder and earn stars
that come blessed with a Lada and weekends at the officers'
club, they are stuck with us in a hole far beneath the contempt
of their peers. They hate us, because we will one day be free
but for them it is a life sentence. I tasted the venom of their
hatred just once and decided that only an idiot would cross
them. Much better to take out my feeling on the puppy fat. I
am hardly the stuff of legends.

Back in the cell Rafael blinks like an ancient goldfish tired
of his tank and asks what the weather is like.

'Sunny and hot, my friend, like always, but the air smells
fresh and that is always the best bit. Did they find anything
interesting?'

He blinks again, betraying nothing, sighs and then lies
back to doze. We are all in this game, playing our part. There
is nothing to say. He cannot. I say it just for the benefit of the
silent listeners, hunched over their headphones wasting their
lives on eavesdropping stale trivia.

I wash carefully and thoroughly, paying particular attention to scraping out my long fingernails with a precious, bent
paperclip. They shaved me very late last night. Having no
mirror it is difficult to know if my face is dirty so I rub and
rub till I am sure I must be presentable. But being accustomed to breathing the fusty air of the dungeon, the walls of
which leak the sweat and piss of a million miserable nights,
I have no way of telling if I smell bad or not. The reason for
this extra care is that today I have a visit. Niara is out of the
country but I have Gilberto and Daniela coming and I want
to look my best. There is a Cuban cookery show on TV with a

Chinese man showing us how to prepare wontons and crispy prawns. Rafael sits transfixed, groaning at the sight of the heaped plates of ingredients while I, cautious dog that I am, sniff my armpits every ten minutes wondering if I need another wash. The morning drags: it is always especially slow the day of a visit, but eventually there is a shout for me to collect my things and go. I take my towel, my underpants, some books and a stack of letters. Although I hand-wash my pants twice a day, after exercise, I always send them and the towel out to be sterilised each week.

With my heart in my mouth, as giddy as a five-year-old, I enter the visiting room and feel a wave of joy and love at the sight of them. I hug Gilberto first, his stubbly chin no higher than my chest, and give his bald head an affectionate polish. Then Daniela. My nose buried in her hair I linger, smelling the extraordinary, complex smells of this woman, and fleetingly I feel that all is well with the world. We sit jammed three in a row on the sofa, an arm thrown over a shoulder, or holding a knee or clapping with laughter. They asked me if I heard Niara and the dancers calling me one night from the street. They were drunk after a pre-tour party and came to say goodbye. So it wasn't a dream after all. Gilberto tells me of his latest attempts at making ends meet in retirement, the reluctant English students and bonsai sales. He recaps the latest humiliations at the hands of his ghastly ex-wife and the relations with neighbours that his bad-tempered sausage dog has bitten. And he never fails to amuse us with an update on his prostate and haemorrhoids. Daniela doesn't play for laughs but talks with a charming vivacity that makes me happy anyway. Nothing heavy, just about the latest gossip at her work, family dramas and mutual friends. They keep it light and funny and fluffy, wrapping up with a summary of messages from family, requests for books and what food I would like next week. It's like an injection of some essential serum, a sort of insulin for mental strength. With a breezy hug and a kiss I wave them goodbye, all of us keeping up the pretence until I am led out of the room. I know for a fact that afterwards they collapse and shiver and cry all the way home. They have ventured into the ogre's castle and part of them must always think, 'Will they take me in for questioning this time?', so when they walk out unchallenged into the sunlight any sadness they feel for their friend must be drenched in relief that they will not suffer the same fate, for this week at least. In its own little way, what they are doing is very brave. It's not only a demonstration of support and faith in me, but it's a statement that what is happening is wrong. And in Cuba the authorities don't like other people making statements.

Halfway back to earth

The family left at the end of June and it's now the middle of October and I'm still here in this dungeon. Nothing has changed except for the worse. Sarah and Adam came to celebrate his eighteenth with me. Poor kid. Other young men get to have boozy parties with their mates or cheesy events organised by their parents. He got twenty minutes with the shabby wreck of his father in a Cuban prison.

My friend the ambassador has left and the new one doesn't want to visit. He sends the consular official once a month. She's nice enough but ineffectual, and hides behind the official briefing. They are doing nothing and offer no assistance other than follow official protocol, which means State Security can hold me for up to two years before they have to actually charge me with anything. Two years.

I think without the visits from my dear friends I would have totally lost it. That twenty minutes of human contact is all that stands between me and madness. They take it in turns to visit and other friends kindly send them snacks and books and messages of hope.

Despite their regular visits I think physically speaking I have hit a sort of plateau beyond which things can start falling apart quite quickly. I have lost all spare body fat and I'm not an expert of course, but I feel that I have been burning up muscle. Since the initial catastrophic weight loss of 20kg in a month the rate of weight loss has stabilised to about 0.25 to 0.5kg a month, so I'm now down to 90kg. So it must be muscle that's going as I have not noticed anything substantial drop off yet. With the limited opportunities for exercise all I can hope to achieve is to maintain flexibility and slow the loss of strength, certainly not gain muscle. The main function of exercise is to pass the time and to keep mental discipline. It also annoys the hell out of the guards when they open the Judas hole and cannot see me because I am doing press-ups. The single home-cooked meal and the dried food and vitamins that come in each week augment the appalling diet that is deficient in pretty much anything useful. I could be an asshole and keep everything I get to myself but I wouldn't consider it for one moment. Old Rafael doesn't get any food. I guess they are so pissed off at all the food he ate at his illegal parties. The combined effects of the poor diet, the lack of daylight, the stress of this never-ending nightmare and the dreadful difficulty of sleeping are taking their toll.

No time to shave or wash, just to grab my pen and paper and off down the dingy cramped passageways and oversized staircase, built for both dwarves and giants. My lawyer is waiting hunched in the chair. He looks pleased to see me but drained and worn out. He tries to get up but I go to him and gently make him stay down. He is excited.

'I have very good news,' he starts, emphasising the significance with a wiggle of his eyebrows.

Then a hoarse whisper in my ear. 'They thought it was a mountain but you are a very little mouse. Do you understand? A mouse! Very little.'

Sitting down I ask him: 'So who have you spoken to?'

Nodding theatrically, he went on: 'Very little! Ivan tells me that you have no problem, don't worry. Be calm.'

'That's nice of him, but if I don't have a problem why have I had to spend eight months in Villa Marista?'

'Be patient, don't say nothing. No trouble please.'

'How much longer, Arturo? I'm not sure how much more of this I can stand. Maybe a month or so, but, honestly I am dying in here. Help me get out, please.'

'Listen, I love your family and I think you are a very good man. Ivan thinks you are a good man. Maybe you made small mistake but he has very good opinion. Be patient I insist.'

'Please Arturo, how can I believe you?' I implore.

'I think they will transfer you soon to La Condesa. This is a prison for foreigners in the countryside. The good news is that you will have exercise and air and other people, the bad news is that your friends cannot visit you. But you can use the telephone.'

And with that the interview is over. I haul him up out of his chair and before he leaves he pats me on the arm and smiles a sad smile.

Going back to the cell I despair. This guy was the prosecutor general of Cuba for years, and he is the best defence lawyer in the country. And so far his strategy just seems to be to tell me not to worry. Still no concrete information about charges. I lie on the bunk and stare at the ceiling in silence. The hours crawl by.

*   *   *

A few days later.

'Collect everything, come on, quick, quick.'

I had been waiting to hear those words for days that have stretched for a grey eternity. Rafael swings himself off his bunk to help. He smiles with pleasure. My few possessions are slipped into a precious plastic bag kept hidden for this very moment under my mattress – flip-flops, paper, pen and letters, a couple of books and a few clothes, wash stuff and a couple of empty Tupperware boxes. We disconnected the little TV and fan. I leave Rafael virtually all of my dried food, my stack of magazines, some writing paper and my best wishes. He helps me roll up my mattress and bundle up the sheet, pillow case and towel. With a quick handshake I was off down the corridor to change out of my uniform into T-shirt and jeans, which had been slowly festering in some locker somewhere.

They hang off me. A few of the guards gave a friendly wink
but most just gave the cold, fish-eyed stare. Then down to the
processing area where I am to be to be processed out together with my few things. There is some paper shuffling by the
duty officer, and my possessions are inventoried and signed
off. I work out later that this is where they probably stole my
razor.

I was manoeuvred into a beaten-up Chinese van that had
been converted into a paddy wagon and handcuffed in the
cage. There is a type of Chinese van that is made from what
looks like baking foil. I am positive that if I had simply stood
up briskly my head would have simply burst through the roof
and I could have been off and away. But I didn't. The three
guards sitting on the bench seat in front were all armed and
looked like they knew what to do. It was only later when I
was getting out that I noticed that the magazines were missing from all of their handguns. As somebody fiddled with the
padlock on the main gate the driver revved the van, slipped
the clutch and we were off like a cork out of a bottle, hurtling through the streets of Mariano. The largest man drove,
the next largest fiddled with the radio and made sure that
whatever else happened one could never complain that there
wasn't adequate reggaeton being played at a more than sufficient volume for the entire journey. The smallest was in
charge and subsequently spent the whole trip telling his pri-
vates about his girlfriend. I could see over their shoulders and
enjoyed watching the world go by for the second time in eight
months. It is a forty-five-minute drive door to door but sadly they couldn't remember where the door was. In fact, they
could not remember where the prison was at all, only that it
was near Güines. So we drove at breakneck speed though the
fields, stopping at villages and asking for directions, finally
arriving about half an hour late. Just to show who was who
they drove past the prison checkpoint at about 50kph with
horn blaring and came screeching to a halt. But they had even

got that wrong and were told to drive round the back where we finally came to a stop. The door opened and a few chickens casually wandered over to see if there was any food on offer. It's at times like these that you wonder how it is possible for these cretins to still control the country. I guess after fifty years they have just got so complacent that they can't even conceive of life in different circumstances. They must have driven their Stasi instructors to drink.

I clambered stiffly out and stood in the blinding sunlight, savouring the honest smell of earth and damp vegetation and the hot breeze rippling off the cane fields. I have arrived at some place halfway back to earth.

Welcome to the spider's web

I sit in a sweaty little room while the paperwork is completed. A handsome middle-aged official with a straightforward smile and a head like a fuzzy boiled egg laboriously handwrote out a receipt for me on the yellow/grey thin paper beloved by government institutions in Cuba. Yes, a receipt. No official document, no computer. That little scrap of paper confirmed that State Security had handed me over to the penal system. While the dust motes danced before the fan in the afternoon sun my eyes wandered about the room taking in a scene that reminds me of every state institution I have visited in the past twelve years. A rusty filing cabinet buried under a towering pile of manila folders. The ubiquitous bust of José Marti frowning at the universe in the corner, despairing that his glorious dreams for the future should have come to this. The little bunch of plastic yellow roses in a delicate earthenware pot, a gift from Cienfuegos. The bottle cap packed with plasticine nailed to the doorframe to make sure nobody sneaked in at night and pinched the roses. The hideous, handcrafted wall decorations of branded wood and leather. The cracked, uneven floor tiles, sunken in places and creating a topsy-turvy landscape where ancient Soviet furniture is put out to pasture. And looming over us all that poster of Fidel, that one where he looks like Moses reprimanding naughty children. There were times in Villa Marista, listening to the life stories of my fellow prisoners, when I thought that the horrifying painting by Goya, *Saturn Devouring His Son*, would be a more appropriate poster.

A pretty but chubby girl in a uniform a size too small for her typed at an ancient typewriter nestling in the shade of her cleavage. She was as pink as a cherub, the tip of her tongue sliding back and forth in one-fingered concentration as she tapped out some long list of prison matters. Under her wonky desk her skirt was riding up and I could see she was wearing fishnet stockings and clumping great policewomen's brogues. She occasionally stole a glance to check me out, I guess wondering what had brought me to this particular room in the middle of nowhere, their standard fare being drug smugglers, people traffickers, gangsters, paedophiles, murderers and rapists. But her eyes were constantly drawn back to Mr Boiled Egg as he theatrically played with his stamps and folders and it was suddenly crystal clear that she was his lover and enamoured with the stars in his eyes and on his shoulders. Everything he did was a little performance for her benefit and this tatty room was his stage. You can put a Cuban in uniform, drill them till they drop and brainwash them senseless, but they can't help themselves. They are who they are, a passionate, unruly and romantic lot. It's no wonder that the entire population drives Raúl to apoplectic rage as they consistently mess up all his best plans for them. The glorious, warm-hearted fallibility of these people is what saves them from taking his regular rants about ill-disciplined workers, antisocial youth, thieving officials and deviant musicians seriously. It's like a bigoted and mean-spirited grandmother being left in charge of eleven million drunken teenagers. I suppressed a smirk and catching my eye she blushed. She knew that I knew what was going on between them but she didn't want him to know that I knew.

The minutes crawl by and then all of a sudden at some mysterious signal the senior State Security guard unlocks my handcuffs and nods goodbye to me. Mr Boiled Egg takes another pair of handcuffs out of a drawer, asks me to put them on myself and then goes back to his papers. He asks me why I am here and the adoring typist shifts her bottom and her words per minute sink to a new low as she concentrates on listening to the drama. I resist the temptation of the obvious answer, which is: 'Fuck me! If you don't know, who does?'

'Mainly illicit activities and something else,' I offer.

'What something else?' he asks.

'Erm, revelations.'

'What kind of revelations?'

'State secret revelations.'

'Ah,' he says, and quickly leaves the room.

The girl glares at me, her worst suspicions confirmed, and she starts hammering away, this time like a machine gun.

It suddenly struck me that they don't know why I've been detained. It seems that State Security send people with a note saying person X has completed a period of instruction and is provisionally detained but they don't say why. It's a secret. The prison actually hasn't been officially told, maybe it never will be. Of course, within a few hours the gossip will flow back and forth over the telephone to Havana. Then later today the cherub, in an offhand way calculated to rub her friends' noses in the fact that she is the lover of a senior officer, will drop the juicy snippet into a chat over coffee. And then it's off the leash and away. Oh well, the whole world will know tomorrow, so I'd better just tell it like it is.

He comes back with a forty-year-old man in civilian clothes, whom I had spotted tinkering with the carburettor of his Czech motorbike in the shade of a palm tree. Wiping his hands on his jeans he inspects each page of my British passport carefully. He seems to be calculating my various trips, indicated by the international visas and Cuban business visas, and getting them into sequence. He is definitely the most intelligent-looking person I have seen all day. So his first question is somewhat disappointing.

'Are you British?'

'Yes.'

Not put off that his impromptu interrogation hasn't yet

yielded any interesting confessions, he tries a different tack.

'Is this your first visit?'

'To La Condesa, yes.'

He gives me a withering look.

'Sorry. No. I live here. In Havana.'

Tapping my passport on my head he sighs and hands it back to Mr Boiled Egg and leaves to try his hand at his motorbike again.

And then I was handed over like a dog on a lead to a very stern young man bearing a strong resemblance to a uniformed shiny piglet. On his arm he had a sort of homemade black leather armband with big pink letters appliquéd in very un-military-looking script. He is the officer of the day. This is not to be confused with worker of the week or playmate of the month; it means that he has the responsibility for the security of the prisoners. If I do a runner he gets it in the neck, so he doesn't let go of my elbow.

He takes me round the corner to a dilapidated hut where I am to be issued with my uniform, mattress and towel. Here I meet a large, angry Cuban who looks really unhappy to see me. I was to find out that this was the hated captain of discipline. The dim hangar smelt of recycled sadness and feet. Huge wobbly stacks of stained foam mattresses, piles of faded blue shorts, mountains of trousers and a landslide of blankets disappeared into the darkness. He assessed my height and build with a practised eye and then stomped about collecting a bunch of clothes and threw them at me. I decided that rather than spend the rest of my life either holding my shorts up or holding my breath, I would try them on. So while he went off to find a suitably musty mattress I stripped off. Big mistake, he came back and went ballistic. Apparently prisoners should not be in their underwear in front of guards and so began my troubled relationship with Captain Simiento. He asked me what my crime was. I had already blown my cover with Mr Boiled Egg so I just came out with it.

'Oh, revelations of state security and illicit activities I think.'

A grim smile lit up his face. Not a boring criminal then. A crime like that threatens the state and everything he has sworn to defend. He is obviously one of that increasingly rare breed in Cuba, a nutcase that actually still believes in it all. It would give him all the excuse he needed to inflict special restrictions and humiliations. Putting my handcuffs back on he loaded me up with my possessions and uniform and balancing a mattress on my head we set off towards the wire and walled enclosure of the compound. He stomped off in the lead with piglet in the rear, having to duck as the mattress swung up and down in rhythm to our marching. So this was to be my new home for the foreseeable future.

I will remember this hundred-metre walk for the rest of my life. This was the first walk in the open air for an eternity and incredibly the first walk where I didn't have to either turn 360 degrees every three paces or stand with my nose pressed to a wall every minute. Going in a straight line and being able to look around me while doing it was the oddest sensation. I could actually look at people. The trees looked more treelike and green than I remembered them, the sky looked clearer and bluer than I could have imagined. Everything was brighter, bigger and more wonderful. The cat licking its paws in the shade looked exotically glossy, and the sparrows squabbling in the dust fizzed with life. It really was like being reborn. Whatever horrors awaited me here, it was a million times better than that bloody dungeon which just gnawed and sawed away at my sanity.

Passing through the Mickey Mouse gatehouse, through the dog run and through the final gate I was met with a sound like the chimpanzee enclosure at feeding time. This part of the prison is for *Severo* and *Medio*. This means where those under severe and medium penal regime were housed together. Three blockhouses each with a barred gate stood in a row.

Watchtowers loomed in the distance and a few bedraggled trusties swept the ground while a work party appeared to be erecting new barbed wire. The entire thing bore a rather alarming resemblance to a Second World War POW camp as seen in a hundred war films, but in concrete rather than wood. The heat was now intense and the bare cement was blinding after all my months of darkness.

A scrum of faces were shouting at me from the nearest cellblock in a variety of languages, laughing and hooting. A single voice could just be heard above the din shouting 'Stephen!' There was somebody in there that knew me. Maybe I wasn't going to be eaten alive in the first ten minutes after all.

Piglet uncuffed me and then just wandered off with Simiento without saying a word, leaving me standing there in the hot sun with all my stuff in a pile at my feet. I looked about wondering what to do. Will they shoot me if I move? How long do I stand here? This was typical, as I was to find out. The guards don't tell you what any of the rules are but any infraction is punishable. It's up to you to find out. Darwin would be impressed. A prisoner, no doubt out and about on some sneaky excuse, came up and explained that we had to put all my possessions in a lock-up and immediately started helping me pick everything up. He had an impressively battered face, a lopsided smile and the most bizarre broken Spanish. While we went round the side he introduced himself as Salim, originally from Algeria, recently from Canada, here for two years and with another six to look forward to. He gave me the first of many gems of advice.

'Very bad people here. Wait, don't speak nobody. Then calm. Some good people.'

Moving the words around like a jigsaw in my head I finally got the gist.

'Don't touch handkerchief. Take handkerchief and take bathroom big problem.'

This didn't make any sense at all until he acted out a little

pantomime. Apparently in this neck of the woods if somebody asks you to hold a handkerchief it means that you are
happy to accept the position of temporary wife and be the
laughing stock of the prison. Dear God, the things they don't
teach you at architecture school. This was rather a lot of weird
information to process in such a short time. Obviously life
at La Condesa was going to be more colourful than at Villa
Marista. It dawned on me that perhaps this piratical-looking
individual had a sinister objective; perhaps somebody offering
to carry your possessions to the lock-up signified something
even worse. I tried to be a bit distant and offhand with him
but it was too late; he stuck beside me like glue. I was to find
out over time that Salim was in fact a very special man, a solid
and dependable friend. A one in a million kind of a guy who
had got himself mixed up in something stupid and accepted
that he should pay the price.

Having signed over most of my possessions, which again
involved a bored official in a hot dirty shed, grey paper and an
extraordinarily long time, we retraced our steps and asked to
be let into our cellblock. A bored guard swings the gate open
and we enter and are immediately surrounded by fifty noisy
faces, all shouting in a variety of languages.

'Where you from, man?'

'Where they catch you?'

'What you do, white boy?'

Salim shouts at them all in Spanglish to go away, adding
something fruity in Arabic to great effect. They wander off,
bored already.

I am shown to a vacant empty bunk above Salim's, which
immediately rekindles my suspicions, and then I am introduced to the guys on either side. On the top left is a tiny
little bundle of knotted wire they call Gadhafi, who vigorously shakes my hand about twenty times, and on the top right a
very smelly Guatemalan known for the obvious reason as Javali (Spanish for wild pig). A smiling older gentleman pops his

head out from beneath a mosquito net, after a lot of huffing and puffing about having his nap disturbed, and introduces himself as Cy Tokmakjian. Mischievous eyes twinkle beneath carefully brushed hair and he is wearing a rather silly moustache. The famous Cy! The top Canadian businessman who disappeared about a year before I was arrested. He welcomes me and says we will have plenty of time to get to know each other. After advising me not to take any notice of the chaos around me he disappears back under his net, which Gadhafi then tucks in with great ceremony. On the bottom left, hopping from foot to foot in excitement, is a vaguely familiar face.

'Stephen, I'm Patrick's father, Matej.'

And then it dawns on me. I remember years ago my son Adam had a mate called Patrick in the same class at international school, and I had met his father a few times. I had no idea that this guy had been taken as well. It was he who had been shouting my name.

So with a sense of great relief I realised that among this horde of murderers and gangsters there were at least a few friendly faces and a few businessmen in the same boat. Salim made us all coffee, in itself an incredible thing after all this time, and they quizzed me while I sipped. After giving them a very brief summary of my case, the clearly unhinged Gadhafi whisked the cups away and then Salim took me on a tour of my new home, my head spinning from the caffeine.

The cellblock is a hot stuffy box about six metres wide and thirty long. The front gate opens on to the communal sitting area, where an untidy collection of plastic chairs faces a TV kept in a barred cage. The TV is officially on at maximum volume between 6 and 9, but in practice it is only off for a few hours in the dead of night. Then there are two lines of twenty-five bunks, a two-metre passageway up the middle and about a metre between each bunk. The bunks are separated by tall rusty metal lockers infested with cockroaches.

Each person has the locker immediately to the right. There are barred windows with moving louvre slats every couple of metres but with no planned relationship to the beds. Consequently a bed with a window behind it is a prized location. Beds on the 'ground floor' are considered the privilege of long-termers or sometimes, at the insistence of the guards, are for the elderly or infirm. Luckily my bunk has a window behind it so I have light to read during the day and some air at night. There is an electrical outlet every so often and people run a collection of battered old fans to keep cool. After the bunks there is a kitchen area. This is a small galley with one domestic four-ring cooker, a sink and a chest freezer. To supplement the meagre rations in the canteen people try to beg, borrow or steal enough bits and pieces to cook a meal in the evening and there is usually somebody making coffee or tea or frying something. Beyond the kitchen lie the washroom, toilets and showers. These are a basic row of sinks with broken taps, then five shower cubicles with tatty curtains, three WCs also with holey curtains and two Turkish-style holes in the ground as urinals. Beyond this is the laundry. This is a roofless small yard just big enough for a row of sinks and for ten people to congregate. Some guys have taken their chairs there and they are sitting around smoking.

It's all too much to take in at once so I go back to my bunk, lie down and try to relax for an hour before we are called for dinner. It is then that I realise just how incredibly noisy it is. You can't hear yourself think. The TV blaring out, people shouting and jeering, competing conversations being carried out the length of the cellblock. What a change from the tomb. After about forty-five minutes of being unable to doze, I get up and go for a pee and to wash my face. Coming back my way is blocked by this huge, tough-looking black guy. He looks at me deadpan, sizing me up. He's got hands like frying pans and exudes an aura of danger. Worst of all, he looks astute. Shit. Big, mean and intelligent. I hope he doesn't have a thing for white middle-aged architects. Nodding his head slightly he asks: 'How's it going player?'

Phew, his opening sentence didn't involve the words bitch, handkerchief or batty boy. Still nervous, but doing my best not to show it, I offered: 'Hi, I'm Steve from England, how's it going?'

'Hanging in there, you know. Welcome to the spider's web. My name is Chino.'

Overplaying my hand somewhat, without thinking I say: 'Chino? Why do they call you Chino? You aren't Chinese.'

He frowned as if it was the dumbest thing anyone had ever said to him, cracked his knuckles and replied, 'Because my mother christened me Chino', then turned his back on me and walked away.

I scarpered back to my bunk and avoided any further casual enquiries until dinnertime. The spider's web indeed.

Football and fighting

It was only a few days after I had arrived, one crisp morning with a slight chill heralding the approach of winter. The sky was tinged a flawless pale violet and the orange ball of the sun was just beginning to show over the cane fields. The teenage guards in the sentry towers were draped in pink blankets with their forage caps holding them in place, looking like extras from some soppy *Star Wars* planet. Hut 2 were lined up, a dishevelled, muttering mob. The guards were shouting at them to shut up and form a straight line. It was still all very new to me.

Then all of a sudden a very thin white guy with a crippled leg steps out of line, lifts his walking stick and starts making machine-gun noises, shooting from the hip, pretending to mow the guards down. In a deranged John Wayne drawl he cries: 'Suck on that you commie bastards!'

Everyone falls about laughing and a Cuban voice rises above the din. 'Oi Stickman, shut it.'

The guy shoulders his walking stick weapon smartly, bows to everyone and shouts at me: 'Limey, one day you will be as crazy as me.'

Cy laughs and tells me as we shuffle to the canteen: 'Ohhh, now that my friend is Stickman, he really is crazy.'

I've got my watch back. I keep looking at it enjoying watching the second hand going round and round, and feeling drunk with the power of planning my time. It's not that I have a lot to do but after the dungeon, where days collapsed into nothingness and minutes ballooned into an eternity, time is starting to establish a simple rhythm again. There was an evil intelligence at work in that bloody dungeon; they pour sand in the cogs of your body clock and then all your mental processes start to fall out of synchronisation.

My embassy delivered the basics to the prison yesterday. A plastic chair, a frying pan, a wooden spoon and plastic knives and forks, plus my allowance of 20lbs of dried food (from an approved list), together with some books and sketching stuff, vitamins, letters and some life-changing phone cards. The vitamins never reached me, stolen I assume by the nurses who had to check them. The need for a plastic chair is a source of wonder to me. They can detain you for two years before they have to charge you and during that time you have to buy your own chairs if you want to sit down. Mine is a nice white plastic garden chair, blindingly white and looking very out of place among the ancient, filthy and much-repaired chairs of the long-termers. How bizarre this system is. Officially we are allowed one delivery a month but they say that this depends critically on your embassy delivering it to the prison gate or on a family visit. As everybody's families are in other countries this kind of limits things a bit. Many prisoners have an embassy visit only twice a year so they have to live by barter, scrounging and thieving. Being Cuba there exists a parallel system whereby certain prisoners get a monthly visit from women from the village who bring vegetables on a conjugal visit, the families of the prisoner wire money to the tart and the prison guards get a kickback. There is a much-fingered school exercise book circulating with photographs and telephone numbers of vegetable ladies. It seems that half the guards are pimping out their relations and the entire economy of the local town is dependent on stuff pinched from the prison or extorted from the prisoners. The hilarious thing is that like everything in this country the black market, even in prison, runs with a cheerful efficiency that the dead hand of the state can never come close to achieving.

If there was one benefit of a second-rate comprehensive school education in 1970s London, it was that from an early age your daytime world was populated by a random selection of humanity and that you needed to learn quickly to survive; a basic rule of life was that if you couldn't get along with most people you would get your head kicked in sooner or later. My school reflected the borough, so it was about a third middle-class kids, a third from traditional working-class families and a third from that peculiarly English class the terminally unemployed and genetically criminal. It was also completely mixed-race, which was unusual in those days. There was a long-established second-and third-generation Afro-Caribbean community, a rapidly expanding Asian community and an everchanging sprinkling of exotic faces. So in addition I had classmates who were refugees from the Biafran War, dispossessed Asians fleeing Uganda, some Cypriots from that nasty little civil war, Arabs and all sorts. Being the initial years of the egalitarian comprehensive experiment we were all mixed up with neither rhyme nor reason and batched into mixed-aptitude classes, to the exasperation of the poor teachers who had been dragged from the certainties of their grammar and secondary schools and told to get on with it. They had to teach woodwork to snivelling accountants' sons who couldn't saw a plank in half without ending up in hospital and then get cretins to try and recite Milton's *Paradise Lost*. Against all this was the underlying cruel violence of schoolboys; officially sanctioned in the bloodbath of rugby and the daily, unofficial battering and torture of the weak. I'm not sure I enjoyed it, but I think it gave me a basic understanding of the pack mentality of humanity in a confined space and how to avoid trouble.

Decompression. It's bad here, but it's better than Villa Marista and that's all that matters for a while. So, I am happy to move, not happy to be here. I'm sitting in a tatty concrete hut that looks like it was designed and built by educationally subnormal children using giant play blocks. Fifty criminals are watching, moist-eyed, *Mamma Mia!* on the telly while the wind gusts in. Huge Jamaican Yardies and evil little Colombian drug smugglers sit spellbound as Pierce Brosnan declares his eternal love for Meryl Streep on an island goat track (perhaps they are reminiscing about goat tracks they have loved). One lesson of the past months is that life can be very strange but people, despite appearances, can be comfortingly similar.

These first few days in 'Condesa' have been a strange return to the surface of the earth. It certainly isn't life as I know it, but it's a quarter of the way there. The terrible sensation of being buried alive has gone now, and that pressing weight on the chest at night has lifted. Being able to breathe the breeze somehow makes it safe to think about things other than surviving without going barmy. In the dungeon any thoughts of nicer things had to be carefully rationed. When all your energy is spent maintaining the defences it was only possible to risk thinking about many things when I was the confident master of my emotions. It sounds ridiculous to say it, but letters that I desperately waited for were left unopened for days until I felt up to reading them.

The companionship between this peculiar cast of characters is almost impressive, like the motley crew of a sinking ship. These are the menacing scum that you would run a mile from on the streets of Moscow, Naples, Quito or Kingston (Jamaica not Upon-Thames). But humanity is flexible. Even the crudest bastards evolve and adapt and so in their shared misery there exists a simple form of co-existence, the fruits of suffering I suppose. It's more than just a 'cease-fire' between thugs, it's a weird community with its own rules based on invisible lines of respect, sharing with mates, preying on the weak and with a hated underclass of the snitches, the '*chivatos*'. Rule number one is don't be one of the weak.

The judges didn't discriminate when it came to sentencing as everyone seems to be in for a fifteen-to eighteen-year

stretch. All equal before the law in a cruel joke. Everyone
has a different story to tell: some hilariously inept criminal
escapades, some tragic miscarriages of justice but mostly bad
luck. Mixed into this convict soup are those like me, 'pending
charges and provisionally detained'. We share every aspect
of the life of the convicted including the attentions of a re-
education officer, the assumption being that everyone is guilty
so why wait for a trial. The four confused businessmen in
my block all share a sense of outrage, injustice and wounded
pride as well as no previous convictions. The king of Canadian
businessmen Cy lies in bed gnashing his teeth or circles the
yard raging against the duplicity, bad faith and gossip that
got him here (fourteen months for him so far). And his hilarious, self-appointed batman Gadhafi, a young Salawhi student
accused of defrauding his telephone card, for which they want
an eight-year sentence.

Nobody else in Condesa had survived eight months of interrogation in Villa Marista, three months seems the average,
so I came here with a certain grudging respect. But a few days
later, during the evening cooking session, I have my first confrontation. The little space where we are allowed to prepare
some basic food ourselves is a madhouse in the evenings: one
four-ring electric cooker for fifty people with everyone having
to get it cooked, eaten and cleared away between inspection
and lights out. There seem to be a few guys who manage to
remain calm and go about it in a rational way and a tidy manner but just as many use it as an excuse to scream and shout
and leave mess all over the place for the next person. If you nip
back to your locker for a forgotten ingredient then anything
left unattended for a second is in mortal danger of disappearing, or worse, some low-life will just take your pot off the
stove if they want to disrespect you. It is immediately clear
why it makes sense to team up with one or two people; you
share everything that you can buy or barter and in return have
some degree of security.

Being the last guy in and not being a black belt at karate,
I decide to wait and see how the pecking order resolved itself.
I wait until the early evening scrum has dissipated and there
are a couple of rings vacant. There are just some little, rat-
like idiots yapping around the feet of their master, this huge
muscle-bound freak methodically slicing frankfurters while
he boils a pot of something. I collect my meagre rations and
implements and dump them down on an empty space on the
tiny shared worktop with a non-committal 'Good evening'.
This is met with a silent stare. He continues winding up his
rodents, one of whom I gather is called X, and I quickly finish
my cooking, dump the slop on to my plate and turn to carry it
and a few things back to my bunk, intending to come straight
back to clean up my mess and rescue my pot. He steps into
my path with his tin-lid knife in his hand.

'Hey, what the fuck are you doing leaving your shit here?'

Instinctively, without a second's hesitation, I put my face
into his, our noses almost touching and shout: 'I've only got
two fucking hands. I'll be back!'

He steps aside. I continue to my bunk with about twenty
pairs of eyes looking at me, my knees turning to water. Pluck-
ing up the courage to go back and wash my pan and clean the
worktop and ring, I half expect to be murdered before I can
enjoy my Uncle Ben's Mexican-style rice. But he just ignores
me. I guess it must mean something, probably just that when
he has a go at me it won't be from the front and it won't be
solo.

The next day, enjoying the sunrise while we line up, smelling the flowers (yes, how Cuban to have planted roses around
the canteen) and later watching cats play with their kittens in
the afternoon dust makes me feel almost normal.

The food in the canteen is really bad. It appears that sufficient supplies are sent to the camp by the central MININT
depot but little actually reaches our metal mess trays. First
off, some evaporates on the journey. Then when they get to

the prison gate the meat, oil, fruit and vegetables and flour are tithed by the guards before they enter the kitchen. Then when they're in the kitchen the cooks and trusty prisoners all steal ingredients for resale later. So when they finally get all the way to the mess hall there is very little left. There is a serving of chicken twice a month, a tiny serving of a drumstick each. Fresh vegetables are served on a limited and random basis and sometimes we get this pickled cabbage. To add insult to injury the trusties keep back the tastiest things and eat them after we have returned to the cellblock. We are all in a perpetual state of hunger and like Bob said 'a hungry man is an angry man'.

I write to my friends. Everything is so strange and disorientating and I find putting the words down on paper helps me to make some sense of it all. I don't want to explain everything, Some of them are worried enough already.

Exercise is compulsory and a welcome diversion. This afternoon there is a football tournament, and the teams are self-selecting on the basis of criminal and national mutual attraction, so we have São Paulo Dealers v. Juárez Rapists followed by Napoli Smugglers v. Montego Bay Murderers. The rare breeds and esoteric crimes have to fit in where they can. So I borrow a pair of plimsolls and play first half for the Napoli Smugglers. Luckily the sole of the right shoe was not properly connected to the upper, which meant I could limp off after thirty minutes with a bloody foot but dignity intact. They all thought it was a passable effort for an old white boy. The afternoon was enlivened by the rather unkempt Guatemalan, Javali. He has a beehive made from an old wooden rubbish bin which he keeps round the back and sometimes he takes it out to the exercise yard, which makes the bees really mad and God only knows why he does it. They chased us all around the football pitch for half an hour and he got stung eighty-seven times trying to get them all back in. Foolhardy and hilarious, he expects honey in about three months.

Weightlifting, using ingenious things made from bottles of

water and steel poles, is diligently undertaken and is border-
line compulsory. If you don't you are considered a bit suspect,
so even the 5ft weedy Mexican engineer is giving himself a
hernia lifting bottles of water on a scaffolding pole for an
hour a day.

On Saturday the finals of the tournament mean a whole
afternoon in the yard for the entire prison. I play my match
and we get knocked out. Two matches later it's the semi-
finals and it's the yellows versus the purples. The second half
starts to get nasty. A couple of people have already come off,
one with a twisted ankle the other with a horribly scraped
knee full of dirt and stones. Tempers are frayed and the yellow
shirts are desperate to get one back and level the score. X, a
talented footballer I have to admit, is twisting and turning
trying to dummy past Salim, who is playing for the purple
shirts. X has been winding him up all game but Salim, who
has no real footballing ability, just a natural athleticism, has
been a solid defender. Scything in to tackle X again, Salim is
rocked back on his feet by a massive elbow blow to the nose
and is momentarily stunned. Before he can tear X to shreds,
a melee of guards and prisoners rush on and intervene. X is
shouting abuse, proclaiming that it's an accident, but all the
while sniggering to his mates. You get extra time if you are
caught fighting so football presents some interesting opportunities to settle scores. If you can pull it off it's a very public
way of doing battle and by its very visibility you are immune
from punishment as long as you dress it up as an 'innocent'
foul. The re-education officer is totally unimpressed but to
cool everything down he tells a furious X that he is banned for
the rest of the tournament and Salim is then led off to the infirmary to be stitched up. The match ends but nobody is that
bothered now; we've had our excitement. The camp is split
between those who think X is an asshole who deserves what's
coming and others who think he is pretty cool for handing out
such a public humiliation.

When we go back inside Salim isn't there. Gossip filters back. Despite there being two doctors, seven nurses and six beds in the infirmary there are no sutures and there's no anaesthetic. It's all been sold by the staff. So they took Salim to the hospital in the local town but had to wait for an hour or so while they argued about whose petrol allowance it would come out of. Dinner comes and goes but still no sign of Salim. Eventually at around eight, that's six hours later, the gate is unlocked and he walks in. The blood has dried crispy brown on his uniform. He has a huge bandage stuck across his face, and one eye is swollen and purple. He needed six stitches in the end and they had to go all the way to Havana to get him seen to. Blimey, what on earth would happen if somebody was really ill or had a bad accident? I guess they would just die.

I have saved him some dinner. Over tea he tells us about the conditions in the local hospital. No X-ray machine. They thought he might have a fractured cheekbone but it's just a badly broken and slit nose, so bang goes his modelling career. It seems that people are terrified of getting sick or injured here. There is a bad history of things going wrong. I get up to take the dirty cups and plates to the kitchen and Salim follows, coming to help with the washing-up. On the way X, surrounded by his gang, confronts Salim and starts abusing him, provoking him to start a fight. I turn.

They exchange a few words and then Salim explodes in fury, moving in for the kill. But quick as a flash Peter, a righteously pissed off yet chilled Rasta, immediately puts his arms around him and holds him back, telling him to calm down. X, seeing his opponent disabled by a peacemaker, moves in to have a go. In a rage I fling the cups to the side, rush forward and wind him with a blow to the chest. I scream in his face in Spanish that I will kill him if he doesn't shut up. And that's it. It's all over as suddenly as it started. I pick up the cups and Salim and Peter go out the back, Salim still shouting and Peter talking him down.

Chino had been watching it all. 'How's it going, player?' he smiles approvingly and laughs at the ceiling.

Lying in bed after lights out, looking at the flickering TV light washing across the ceiling, I replay the whole thing. That was totally instinctual, real beasts of the forest stuff. I can't understand why, but I think this evening is a turning point. From this moment on I guess that means that as far as the rest are concerned we are now in a gang that will defend each other. A totally pathetic gang it has to be said, comprising a seventy-three-year-old Canadian businessman, a sixty-year-old Slovak misery guts, a forty-year-old Mexican telecoms engineer, a fifty-year-old English architect and a forty-year-old Algerian security guard, but it doesn't matter. Together we are stronger and our lives will be a little less miserable because of that.

One of the first things I did when I got here was to request a family visit. My mum and Sarah will come. I hadn't seen anyone for ages. The approval takes the authorities around a month to organise for some bizarre reason. This means that organising flights is messy and all done at the last minute. So many things about the process are awful but the visits themselves are arranged in a very humane way. You are, of course, all locked in but you are given private time with up to four family members for three hours. For an international visit they allow three visits in total. It's a hell of a long and expensive way to come for nine hours' company, but by God it's worth it. There is no guard sitting there, no chains, no glass screen and no microphone. It is one of the few aspects of this prison system that I think is good. It makes such a difference to be able to hold hands, hug and chat freely. Sure, the guard pops his head round the doorway from time to time, but he's actually respectful of our privacy.

The other thing I did after I got here was to go and see the re-education officer and explain I wanted to teach an architecture course. He smiled his inscrutable, mocking smile and said it should be okay but he needed to get approval, which could take months.

Every weekday at 10.30, thirty minutes after the second exercise period, prisoners got called out and trooped off to join classes, with the sweat from the yard still drying on their backs. There are three levels of English and Spanish, a course on business marketing and, for the really insane, Cuban political theory. The English courses are taught either by polite Canadians or, bizarrely, an unpleasantly hairy Ecuadorean drug dealer with only moderate English.

The one that made me chuckle was the marketing course. This is run by some pathetic songbird who had apparently managed to get fifty-three Cubans and several foreigners arrested as a result of his denunciations following his arrest for corrupt activities. Some bad-tempered and unforgiving Cubans are probably planning how to kill him at this very minute. I was tempted to sit in and listen to how he weaves his peculiar brand of marketing into some kind of serious lesson. In truth he has the pendulous lip of a self-pitying tapir and he leaks an invisible cloud of rat pheromone and so the idea of spending time in his presence makes me feel sick. Thank God he is in the other cellblock. Actually I think they did that on purpose, as according to my new friends it was he who had been cheerfully telling inmates that he had denounced my boss, and thus I could reasonably conclude that my personal chain of nasty events started in some fashion with this jerk.

* 　 * 　 *

Finally the day of the visit comes and I couldn't sleep with all the thoughts racing through my mind. How will they be? What will they think of this place? What has the lawyer said to them? What food will they bring? I'm sitting on the dwarf wall by the visiting area enjoying the feeling of the winter sun on my legs when some metal on metal squealing announces that visitors are passing through the dog run. And there they are. Both of them looking great. They in turn have checked me out in a millisecond and are happy to tell me that I look thin but normal again.

We are locked into the partially derelict visiting room and the hours fly by. I hadn't realised but I suppose my physical recovery must seem miraculous. When they had last seen me I was transparently pale, skeletal with shaggy hair and stinking of confinement. I had been suffering from tinnitus, a thumping head and badly blurred vision and by all accounts my conversation had swung from totally vague to hyper and back again in a few sentences. In short I had been a complete mess. And three weeks of regular sunshine, exercise, air, companionship and space had transformed me. My eyesight was perfect again and although I was still physically weak I was improving each day.

On the third day we are allowed a conjugal visit. At six in the evening I am led out with a bag containing a spare blanket (I hear it is cold) some soft drinks and my wash things. I meet Sarah under the floodlights by the visitors' centre and we are taken to a small room with a rickety bed and a little primitive bathroom. The trusty has left a rose in a yoghurt pot on the bedside table. The guard locks us in and reminds us that she has to leave at 5.45 a.m. Sarah has bought a simple supper and we eat, nervously chatting away as if the past nine months had never happened. We tiptoe around the mountains of hurt and try to keep the mood buoyant.

'What an adventure, a night in prison.'

Catching up on the news about all sorts of people and the minutiae of home is infinitely comforting. Later, in the dark she asks me about what it was really like in the dungeon. I can't bring myself to talk about it. It will take a few more visits before I will feel strong enough to even think about it. And I ask her what it was like for her, in the hospital and then the long recovery. But she can't bring herself to talk about it either.

'I'm much better now, sweetheart, and that's all that matters.'

We lie side by side on the ancient bed, trying to get comfortable under the scratchy blanket. The reduced meds take effect and she is soon away with the fairies, but for me sleep is elusive. Despite the physical intimacy, a gulf of solitude separates us. The sodium lights left on all night to illuminate the perimeter wire cast tangerine shadows on the moth-eaten, flowery curtains and the sounds of a prison going to sleep fade to sighs and take me with them.

In the chill morning, we have a hurried lukewarm coffee from a flask and a cold bucket shower. Before we know it there is a hammering on the door and it's time to leave. We part at the dog run gate, a snatched hug and then it's over.

By mutual, unspoken consent we chose not to reveal the extent of our individual suffering until it was all over.

Anyone for tennis?

We moved huts today as the place is being renovated to bring
it back up to the standard of the pig farm it used to be. This
was an extraordinary spectacle of politically correct misman-
agement. Randomly selected bunches of prisoners do all the
work. The only common characteristic of the Canadian kiddy-
fiddler, Dominican smuggler and Colombian loony who are
currently rebuilding the perimeter fence using Frankenstein's
electric arc-welding equipment is their complete lack of
knowledge and experience of welding. Supervised by two majors, four captains, ten lieutenants and about twenty guards,
they proceed at a snail's pace in a shower of sparks, cursing,
collapsing poles and general mayhem. Significantly the only
person missing from the supervising team is a doctor with a
defibrillator. I was told to unload a lorry of bunk-bed bits and
assemble them. A relatively harmless task made interesting
only because half the nuts and bolts and the spanner were stolen. So we are all sleeping in a state of nervous anticipation.
One careless fart could trigger a general collapse.

I have made a French friend, JL. JL runs the library, which
is a converted cell off the exercise yard, and I like his cocky
Gallic style. There is his desk with a pencil and an exercise
book for logging books in and out, and about six plastic chairs
with people either dozing out of the sun or huddled around
talking about their cases. The books are arranged on sagging,
termite-riddled shelves by language, the range of nationalities
and their vintage, a living fossil record of the various people
who have passed through La Condesa. Whatever the critics

may say about the literary merits of Stephen King and John
Grisham they are avidly read by the strangest collection of
people in the strangest of places. They are certainly popular
with criminals in Cuba. Not really my cup of tea, but then
nothing much in my life is at the moment.

I had heard of the case of JL but not paid much attention
to it before. He told me he had met me at a social event ten
years ago. But then, as most social events seem to have been
conducted in a haze of rum, it's not surprising that I couldn't
remember him. He's a small, handsome, middle-aged man
with a neat parting and the Coq Sportif walk of a prize ban-
tam. I see him pass by the cell window each day with his
tennis racket in his hand, eyes fixed on some dot in the far
distance. His release date probably.

He told me his story. Interpol and the French government
had both repeatedly confirmed his innocence of international crimes but he had been charged for them here in any
case. He had a very particular hatred for the jealous son of a
famous Cuban politician, who he felt had a hand in his fate,
and had nothing but contempt for his notoriously inept prosecutor, Duma. Word on the street was that Duma had famously
arrested and then charged the wife of the Ecuadorean ambassador with money laundering after she had taken her husband's
monthly salary to the bank and asked to change it to local
pesos. Fired with a furious passion for punishment, he is apparently a modern Robespierre but with the IQ of a baboon. Poor
JL has been rotting in here for almost four years and apparently
has at least another six in front of him. Apart from being the
king of the library, he was also one of the top tennis players.

The only good thing about this dump is that there is a
tennis court. Well sort of. It's a large concrete rectangle oc-
cupying one quarter of the wind-blasted yard. It is wider and
shorter than a proper court and with a very uneven playing
surface. One end is definitely the crap end as the prevailing
wind is against you, the sun is in your eyes and it has cracks

like an elephant's arse. But it does have some lines painted on it and, incredibly, a rather droopy net extensively repaired by the fishermen prisoners. Not too many people are that interested in playing: too much like hard work and not much excuse for a punch-up. So I can pretty much guarantee a game every day. I borrow a racket and balls until my family can send one. The position of top dog is a hotly contested one. JL and Jamaican Jay have a long-standing and simmering battle for supremacy. They are both excellent. JL is always crisply turned out in proper whites, the sun glinting off his matching teeth, and Jay in tattered rags with dry eczema patches from long-term vitamin deficiency. People actually get scurvy in here.

JL is too busy and anyway he is in the wrong cellblock, but Jay has time on his hands so he agreed to teach me tennis. Jay is a well-read, skilled engineer from a good family so God only knows how he ended up here. He told me his story one night. I believed about 10 per cent of it but that doesn't matter. He's a good man and had been a bit of a local tennis champ in his youth.

Like most long-term prisoners he is clearly suffering from depression and the catastrophic separation from his family. So to give himself something to do he is reteaching me tennis. In return I give him my books when I've finished with them, and food. He particularly likes the P. G. Wodehouse ones.

JL has read the entire penal code and all the relevant law books and is a mine of rather depressing information. He has also studied all of the cases passing through. He presents an alarming analysis of Cuban law, one that is just too ghastly to want to dwell on.

'Zis starts with ze basic presumption in ze law. In France, and even in England, everything is legal unless it is specifically stated zat it is illegal. In Cuba, as with Mister Stalin, everything is forbidden unless ze law says you can do it. Zis is a scandal, zis is an inversion of natural law.

Zis means everyzing can be illegal if they say so, non?'

So far so depressing. The only thing I could think of to say was 'Fuckkkkkkk'.

'And then they 've ze *conviction morale, tambien.* Zis is zere secret weapon!'

'And that is . . . ?'

'*Conviction morale?* You do not know? *Conviction morale* is where zee instructor believes you are guilty but ee 'as no evidence. If ee thinks you are guilty zen ee does not need to 'ave evidence to get a conviction. Voilà. End of story. So, do not expect anything good my friend. In my case zay 'ave five thousand pages and no evidence. Paah.'

'Fuckkkkkkk.'

'Exactly. Well actually we 'ave it in France as well, but we 'aven't used it since Napoleon. N'est- ce pas.'

Fuck. So it's the Frenchies' fault after all. Bloody typical. After this brutal summary I decide for my mental health that our conversations going forward should be about tennis and the rugby results. It's just too damn depressing to have an intelligent analysis of the situation served up. I shall just have to concentrate on my backhand.

With his trial long past and the only hope of salvation a prison transfer back to France, JL's family started a media campaign. They have thousands and thousands of people on a petition and all sorts of media and political support but he is sanguine about the possibility of any success.

'If it 'appen it 'appen,' he says.

We discuss the relative merits of making a big stink in the press before the trial. His view is that it will not hurt me and that what will be will be, but I disagree. I think the Cubans react negatively to bad press. It will probably make my situation a lot worse, as they will invent something new to justify my detention without trial. So I have told the family to say nothing to the press and to rely on diplomatic pressure no matter how ineffectual. In fact the diplomatic pressure is not that applied by HMG's half-hearted efforts but by the network of family contacts in the diplomatic community in Havana. My fate is the subject of a lot of unofficial questions and from what I hear the foreign community is now very concerned about the safety of foreign executives in this sinister witch-hunt. A lot of people have left and offices have closed down in the last six months as more and more people have been arrested. So my strategy is for me to become a real inconvenience to them, not to antagonise them. They haven't been able to find anything dirty on me, as I am clean, of that I am certain. But from what I see around me, falsifying evidence and listening to fake denunciations is part of their modus operandi so I am not going to start poking a stick up their arse in public. Hopefully they will be content with simply stealing the assets of the company and let me go.

Letters from home have been variously hilarious, touching, informative and illegible, but they have all been gratefully received. They are not the difference between sanity and the psychiatric ward that they were in the dungeon, but they remain a lifeline to a normal world. The routines of this place are now familiar and all things considered life has improved for me and I now feel I have the energy to start to get to grips with this bizarre society.

The currency in here is tobacco. Cartons of very British-sounding H. Upmann are the price of anything from a haircut (choices fairly limited) to the monthly rent of a spoon. Actually, the local pronunciation 'aitchiupma' perfectly describes a product that produces plenty of phlegm and a hacking cough. I have discovered a market for my meagre talents as a painter. My portraits of prisoners' wives are in great demand now that Xmas is coming. It's actually touching how many say when presenting a photo of an overweight, snaggle-toothed hairy beast that she actually looks more like Jennifer Lopez, Beyoncé or Shakira. I also have a sideline in tasteful erotic nudes (ladies only), but I refuse to combine the two subject matters as it would inevitably lead to unfortunate comments, plus the thought of the details would put me off my bean soup. So after three weeks of pre-Xmas rush I have used all my paper and amassed a small fortune in 'aitchiupma'.

I am slowly beginning to understand some of the differences between the various gangs in here and I finally twigged the difference between the Caribbean drug guys and the Latin American ones. The Caribbean ones all got caught in boats or planes with tons of stuff in chases involving helicopters, gunfire and mayhem. Basically they are pirates, which demands a relatively normal IQ, if not a normal moral compass. The Latinos in here are without exception mules; people gullible or terrified enough to eat twenty condoms of cocaine for a pre-flight breakfast or pack a brick of hash with their underpants. Morons to a man. Not being content with being stupid enough to get caught, they do daft things in prison. They have a very bizarre hobby. They insert pea-sized plastic balls under the skin of their penises, using a sharpened biro tube. The prison shoe mender then sews it up. Israel from Ecuador apparently holds the record of seven and he tells me that he has done it to surprise his wife when he gets out. Now that's stupid. What's wrong with a bunch of roses?

The Jamaicans have robustly old-fashioned views on the Old Testament, which is conveniently silent on the subject of drug smuggling and firearms, and so there is no sign of any batty boy behaviour at their end of the cell. There are a few preening Latino bodybuilders who spend a suspicious amount of time blending each other's banana-flavoured power drinks, but in general the love that dare not speak its name keeps its trap shut. The random inspections are rather annoying. The main purpose of these inspections is to keep the guards happy and stamp out the vile crime of keeping sardine tins in your locker. The main purpose of the sardines is to use the lid, folded in half, as a knife for carving your initials in the prison bread etc. I have seen the documentaries about

Mexican prisons where the inmates hide their knives up their rectums. Luckily this is Cuba and the guards (unlike in Mexico, obviously) have no desire to look up convicts' arses, so the informal arrangement is that everyone leaves their tool under their mattress. A solution which greatly relieves me, although I dare not make my own knife just yet as it seems that the captain is on my back for some reason. Yesterday I got bawled out by Simiento for having a photo of my family inside my locker door. He shouted that it was forbidden and that if he saw it again I would be in serious shit. Nodding vigorously and accepting my heinous guilt I could not help but notice that everyone in front of me had photos on their locker doors. Simiento gave me an extra hard, final glare and stalked off to inspect the toilets.

My Friday supper club for business-class passengers is going well. Last night I did Chinese, although to be fair the only Chinese thing about it was that it was cooked in a communist country.

Thankfully, tennis, football and chess now seem to take up lots of time. It's like being retired except without the G&Ts. I'm generally pleased with progress, having moved out of the realms of the pathetic in all three sports to the merely hopeless. The footie is hotting up as the season draws to a close. I recalled the story of the Colombian goalkeeper who was shot the day after his team lost in the final. Well 50 per cent of my team are Colombian criminals and I am the goalie. Hence the slight nerves before each match. Our inspirational captain got very emotional today as we lost 9–5 (he missed three penalties!). Despite the final score I didn't embarrass myself too much and was encouraged by a lone voice from the touchline: 'Lord Stephen Regal (an old dancehall singer I gather or maybe a wrestler) ya pussy man.' Actually the only thing warranting a yellow card is playing like a sissy, and a serious foul is basically either punching the ref or trying to escape over the wall during half-time. Robust play is expected but the beekeeping berk Javali lost it yesterday and in the final seconds of injury time ran on and laid out his own forward. Then he fought with the guard who ran on to congratulate him. His judgement must have been impaired by the bee venom as last night he made a disastrous attempt to harvest his honey.

It was dark and the cellblock steel gate was locked. After a bit of banging and crashing round the back Javali suddenly appeared wearing the wire cover of an electric fan as a hat and swathed in an old, holey mosquito net. He ran through the hut to the laundry at the back waving a bucket with a mixture of honey and shattered bee hive in it and shouting, 'Look, I have honey!', closely followed by 2,000 angry bees. Total pandemonium broke out with everyone hiding under the sheets and running around swatting bees. So today, with his head swollen to about double its normal size, some irrational behaviour was to be expected.

Apart from a few humorous interludes life is crushingly tedious and there is absolutely no news about my case. Still no formal charges and still a secret file that my lawyer has no access to. I've had some time to reflect and an opportunity to discuss things with the other businessmen here and as a result a few things have become clear. It seems that the reason I was detained was because of the malicious denunciation of my business partner by a competitor of his. It is also pretty obvious that the reason they kept me in the dungeon for eight months was to try to get me to denounce fresh victims, which of course I refused to do. One day they will have to charge me or release me, but they have two years in which to present charges. Yes, two years in exactly the same conditions as convicted murderers. Making fun of the whole thing is my way of coping with it, but the underlying reality isn't amusing whatsoever.

Yesterday I found an interesting book in the library about Spanish history. The bit about Cuba I knew: Columbus lands in 1492, bla bla. Hatuey the leader of the Taino Indians is burned at the stake in 1512 but it doesn't matter, they named the beer after him. By 1557 there were fewer than two thousand Tainos left out of three million. Bla bla. By 1774 the population was 172,000, of which 44,000 were African slaves. So far, so genocidal. Where the book gets interesting is when it starts talking about the Inquisition and I begin to see some parallels. I knew the Castros had received a good Jesuit education and had been enthusiastic students of the methods of the KGB and later the Stasi, but I had no idea that the methods of dealing with threats to state orthodoxy were so engrained in Hispanic culture. It seems that the Inquisition, which came to Cuba in 1613, has never left.

I make my notes. 'Edict of Grace'. The congregation were encouraged to relieve their conscience and denounce sinners. Sounds like Ivan asking me to rat on people. 'Promise of Tolerance'. The inquisitor would show leniency to those who denounced other sinners. Interesting, JL had explained clause 52(ch) of the penal code to me. If the instructor wishes to apply this clause it will come with the words, 'the accused has shown a positive comportment and has collaborated during the investigation'. This is the roundabout way of saying it is the rat's reduction in sentence.

Apparently the Inquisition was self-financing and it relied on confiscated property to survive. Surprise, surprise! Some robed dude in Toledo had ruefully written: 'If they do not burn they do not eat.' Well, that pretty much sums things up, doesn't it?

And then the details just started to get bizarrely conjoined. Detention for up to two years before the 'Qualifiers' (now there is a suitably abstract title) determined if heresy had taken place. 'Detention entailed preventative sequestration of property'; oh, doesn't it just. And they targeted the wealthy because there was more to confiscate. 'Entire process conducted in secrecy and the accused only being told of his supposed crimes at the last moment.' Well I suppose the prevailing opinion must be that if it works don't mend it.

And then, finally, to prove my paranoid theory, 'the trial was conducted by the Fiscal'. So four hundred years after the Inquisition exactly the same methods are used against me. Ivan should be wearing a black robe and a pointy hat, not badly pressed nylon fatigues with a shiny bottom. Bloody hell, it's a good job I didn't read this book in the dungeon. I would have freaked out. At least here I have some friends around to laugh about it and tell me I'm full of shit.

In the interminable evenings we go out to the back, smoke, rinse socks and rerun our back stories. Combing back and forth to try and work out where we have gone wrong. It's a boring but strangely comforting ritual. It's a game of sorts. As somebody explains the whole story from beginning to depressing denouement, everyone listens patiently and then we try and deduce at what moment it was already too late and the traps were sprung.

Christmas comes but once a year

The week before Christmas my wife, one son and both daughters will come to Cuba. I am to be allowed to see them three times for a couple of hours and Sarah will get to stay over for one night.

The day of the first visit dawns and I am nearly sick with anticipation. I skip exercise in the morning as I want to check over my letters again. Some I hand over to the re-education officer so he can copy them and read them at his leisure, others I fold carefully and put inside the rim of my jungle hat. I will pass them over accompanied by some conspiratorial eyebrow waggling to my kids to smuggle out in the dirty lunch things.

Luckily the officer handling visits this week is a very nice guy and lets them bring in way over my allowance of food, plus all sorts of prohibited items. I skip lunch because they will bring something tasty with them. So after a cold shower I wait impatiently for the call while the rest of the cell dozes. I have a bag ready; cups, a flask of tea, plastic plates and cutlery, some tissues and some cold water. The visiting rooms are in the same block as the library and shop but with separate access via a gated, central corridor. They are nothing more than doorless cells, with a dirty table and a few chairs. The floor is bare, dusty cement, the grubby walls covered in flaky paint. The lights don't work so we shall dine in soft light from the barred Miami blinds. These rooms are full of history. It wasn't always a prison for foreigners. After conversion from a pig farm it was for a while a high-security place for big fish. Ochoa, the celebrated general executed for treason after the Angolan war, spent his last night in one of these rooms. Maybe it's this one we are about to have lunch in. The real reason for his elimination was rumoured to be jealousy, pure and simple. After all, this is a country where there are only ever two stars; a giant supernova called Fidel and that sneaky little red dwarf Raúl.

So in a flurry of hugs and kisses we get locked in and then we unpack the salad, potatoes and roast beef and toast each other with fruit juice. This is Rosy's first visit and she is wide-eyed with curiosity and fear. While standing in the sun waiting to get through the dog run, fifty pairs of wolf eyes had been picking them apart. Another cellblock was exercising. It must have been a scary experience for young girls. The food, forbidden but not forgotten, tastes wonderful. But I'm not paying much attention to it, I'm just basking in the sensation of family. The hours fly by and before we know it, it's over. We hastily pack up the first instalment of ingredients for my Christmas lunch that the guard had kindly overlooked with a wink. I will have to sort him out later and post something tasty out of the window. And then we part; me back to my cellblock with my cellmates and them on the long road back to Havana with their thoughts.

The next couple of visits pass so quickly I don't have time to savour the moment and before I could say all the things I wanted to say they were going for the last time. Hugging goodbye and watching them troop out with glistening eyes was heartbreaking.

Christmas Eve turned into New Year and the temperature dropped to new lows at night. Steam came off our midnight piss and despite the forced, festive activities everyone's spirits sank faster than the thermometer.

I decide to try and snap out of it by writing a New Year letter to my chums overseas:

7th January 2013

Dear all,

The world can be safely divided up between those people who can think of nothing finer than spending Christmas and seeing in the New Year with 49 convicts in a draughty concrete hut and those who would prefer the comforts and company of home. It was obvious to me that the penal system was going to go the extra mile to make it a dismal affair and that I was going to have to summon up all my 'ho ho ho' reserves of festive cheer to make it bearable. Luckily when things are looking rather bleak or boring something bizarre or ludicrous pops up and things look a little brighter for a while.

The week before Christmas saw the prison shoe mender rushing out some last-minute 'special alterations' that I described before. Sarah brought Oscar, Naomi and Rosy over and she was pleased to find out that the only surprise I had for her was a painting. The visit was my Xmas present, and a lovely one it was too. We even had a turkey lunch, which despite the lack of booze and roast potatoes was very Christmassy. The only other pre-season news was that the administration decided to kill all the bees. As you can imagine we have had a very depressed Guatemalan mooning about the place ever since.

One of the business class inmates is a terminally miserable Slovak called Matej, who has an irrational nervousness about black people with loud voices. As that covers about 30% of the people he sleeps, eats and showers with you can imagine his face. This Matej surprised our fellow dining club members by offering to give us a traditional Slovakian Xmas meal at 6 p.m. on the dot Christmas Eve. As I was supplying Christmas breakfast (smoked salmon, toast, juice and coffee), Christmas lunch (turkey, stuffing, spuds, carrots, gravy and cranberry sauce), Christmas pudding (plum dumplings and custard), mince pies and Christmas cake all to be swilled down with 8lt of real Coke this seemed only reasonable.

Summoning every ounce of courage Matej spent 3 hours fighting in the kitchen with the Jamaicans and emerged triumphant at 5.45. He presented us with a plate each on which sat 10 crackers, a dollop of honey, 10 garlic cloves, an apple and a rather long prayer in Slovak. So on Christmas Eve we went to bed at 10 p.m. as usual with hunger pains and foul breath. At 10.30 p.m. the lights came back on, and as a special treat we were allowed light until midnight.

The commandant had been infected with the spirit of the season and his gifts to us were new padlocks on the barracks and a snazzy new pepper spray for all the guards. He gave us a quick 'feliz Navidad' and then scarpered before we found out that the Christmas breakfast served officially was in fact to be absolutely nothing. At the best of times it is simply bread. On Christmas day it was just no bread. So you can imagine when my four friends and I tucked into our salmon etc. . . To make amends I distributed the contents of a huge tin of chocolates I had received. Christmas dinner, the contents of which I have already bored you with, went down very well. Again surrounded by slavering wolves. We had a spirited game of footie with no injuries, plenty of cheer and head hit the pillow as usual at 10 p.m.

Since then we had New Year's Eve, noteworthy only because they turned the water off and then life has settled into its normal round of inspections, lining up, cleaning lockers, eating biscuits, etc.

The big news is that they have introduced 'bolas criollas'. This sounded like a sexually transmitted disease from Mexico and when they asked me if I wanted to sign up I refused. But, it turns out that it is a perfectly respectable game played by old gentlefolk in parts of Spain and the former colonies. However, and this is where we have a big however, I think it is highly unlikely that there is a maximum-security prison in the UK where they give 2 sets of convicts 10 cannonballs each and

expect them to throw them at each other without incident. The
potential for foul play, gamesmanship and evil is enormous and
the league is even more savagely contested than the footie. In
the footie we are doing well, we have won as many as we have
lost. The last match saw me off the pitch inside 10 minutes
after receiving a volley at short range in the upper section of the
trousers. No permanent damage.

And that my friends is that. Don't bother asking about
lawyers, trials, dates, etc. as the situation remains the same.
When there is something concrete you will hear.

Lots of love
Stephen

What I don't tell them, of course, is how depressed I have
been after the family left. On New Year's Eve I stood in a
small clump of guys waiting in the damp midnight air to use
the telephone to try and phone home. The coronel had made
a big song and dance about giving us special permission. The
ghostly orange light of the yard floodlights turned all the
shadows purple black and I suddenly felt very lonely and a
long way from salvation. When my turn came I couldn't get
through to home and then, desperate to speak to a voice from
the real world, I started calling all sorts of friends. But they
were all engaged, or out having fun, or didn't want to pick
up to some unknown number. So after a fruitless ten minutes
leaving faltering answer phone messages I slammed the handset on to its cradle. Hating the whole universe I stomped off
in a filthy mood to bury my head under my pillow.

Battypaper

In the classrooms there were dusty piles of senior school chemistry, physics and maths textbooks: mildewed traces of tutors who had gained release. The rooms were locked with ancient padlocks and for some reason almost half the prison population had a key. There were also some old paintings. At some point an artistic prisoner must have found the time and materials to teach painting. But clearly this was a long time ago, under a previous, more humane governor. There were two classrooms set back behind cellblock 3 in a row that included the workshop, the dentist and, at the far end, the hospital. The workshop was interesting. Whenever I went past the door was always open and two or three trusties were busy behind wobbly benches piled high with a tangle of electrical bits and pieces, scrap wood and primitive tools. The main function of the workshop was to provide a free repair service to the guards who would bring all manner of things in from home for mending. In their spare moments the trusties would try and repair fans or watches for prisoners. I loved to pause and watch the tragedy unfold. The repairer, brow furrowed in concentration, would be staring angrily into the microscopic bowels of a five-buck copy of a Rolex, the air bitter with the smoke of the flux boiling off his homemade soldering iron. A Bronze Age tool was poised in mid-air, waiting to administer the blow that would either bring the ticker back to life or consign it to scrap, the watch owner praying that all would be okay. Not surprisingly, this procedure was normally fatal to the watch. And so having handed over two packs of H. Upmann for the failed repair the prisoner would glumly go back to his cell with a pocket full of fragments and the sobering thought that for the remaining twenty years of his sentence he would have to ask other people: 'How much longer?'

I went to the dentist for a check-up. The prison dentist was a source of much speculation of a sexual nature. She came twice a week in the mornings. A cry would go up from whoever was hanging off the bars on the cell gate and a small crowd would quickly rush to cop a view. She was an unremarkable woman in her mid-thirties, her white coat taut at the front and loose at the back. The brutal consensus was that she had great tits, no ass and probably had bad legs. She always had a blousy-type blouse fluffing out of the cuffs and cracks and slacks worn with stack-heeled shoes. She knew she was the object of intense interest to the 150 pairs of eyes that followed her 'tic, tac, toc' walk past the cellblocks to the infirmary. She had an interesting routine. The major would be her first patient. No sooner had she disappeared from view in the direction of her chair than the major would come past at a brisk canter in his best khakis, with a cheery good morning to whoever was in his path. It was the only time he ever seemed happy. Then half an hour later he would saunter past, his silly cap under his arm and his shiny nylon uniform alive with static. If he had any hair it would be standing on end. Apparently his mysterious dental condition had required two sessions of mid-morning treatment a week for the past year and there was no sign of improvement. As the infirmary had no anaesthetic it was safe to conclude it was not root-canal treatment he was getting. When I was called, it was totally out of the blue. I eventually found her chamber: whether it was of love or torture I never found out. Lying back on the cracked Soviet vinyl chair, with the huge blind eye of the broken lamp staring at me, I was intoxicated by the perfume and nearly passed out at her touch. I could sense a woman's body close and felt her warmth underneath the stiff white cotton of her sleeves.

Oh lucky major. Closing my eyes and opening wide, I could feel the scratchy point of her stainless steel probe tapping each tooth in turn. She counted slowly while I controlled my gag reflex and tried to look manly.

'Thirty-two,' she concluded, to nobody in particular. 'You have nothing wrong. Goodbye.'

And that was it. I turned to give her my most alluring: 'Goodbye, señorita. Until next time?' But she was busy writing down the number of teeth I had and ignored me. The bitch.

Most people seemed to attend at least one class a week. Soon after I had arrived Salim explained that this was because there was a points system. To get a good-conduct write-up at the end of the year and qualify for the 50 per cent rule you had to do three things: participate in exercise, work and attend lessons. Of course I loved doing the exercise but the idea of going to ghastly lessons or, worse still, working for the bastards was very unappealing. Out of boredom I had volunteered a few times to do things like knock walls down with a sledgehammer, but hard physical labour in this heat and on these rations was a path to an early grave.

Finally the re-education officer tells me I can teach architecture. I spend a few days planning the course. It's an interesting challenge because of the huge spread of character and education of the guys who have signed up. They varied from people with tertiary education, degrees and things, through to skilled artisans and all the way down to the barely literate. Some of them have signed up because they are bored and anything that gets them out of their cell for a few hours twice a week is worth the effort. But I have decided to make it difficult for them. I plan to set homework once a week to be done over the boring Sunday, and to make the lessons as proactive as I can.

My general idea is to make it a three-month endeavour. The first month I will be teaching the basics of drawing conventions so that they will be able to read technical drawings and then actually start to prepare them. By the end of that they should be able to understand and prepare a simple plan, section and elevation and then some axonometric and single-point perspectives. The second month will be devoted to setting a brief for a dream house on an imaginary Caribbean plot and getting them to start imagining concepts. The third month they will be asked to prepare some presentation drawings. I have become totally absorbed by the planning of it. Then one day my supplies were delivered and so I could start.

Unlocking the wooden classroom door was always a strange experience. Twice a week I actually got to unlock and open a door with my own hands. The feel of a poxy padlock yielding to an illicit key was so alien. It was always baking hot outside and deliciously cooler inside. The swing of the door would send a gust of turbulence into the dark interior. Billions of specks of chalk dust from a million erased lessons would swarm in the razor-thin sunbeams that pierced the metal window slats. The smell was of wooden chairs and wasted schooldays. Dumping my collection of pads, rulers and set squares on a desk I would wrestle the ancient Miami blinds open and let the sun flood in. I cleaned the blackboard while the students trooped in, argued about chairs and exchanged gossip between cellblocks.

At the beginning there were not enough desks for the students, but within a few weeks, as the intellectual demands of the course started to kick in, the class rapidly dwindled to eight, and then to seven when Chino finally got his transfer to a prison in the Bahamas.

A friend from home had sent a few scale rulers, some pencils and rubbers and a few rolls of butter paper, and sure enough about a month later they arrived and the classes began. When I explained butter paper everyone just fell about laughing: 'Haha, battypaper man.'

It was fascinating to see how men with no background in design learned to manipulate a pencil, began to think about three dimensions and developed the confidence to talk about it in front of others. What I found surprisingly touching was how they found some kind of hope in the class.

All of us with families succumbed to mawkish sentimentality from time to time. So finding something to occupy our brains other than the damn prison system and survival was important. We need something to hope for other than the inevitable reunion with loved ones, a decent steak, a few cold ones at a bar with some mates and getting back to work. Something to dream about other than bloodthirsty revenge, everlasting sex and a swim in the sea. Without planning it, these silly lessons gave a few of us something to lose ourselves in. It takes us out of La Condesa and to a brighter future.

As the weeks passed and the flaky students fell away, the remaining students started to fall under the spell of their imaginary dream homes. The first tentative sketches slowly came into focus, and they developed some confidence in their hands. Chino went for a relatively sophisticated steel and glass, luxury Miami look. His decision-making process was logical, swift and final, as befitted his criminal occupation. In his house, the world could see in and he could see out. It was straight out of *Yachts International* magazine and screamed money. Jesus shuffled and fidgeted his design into life, each week moving a grid here, smoothing back a surface there. A patient and solid white volumetric building that could only be post-modern Mexican. He felt comfort in the church-like solidity and the calm, internal spaces. Panama wanted a huge three-storey neoclassical plantation-style house in wood. The kind of thing rich folks back home had.

A new businessman arrives. He is from Argentina and is in the oilfield supply sector. He was provisionally held for over a year in VM for sabotage. He puts up a good front but something is broken inside. It's actually amazing that he isn't in the mental hospital, because to have survived VM for a year takes exceptional mental and emotional strength. His arrival has kick-started the eternal cycle of each of us repeating our history. Naturally, after explaining his misfortunes he is anxious to see how he fits into the pattern and so during the long evenings we reciprocate. His story was pretty short in the run-up. He was country representative for an oil-services company and had sold some lubricant for deep-well drilling. The idiots using it didn't read the instructions and broke a drill, thus ruining a particular well. Rather than admit they had made a mistake they accused the poor guy of sabotage. He had been in the country less than a year.

*　　*　　*

My own story was a bit more long-winded.

In the early years, working on the first projects, I had felt that I was actually part of something positive, something more than just a mad job in a funny country. It sounds slightly daft in retrospect, but I felt I was doing something other than just adding to a developer's profit margin. I was a tiny part of a move to create a more liberal society in a beleaguered and bullied backwater. I will never forget one of our early employees telling me that with his initial pay cheque he went and bought a glass of milk, his first milk for five years. The foreign investment laws were freshly minted and the attitude of the officials we dealt with was to welcome us with gritted teeth. Our local counterparts were very tough negotiators. One rather unpleasant old lunatic in charge of investment in old Havana told me during a heated argument about the cost of plumbing that he had enjoyed killing people like me in Vietnam. At the time I was surprised not by his negotiating style but by the revelation that the Cubans had in fact been up to no good in that part of the world. Generally speaking, all these reluctant *hombres de negocios* had were dusty title deeds proving no US claim on their prospective projects and their principles, and so contracts were honoured to the letter. It was as simple as that. In that honeymoon period we trained up the engineers and architects, computerised offices, brought all sorts of new construction technologies to the country and people were happy to see us. We actually did things that changed Havana for the better in countless ways. We built the finest hotels, ran factories, funded everything from kids' milk to motorbikes, made feature films and collected contemporary art. And best of all during these years, we supported many hundreds of people and their families.

My view of the embargo on Cuba was coloured by the outrageously provocative behaviour of the local USINT. The quasi-ambassador pulled off stunts like a pre-thanksgiving press interview when he introduced the journalists to his two doomed turkeys; the male one called Fidel and the female Raúl. The argument between the governments seemed to be caught in a surreal vortex of childish tit for tat. The Cubans painted huge cartoons of Bush with a Hitler moustache on the roads outside the USINT. The Americans had a techno retort in the form of a giant electronic billboard on the façade showing anti-Cuban factoids. The Cubans' brilliant but ultimately ridiculous reply was to erect a giant forest of flagpoles to fly huge black flags. The overall effect was as if somebody was expecting Darth Vader to give a speech to the troops. Then in an astounding act of hypocrisy, something that the US seems to specialise in, they allowed American exporters of food and medicine to export to Cuba for cash only. This ballooned to such an extent that a year ago they were selling $700m worth of goods a year for everyone from Cargill, Inc. down to mom and pop operations. So basically the wrath of the OFAC, or Office of Foreign Assets Control, can fall on the head of anyone in the world for dealing with Cuba but it's no problem if you are in the frozen chicken business in Texas. Can anyone justify this nonsense?

Then there was a time when sitting with my family waiting for our Texan chicken and beans in the famous Aljibe state-owned restaurant we saw the garage door of a US diplomatic house open and some guys start handing out box loads of transistor radios pretuned to the Miami exiles' propaganda station, Radio Marti. It turned into a mini-riot before the police came to break it up. Things took a sinister turn for the worse when a group of dissidents were arrested after regularly attending the USINT for meetings and cheerfully receiving computer equipment, phones and funding. The fact that half of them turned out to have been Cuban agents is irrelevant: it was an outrageous piece of cynical provocation. I love the US, but for some reason if anybody says the word 'Cuba' US officials start acting like the girl in *The Exorcist*.

To add petrol to the fire certain EU embassies triggered the 'cocktail wars' by inviting celebrated dissidents to national day parties, which senior Cuban government officials tradition-ally attended. The Cuban response was simple. They ceased to have any kind of interaction with the European embassies on anything other than consular matters for years. This was considered a great success by the Cuban government, since it meant that they could simply ignore tiresome questions about human rights, and a tremendous result by the European diplomatic community, because they could get down to the serious business of going to the beach and making up reports without having to have any contact whatsoever with any Cu-bans but the maid and the driver. It seemed to me that the only people actually making a positive and collaborative con-tribution to Cuba's problems were some ballsy international investors like us, the UN in its various mutations and some downtrodden NGOs.

Our judgement was clouded by a great lifestyle. Based around the needs of four young kids growing up in a tropical funhouse, we had become addicted to it. A place like Havana attracts dreamers, crooks and empire builders, together with all those terribly serious representatives of multinationals. And, of course, as the world was expecting Fidel to pull a rabbit out of the hat, it was infested with journalists. Con-sequently there was a merry-go-round of fascinating parents from all over the world to mix it up with the Cubans, who proved themselves to be the most quixotic, infuriatingly loveable and interesting hosts. Some of them became the best friends one could ever wish for. My wife concentrated on four kids, the youngest of whom was only six months old, when we moved here. In time she became the chair of the PTA and found time to start a choir and take up some bizarre Peruvian hobbies, but every weekend the population in the house seemed to double as we acquired all sorts of stray children. The weekends passed in a blur of smashing crockery, screaming in the pool, football and finger painting. The only thing I hated about it was having to make a pile of pancakes on Saturday morning. I hate pancakes. Sadly, the mood gradually soured and we found ourselves in an increasingly difficult dilemma: Should I stay or should I go? as The Clash sang. It had become obvious that there was no future for us in Cuba. They didn't want us any more and the state mood was getting increasingly xenophobic. Finally we decided that we would leave at the end of the academic year, when Adam had finished his IB exams and Oscar had taken his IGCSEs. We would pack up our hideous collection of art deco mahogany furniture and dreadful paintings, return to the damp suburbs and try and get back into the groove of life in the real world.

From a work perspective it had been a slow, jerky descent into cynical acceptance that the country was changing for the worse. The first wake-up call was the plastics factory. We had some South African friends, definitely in the dreamer camp, and they were slowly coming to the conclusion that the wreck-salvage joint venture they had created to discover Spanish treasure was just a rather elaborate Cuban joke. They had a farewell party and I met another dreamer, this one a Turkish refugee from Sweden who had a dream to open a plastic bottle factory in Cuba. One thing led to another and within a year we were slowly but surely cornering the market in domestic plastic bottles, blown in high-density polyethylene out of

French machines. They were just the job for cooking oil, vinegar and cleaning products. I knew nothing about factories or making plastic bottles; my job was to try and make the business profitable. My partner, being the shouting species of socialist, was happy to leave the business bit to me while he concentrated on the technical side. It soon became apparent that his expertise came out of a book, but he was a fast reader and we had an enthusiastic workforce so things worked out very well. Incredible really. The JV was with a state plastics company. They had a draughty Russian factory building with a lot of scrap machinery, and a workforce that came to work and waited for lunch and then went home again on the ancient bus. And they had the director in his office with his Lada parked in the shade.

My suspicions about the director were initially raised during a meeting early in our relationship. We had built a male and female toilet in the factory because the existing one had been dismantled and stolen and as we were attempting to produce a domestic product in hygienic conditions a toilet would come in handy, but he was furious. How dare we build a toilet! My partner pointed out with characteristic bluntness that until now the workforce had been forced to shit in the field behind the factory, hardly ideal for the modern worker. But the director was having none of it. We had to take it down. When he opened his briefcase and then slammed it shut I caught a glimpse inside, assuming it contained files, a tape recorder and his lunch. It was empty except for a comb.

By the time we had stabilised production, sales and collections for the two machines while at the same time ignoring calls for the destruction of the toilet, we were planning the next phase of production. This entailed ordering some new moulds for 1-litre bottles. When they came we tested them and they came up at about 8 per cent less volume, which meant they were useless. However, when we explained the problem to the director he was overjoyed. His reasoning was that we would sell them for the same price but use less material and buyers of the bottles would be happy because they would sell their products as if they were 1 litre but actually use 8 per cent less. Everyone would be happy except of course the consumer. And this is exactly how these state managers get rich. When we refused to make use of this God-given right for him to line his pockets I think we made an enemy for life. A year later, after we had a second line operating in retractive film and the business was going gangbusters, we had a mysterious theft. All our raw material was stored in a warehouse, hundreds of tons of bagged, plastic pellets. There were two keys, held by the warehouseman and the director, and there were security guards posted. One Sunday the plant was closed for a public holiday and when everyone came to work the next day the warehouse was empty. Not a single pellet left out of many container loads of material. The police came, went through the motions and closed the case within a few days, saying it was a mystery. This was not somebody putting something in the back of his car or in his lunch box. This was industrial quantities requiring a team of people, plenty of time and a couple of articulated tractor units. My partner, incandescent with rage, demanded a meeting with the minister of light industry. The week after he had his visa revoked and was kicked out of the country, leaving me to close the business and turn the lights off. To this day the building lies empty, the workforce is idle and the country is importing bottles at double the price. There were so many levels of 'wrong' about what happened to this business it told us all we needed to know if we were prepared to listen, but we didn't.

* * *

Of all the back stories, the one that gave us all the most entertainment was Cy's, especially when he told it. His story was a tragic farce with lots of treachery and double standards on the one side and a great deal of generosity, dignity and humanity on the other. What made it extra spicy was that he had been so intimately connected to the Royal Family and their favoured few. I think this was why he used to work himself up into a raging froth of injustice whenever he had an opportunity to tell someone about his case. He would curse the Castros and their henchmen in four languages and threaten terrible, worldwide retribution. That and the fact that he refuses point-blank to wear prison uniform, and has thus been given about 200 extra years by Simiento, means that he is loved and respected by pretty much everyone in here. He also tells hilarious jokes, which always helps in dire circumstances.

I pass many a night reviewing his case notes with him, and discussing strategy to get him out. But his default position is always: 'Fuck them and their mothers. I will never say I am guilty of anything and I would rather rot here for ever than they have one cent.' We had to restrain him on the day he heard from his son that they had been approached by a senior official and told that they could have their father back for $50 million. I thought he would tear a guard apart with his bare hands. Interestingly, that is precisely how Raúl started funding the revolution all those years ago in Mexico; kidnapping people for ransom.

My fifty-second birthday came and went. I haven't really enjoyed my birthday since I hit forty, so it would be hypocritical to grumble about this one. Sarah and Mum arrived in Havana that weekend and so I was able to enjoy three hours with them in the afternoon over a delicious lunch of steak and roast spuds, which they smooth-talked in past the guards. We caught up on all the gossip and news and they delivered a ton of mail, which I have slowly and greedily read three times.

It's football again. We are doing pretty badly, but we aren't the worst. Today we play the yellows. I'm not looking forward to it, as there are a few pretty nasty guys on that team who don't like me, and as the keeper I always seem to get into rough stuff. But I'm way too old to go chasing around after a bunch of twenty-year-olds in this heat, so it's better than a heart attack.

Half-time and we are actually ahead. They decide on a change of plan. Long balls up and crowd the box trying to rush a goal in the melee. Santiago, the muscle-bound small-time gangster who confronted me on the first day, is standing with his back to me, right on my toes, waiting for the corner. The corner's taken, too much height and it sails over. He stamps hard on my foot and without thinking I punch him. It just sort of bounced off, like a pea off a tank, but he stopped and turned in angry surprise. 'You punched me?' The ref started blowing his whistle before anything happened but I have a really bad feeling about this.

Elroy's story

There were high expectations early this year that Raúl would once more announce that, for reasons of humanity, he would release a lot of foreign prisoners as he had done in January 2012, when 30 per cent of the convicts at Condesa were sent home. The weeks and months had passed with no news and prisoners were on the verge of giving up all hope for an amnesty this year when it became known that the little chap would be making a speech on the subject of justice and crime in Chile. The day has arrived and seating in front of the TV is at full capacity, the atmosphere pregnant with happy expectations. First the president of Bolivia gripped the lectern. His plan to legalise the growing and selling of drugs generated a heated debate among those gainfully employed in the industry. They were split pretty much half and half. The crowd settled down to hear Chinita. After boring the pants off the conference hall with a highly dubious account of the triumphs of the past fifty years he came to the subject of law and order and prisons. Instead of a proclamation of clemency he stunned the floor by announcing that he was considering introducing the death penalty for drug smuggling, This was met with complete silence from all except Salim, who slow-clapped and shouted 'Bravo!'

That night there is a brisk trade in Bible rentals and Salim sneaked an official-looking paper on to the cellblock notice board announcing that executions would be done strictly on an alphabetical basis. After breakfast the paper was spotted and three of the dafter convicts thought it was real and burst into hysterical shouting before the guards removed it.

Winter has definitely ended here; the concrete box is starting to heat up, the mosquitoes are getting frisky and the flies
are now forming blizzards. The management have decided to
make all sorts of rather random changes to our tiny lives, so
the ventilator fans on the ceiling are turned off for the hottest
part of the day. The water is often turned off when we wake
up and want to brush our teeth and after exercise when we
need a shower. They are either totally retarded, or there is
some fiendish psychological game going on to punish us. The
jury is out on this. Having made us buy our own chairs they
have now decided to ban them. Grudgingly they accepted the
possibility that some people would want to sit down, so five
banks of bus-station seating were plonked down in front of
the telly. If you want to sit anywhere else you have to use your
buckets. There have always been a lot of cats and perhaps the
greatest punishment has been handed out to the prison tom.
He was a huge, black cat with balls down to his knees and a
rather self-satisfied look about him. He led a happy life surrounded by his large, hairy harem and numerous offspring.
One day last week the guards took him away and the rumours
are about that he was killed. Elroy is very upset about this.
Elroy is an extraordinary man.

When Elroy cleans he cleans like a sailor, scrubbing and
scraping and leaving it spotless. Without Elroy and his cats we
would be totally overrun with cockroaches and rats. He cleans
the cellblock simply because he sees that it has to be done.
He doesn't clean because the guards tell him to, he cleans out
of the goodness of his heart. So I think I will propose Elroy
for the next Pope. Sitting on a cracked, upturned bucket and
flossing his teeth with a strand of plastic twine from a cracker
sack while staring vacantly into space, he looks an unlikely
sort of potential Pope. It's not that I see him dispensing a lot
of divine judgement in his Jamaican fisherman's patois. He
never pontificates. And he certainly doesn't talk much, not

unless you ask him about the mysterious lives of the fish he has spent his life catching in the vastness of the Caribbean night. Did you know that it is possible to bait fish traps with rotten papaya or soursop? I thought not. From the depths, when the moon is full and the night tide flows strongly, snapper are irresistibly drawn to the smell of the fruity decay. And then, once inside the wire and bamboo cage they frantically dash their heads against the empty promise: there is nothing to eat, no plump carcass of baitfish, just a mush of tasteless, pale skins. Confused, the snapper rips into fruit husks, releasing a fresh cloud of minute, aromatic particles that fall like snow into the void to whistle up the next victim.

For an inveterate rod-and-line honky fisherman like myself there is much to savour in these gems of information. How crude and inelegant my attempts to fool a fish have been. Even the supposed fine art of dry-fly fishing on a wild Scottish burn is mere simple deception. And as for the deep-sea fishing beloved by shiny holidaymakers, well it really is hunting at its most basic. Just a stupid plastic and steel lure trolled hour after hour behind $200,000 worth of fibreglass. It's no wonder success was as infrequent as it was unfulfilling. It is simply a matter of time invested in beer drinking before the flashy, alien object travelling at unnatural and unvarying speed finally annoys some bored specimen into attacking it. And then there is that awful moment when you have to batter the thing to death with a baseball bat while it stares right back at you with its huge wise eyes.

Elroy has learned the weakness of fish, he has a priest's understanding of the desires they cannot deny. And with the detachment of a hypnotist he enlists the help of each fish in the capture of the next. He couldn't be further away from his little boat now when he talks of fishy things, or further from his dusty yard when he recites a list of strange fruits and their even stranger properties, but he has the power of being able to transport the listener to other more sunny places. Cubans are a superstitious lot and the guards are no exception. So even the most brainwashed cadre or cynical, hard-bitten hustler senses that Elroy has some elemental connection with nature and they don't try to coerce, bully or abuse him. In Cuban folklore the sea exerts a mysterious power. It is the home of the ancient gods Elegua and Osa: from the sea the terrifying hurricanes blast great swathes of destruction across the land, from its dark and treacherous waves the Virgen de la Caridad del Cobre has plucked lost souls. The sea is not just the benign and balmy turquoise sold by Thomas Cook, for Cubans the sea is also the iron-grey monster that guards the island and keeps them all prisoner. Heaven for Cubans is beyond the sea, not above the sky. So any unlikely spirit like Elroy, who has lost their fear of the deep, who can appear at will from the vastness of the sea and who can skim before the storm, is treated with a certain respect.

He reads his Bible every day. Sometimes after lights out, when the last illegal poker players have folded, I need to get up to creep to the bog for a pee. A dark shape by the locked gate has one hand extended into the pool of light cast by the floodlights. Rocking back and forth to the rhythm of the verses, it is Elroy fishing for comfort, refuelling at sea, and he is a long way from a safe shore and a cold beer. I asked once if he enjoyed St James's words. 'He he, sometime, but no bother I gets de meanin.'

Elroy was convicted of international drug smuggling and is two years in to a twenty-year sentence. His two pals got life. Real life. The 'shot dead in a hail of revolutionary justice fired by nervous conscripts' kind of life. But I'll leave the details of that for later. It's enough to know that Elroy came from the sea and has a practical understanding of luck, crime and punishment. I only saw him lose his temper twice and this is a place where everyone's temper is constantly simmering away, waiting for that small provocation that will release all the thousand frustrations in a few seconds of operatic violence.

Once when for the umpteenth time some selfish idiot dirtied the stove minutes before lights out, after Elroy had painstakingly spent an hour rubbing it clean with soap and a fragment of aerated concrete block. And once when a really nasty piece of work threw some trash on Elroy's bunk bed.

This nasty piece of work has a name of course. Werner. No doubt he is a victim of circumstance, and deserves pity: by all accounts he is an orphaned street kid from Colombia raised on a Latin diet of neglect and the wilful abuse of power. But when you are trapped in concrete with these kind of people it's difficult to give a damn about that. Because the point is that he is totally twisted as a human being and everyone locked up with him has to live with it. With a strangely cherubic aspect, a gym queen's torso set off with lascivious choirboy lips, he is the imbecilic muscle in a nasty little three-man gang of low-life Colombian street scum. You don't need to see his arrest sheet from Cartagena to work out how he made money on the street: cheap gay hustle and knife work, robbing old people in their beds, snatching bags from confused tourists and doing favours for the drug men. He has a very odd, badly executed tattoo across his back, extended girly angel wings the significance of which is a mystery best left unsolved. This band of charmers had been arrested at the airport, one after another, each one telephoning the next from the holding cell to give them the 'all clear' to take the next plane in. The leader styles himself 'Don Jose'; mafia pretensions I guess. He is a myopic diabetic who looks like an ancient, but very malevolent, koala bear that has spent a productive forty years drinking urine. It seems he was the first to be nabbed at the airport. Being a certain kind of guy he readily agreed to call his next courier in exchange for the promise of less time, and so the Cuban police used their connoisseurs' appreciation of the psychology of trash and the whole gang was snapped up one by one. Instead of being outraged at this betrayal, Don Jose's bitches seem to consider this totally acceptable behaviour and just a simple risk of doing business and being under the koala's protection. This gang mystifies me, its food-chain morality as practised by morons no different from the fish in Elroy's trap.

The other guy in the gang, Juan Carlos, is both Werner's 'husband' and unsuccessful pimp. No takers for Werner in the showers during my seven months in La Condesa, but I heard plenty of stories of Venezuelans who crept about after lights out. Juan Carlos is a common enough name in Latin countries and in La Condesa it is commonly reduced over a low heat to the abbreviated Juanca, which to the delight of all English-speaking nations is pronounced wanker. Never was a name so richly deserved. Juanca is short with a rather complicated religious-looking tattoo and another of a scorpion, which I gather indicates some sort of sinister brotherhood. He lets it be known that he is a practising member of some obscure cult and savage gang, which may explain his very odd haircut: shaved all over except for an equilateral triangle pointing towards his nose. I suspect the real reason is to remind Werner which is the front and which is the back.

The three charmers stick together in close formation, the koala bear in front with his two wingmen flanking slightly to the rear. They spend most of their spare time hatching plots against prisoners they feel have been disrespectful. They would be laughable if they were not so dangerous. The danger lies not with a direct attack – it's never a frontal assault despite their pretensions of honour and respect. Instead they attack in the dark and from behind. They rarely attack with force or physical menace. Their preferred method is to gather snippets of information, spread malicious gossip and denounce prisoners to the re-education officer or fat Simiento, the captain of discipline and thus the most feared official in the camp. They are not alone in this devil's work. These '*chivatos*' live in evil symbiosis with the prison system. For a pat on the head and the right to have an extra bag of food a month they supply the penal system with ammunition to use against fellow prisoners. I was a victim of this: the koala denounced me for illegally bringing meat into the cell, a crime punishable with an extra two months' of prison time. The facts are irrelevant to Captain Simiento, who enjoys letting you know that he knows it's all made up but that he doesn't care and it won't change a thing. So before I am even charged they are starting work on adding time to my inevitable sentence.

I become sidetracked. With eternal days it's easy to meander off. I wanted to make a record of Elroy's story, basically because nobody in the whole world seems to care about what happens to him and because, despite making a few deadly mistakes, he is a great man.

Elroy had a fishing boat. One night a great storm blew up and the small, open fishing boat quickly started shipping water. The electrics blew, water got into the carburettor and the engine failed. The boat flipped and sank, leaving Elroy and his two friends in the water miles from land and hours from daylight. Later the next day Elroy was spotted dehydrated and barely conscious and was plucked to safety. They never found his friends.

A fisherman with a family and no boat is about as much use as tits on a goose. Elroy needed to get the money for a new boat. So when he was asked if he wanted to do a small favour, a simple nocturnal landing to collect something that had been left behind by somebody, he weighed the risks of failure against the certainty of shorebound poverty and said yes.

He set sail for the rocky coast of Santiago de Cuba, with two friends. The plan was to anchor a few metres off the low cliffs and take delivery of some bales of marijuana that had been dumped by a smuggler escaping the clutches of the Guardia Frontera. But there was a platoon of soldiers waiting for them. As soon as they dropped anchor the military hit the searchlights and opened fire, killing one deckhand immediately. Elroy, with an AK47 slash across his leg, and the other deckhand rolled over the blind side of the boat into the sea. He swam into the darkness, found some cliffs and then shoeless went on the run in the waterless bush for a day before giving himself up. He got twenty years. At the trial there was no mention of the lethal ambush, no mention of the two dead friends and no bodies were returned to grieving families. Nothing. The only epitaph was a bullet scar on his leg and the faces of two more dead friends to haunt him. That is Elroy's story.

He doesn't say much at the best of times, preferring the conversation of his cats and the words of the Bible, and when I ask about his little girl and his wife he can't bring himself to say anything. They are too poor to visit and too poor to even call very much. It will be at least ten years before he sees them. His hearty laugh and tombstone grin hides a bellyful of hurt. I cannot even begin to imagine how it feels, and I am ashamed to moan about anything at all in his presence. So when we talk we talk about the sea, we talk about cooking dorado on the beach and we talk about whether Judas was a man or perhaps a fish.

Enough of this gloominess, I need to write to my friends. There is a diplomatic visit from Slovakia tomorrow and I can get a letter out.

I spend a couple of hours writing and rewriting the letter. Finding the right balance between honesty and a stiff upper lip is challenging and I find I have to be in the right mood. Better not to write when I am depressed. I am well aware that people have limited patience for the misfortune of others; sympathy is not infinitely elastic after all. And of course I really don't want to freak my family out by telling them either my grave misgivings about how long this could be or how grim things can be at times. So I try to keep up the light-hearted style I employed from VM. Halfway through I allow myself a rare moment of introspection and mourn the loss of tenderness.

Some of you have asked what I miss most, well obviously alcohol, nice food, work, friends and family (not always in that order). And of course all those abstract thingies like 'freedom'. But I have realised that one thing I really miss is the touch of another human being. Obviously a brisk punch on the nose is available quite readily. I mean the gentle touch of someone you love. With no touch in your life you start to sort of shrivel up and harden on the outside. We slowly turn to stone. Just think for one minute how often you touch somebody every day, and then imagine not doing it. Strange isn't it? People go and see the prison dentist (who has no anaesthetic) just to feel the sensation of somebody touching their face.

Finishing my letter I sign and date it, with the depressing thought that it is fast approaching a year since my rather dramatic change in social life.

And so the letter leaves, to find its way through many hands to home. Home, where everybody's life is lived at a frantic messy pace compared to my world of the living dead. The replies will filter through and I will hear of shopping and studying, beating cancer, getting laid and getting laid off. I love reading about the beautiful crap of normal life, but each letter reminds me that normality is slowly drifting away and one day it will be just a tiny speck on the horizon, way beyond the camp wall and the ocean of cane fields that I am slowly drowning in.

My Mexican friend had his show trial and got five years. It is difficult not to be completely cynical about the whole thing. I asked my lawyer a few weeks ago how many people go to trial and are found innocent. He looked rather sheepish and said 'well actually zero'.

Stickman

There were mutterings of an insurrection yesterday. The re-
education officer had demanded that the model ships that the
workshop crew had meticulously made over the past months
were to be handed over. It was a prison custom from time
immemorial that guys in the workshop would make models
that they would either sell to the rest of us or send home as
gifts. And whether you bought it or made it, it was a mute
symbol of love for somebody a long way away. A wonky little
varnished galleon twelve inches long from Daddy that said:
'I haven't forgotten you, forgive me.' So when the officials
said that they would all be confiscated and be sent to a national competition between prisons everyone got very angry.
Whether it was true or not, the suspicion was that the guards
would simply sell them and keep the money, or if it was indeed true they would disappear forever. Most people preferred
to smash up the boats rather than hand them over. And the
re-education officer went nuts over this breach of discipline.
The commandant has ordered the workshop closed until further notice. The workshop trusties were bitterly angry and
now there was nobody to mend the guards' home appliances.
But the handful of trusties who had been selected to do some
quiet building work in the homes of senior officers still slipped
out, so for them it's business as usual.

The Sunday morning English conversation class I do with
a few of the guys has yielded some interesting 'back stories'
from some students. Today William from Venezuela told a
sad story about being coerced into the drug business and the

terrible impact on his family. He is desperate to get transferred and is clearly on the edge of doing something silly. But
the mood soon changed, and I nearly fell off my bucket laughing, when during a discussion about religion the beekeeping
berk Javali told us that he was Jewish. His story was bizarre.
Apparently, when he had reached the tender age of thirteen
some Zionist missionaries arrived in his Guatemalan village
and offered to pay for youngsters to go on an 'educational trip'
to Israel. As his mum had no idea where Israel was and the
small amount of money they offered would pay for a new pig,
off the infant hero went. He returned a fortnight later with
a pile of religious literature but minus his foreskin. A most
unlikely Jew.

Other more secular recent revelations are that one chubby,
gentle fellow with a ready smile and good manners is in fact
a contract gunman. Another surprise has been about one
of my chess partners, Taz, who has a face like Snoop Dogg
and eye-watering varicose veins. He is in fact wanted for the
cold-blooded murder of a rival gang member in Jamaica. It's
unnerving in a way, because if I don't accept that they are cha-
meleons hiding a cynical savagery under a cloak of normality
then I have to conclude that we are all capable of committing
such crimes, and it is merely a lethal combination of crappy
circumstances. These dualities of personality are child's play
in the relatively sane but are alarming in the nutcases. Long-
term prison sentences and cruel treatment really do seem to
trigger the worst in some people, especially when the paranoia kicks in. There are a few lunatics here. Alexei of course
has his moments, but the weirdest guy here is a legend in the
penal system, Stickman.

I was accelerating past the back of the storeroom, the only
shade in the yard provided by twenty square metres of tin
lean-to roof. This was the place with the worst karma in the
yard because this is where the guys who never take any exercise
hang out. This is where the living dead and the pederasts loll

about on plastic chairs watching the rest of us take exercise.

There was Pablo, a poor old man who had been given a colostomy a year back. He is cadaverous and yellow with a bulging plastic bag hanging from a string belt, the catheter just sticking out of a barely concealed stoma. Watching him stagger about with the contents sloshing and slopping down his leg was just about the cruellest thing I have ever seen. Then there was another Mexican guy, with strangely Nordic tattoos all up his legs. Apparently he had been a proficient rapper when he arrived, a quick-fire wit with all the fancy moves. Now he just stares in a fixed trance, wandering about with limbs in perpetual slow motion as if he is wading through a chest-high flood.

It was also where the kiddy-fiddlers hung out. There were two, a Belgian (surprise, surprise!) and an Italian. What is it about Belgium? Is the child catcher in *Chitty Chitty Bang Bang* a role model?

Our nonces are both well-educated and over sixty. One professes to be a professor and the other an office worker. The office wallah is so well camouflaged you would never guess. He talks to nobody under the age of thirty, plays a good game of tennis and keeps his nose in a book. I suspect with him it was little girls plucked from the street when nobody was looking. The professor just cannot help himself. There are a few handsome young Latinos, totally immoral, functionally illiterate and as crafty as slum cats. Within a few weeks of being here he has accumulated a little group of friends who sit around him listening while he lectures them on the glories of ancient Greece. They sit nodding and making jokes; it will be grease on his glory hole later. For this weird relationship they are paid in biscuits. Some days I have fantasies of mass executions. All these people are so irredeemably awful the world would be better off just snuffing them out. The professor is the more morally warped of the pair: he justifies his perversions as a reward for educating the young. But perhaps he is less dangerous than the Belgian. The Belgian can hunt without attracting any notice at all. He is just pale grey, respectable wallpaper. Interestingly, they don't try to get transferred back to their home country. Back home they would face the daily threat of death or disfigurement at the hands of other prisoners. One of the peculiarities of this international jail is that there are no ordinary honest crooks; no bank robbers, burglars, cheque kiters or plain vanilla murderers. Apart from the innocent and the dodgy businessmen they are all guilty of fairly depraved crimes. That and the total lack of any social norms means that the paedophiles are not mistreated by their fellow prisoners.

So that is why I accelerate past the lean-to, with its seedy collection of pederasts and human wreckage. It is also where the guards sit, scratching themselves and tapping the ground with their truncheons. Safely past, I drop my speed only to find Stickman at my shoulder. Damn, he slipped out of the shadows on my blind side.

'These fucking Cubes man,' he mutters darkly. His version of: 'Good morning, what a splendid day, did you enjoy breakfast? I thought the bread roll was particularly tiny today.'

Stickman is one of the more extreme characters in the place. He is in another cellblock so we only bump into each other on Wednesdays when everyone from *Severo*, *Medio* and *Minima* is given '*terreno*' together. The other time is when the lines pass trooping to and from the mess. If I had to deal with him 24/7 I am not sure what I would do.

I would definitely hesitate to use the word friend for someone so totally off his head and bad as Stickman, but he is good value for money in short doses. His life story was more than average extreme. He is a Texan who was born into a naval family, which meant enduring a childhood shunting about tropical ports. Clearly intelligent, he did a rather silly thing and joined the marines. Whether he left of his own devices or was cashiered he glosses over, but then fate took him to the Caribbean where he led a seafaring life doing, in his view, a relatively innocuous bit of inter-island drug running and selling guns. Trips to Central American ports for stock increased his appetite for female company, so he moved onwards and upwards into his final career: he supplied young Latina and Caribbean chicks to strip clubs and brothels in the US. A people trafficker is the accurate terminology I believe. He would get a shopping list and go and fill his yacht up. He got caught in Cuba trying to leave with some girls. Once they found out he was an ex-marine they threw away the key. He's been to pretty much every prison on the island, and has spent a year in solitary and been beaten, abused and neglected, but there must have been something in his training because he will never give up a chance to annoy them and they have given up trying to get him to shut up. A number of the Caribbean drug dealers have bumped into him over the years, so his epic history has been verified.

Physically he wasn't impressive. From Scottish/Irish stock, his white freckly skin was burned and angry-looking from years of solar abuse. Somewhere along life's path he had been attacked by a shark, hence the name, and one leg had most of the calf missing and stitch marks running to his hip. Thin as a stick, he was surprisingly strong. He would limp over to the pull bars, flip himself upside down and do thirty inverted pull-ups. Nobody else could do even one. It wasn't even his power-to-weight ratio; he could lift the heaviest weight in the gym along with only a handful of prisoners. Incredible.

He had a fine mind. His appreciation of literature was deep and subtle, his knowledge of history encyclopaedic and sometimes you could even forget he was a bad guy suffering from advanced but justifiable paranoia. I would lend him a book by some tweedy, camp intellectual like Somerset Maugham and he would say: 'Thank fuck you're here man. At last. Someone who thinks like me.'

A worrying thought. Perhaps I will bug out like him after all. He was convinced the Castro brothers were in partnership with the CIA and was always trying to get people to smuggle out loony letters to various public figures in the US: pages of tiny handwriting with the occasional word in huge capitals. BRAINWASHINGTON was his favourite.

So up pops Stickman. 'I've been thinking man.'

Oh dear. It isn't going to be an interesting chat about the closing stages of the Second World War and why Stalin declared war on the Japs at the eleventh hour. It's going to be one of his rants.

'There are three separate races of human being right? White people like us. Then the blacks. And at the bottom are the Latins. It's genetics man, a proven fact. The Cubes and Venezuelans are the fucking pits man. They don't eat right, they don't think right and they don't shit right. Fuck they can't even run a prison.'

Well it's one version I suppose. Most nutcases think humanity is divided along racial lines. And he's off on one of his rambling non-stop stream-of-consciousness blathers. His mouth in overdrive, dried spittle on his lips, he pings from thought to thought.

'Neurones . . . brain density . . . cannot digest complex proteins . . . cultural supremacy . . . Darwinian theory . . . Nobel prizes . . . Clausewitz, . . . particle accelerator . . . the CIA and the Castros.'

It would not be a conversation with Stickman if the bloody CIA and the brothers didn't pop up.

'Who shits in the showers . . . bananas, . . . vitamin D . . .'

He's flying today. I am a polite guy, especially around deceptively strong, crazy people, but I'm tired of this after two laps of the yard. Nodding at every point I slowly pick up the pace. I have developed a rather sneaky way of getting rid of the cripple. I would simply just start walking faster and faster. Sure enough after another five minutes he pants: 'Fuck. You limeys walk fast. I'm done in.'

Nodding his head in rapid fire he told me to 'take care' and went off to finish embroidering the Marine Corps emblem on a handkerchief. And so with that I could drop a gear and coast round the bend towards Salim's beach and comparative sanity.

Salim is in so many ways a natural genius. He has a gift for survival and is a realistic optimist. He decided that once a week he would go to the beach. His logic being that he was in Cuba, and if you lived in Cuba you would try and go to the beach once a week. The fact that he was in prison was irrelevant. Once a week, sometimes Wednesdays but more often than not Saturday afternoon, he prepared a bag: a rolled-up towel, a flask of black tea, his chess theory book and his CD player of Algerian pop. In the yard there was a few square yards of raggedy grass, right at the back next to the gym. He would act out the entire thing as if he was at the beach, choosing the best spot to place his towel, stretching and examining the view as if there were yachts on the horizon. He would lie sunbathing and making contented sounds as if he was chatting to his wife. He would call out a cheery greeting to all who passed and invite friends to sit and drink tea. The entire performance is always exactly as if he was at the beach. Then on the march back to the cell he would say: 'Lovely day at the bitch, very relax.'

But today I declined tea and kept on going, I had a routine of doing exercise without fail during the '*terreno*' sessions. We had enough time for drinking tea and lying around. I was about to start my final ten minutes of running at a shambolic trot when the shout goes up that I am wanted on the phone. I go scampering off to the phone which is screwed to the wall of the cellblock. It's a terrible line but I can just hear my old friend Giles calling from reality.

'How's it going nigga? Been bummed in the showers yet hehehh?' This is his warped sense of humour. We talk about family, and this and that and finally it is time to go.

'Happy anniversary mate,' he says earnestly.

'What do you mean?'

And in a thick Irish accent he says: 'Ye daft cunt, it's a year since ye was nabbed by the helmet boys. Nu fuckin' surrender Billy boy.'

We laugh and the line clicks dead. So it is, exactly one year since I was taken. Well I'll be damned. So, according to the law they can still keep me another year before they have to charge me with anything. I'd better call my lawyer tomorrow and see what he has to say.

William came back from the prison hospital at Combinado Matanzas today. He looks terrible. Skinny as a rake, he is a ghastly colour and his breath stinks to high heaven. I ask him how he is.

'Not too good, but happy I'm back.'

'What happened?'

'Well, they let me be for a few days and asked me to reconsider. Then they started force-feeding me a couple of times a day with a tube down my throat. I'd vomit most times. After two weeks I gave up. If I can't die I don't want to be a cripple. So I am back.'

'You need to take it easy brother, try bland things first. Do you have any money?'

'No.'

At exercise I went to the prison shop and bought a kilo of milk powder and left it and a bottle of vitamins under his pillow. He was a nurse from Venezuela who had got into debt with a gang. They gave him a simple but brutal choice. He loved his daughter so he took the trip to Cuba and got caught. A month ago he got his sentence. Twenty years. So he went on hunger strike.

'Hakimatti'

I've been talking to Shagga about him setting up a boat-repair business when he gets home. It's as common as a car-repair shop in the Bahamas. Everyone needs a boat. This is his first time inside and it's enough for him. He did something stupid and got caught and now he's anxious to show his family he has a plan for his future. He has a cop for a sister and his aunty works in a bank. They are good folks and he knows he brought shame on them all. I've shown him how to put a business plan together for a bank loan and together we wrote a proposal. Maybe they are just crazy enough to do it. Anyway, today his consul is coming and he wants to send it out so we do some last-minute changes. He thinks it may help his case for transfer.

This afternoon the rain came heavy and grey, hour after hour. I stood near the kitchen where the slats were still open, watching a cat hesitate to leap on to the pathway from the window of cellblock 2. It would be months before the work party finished remodelling cellblock 2. The camp commander had decided that he wanted everyone in '*régimen máxima*' to be confined under lock and key for most of the day. Thus the guys serving the first third of their sentence would be locked in a four-man cell and not in the fifty-man barracks. Anyone in preventative detention, in other words prisoners like me who had not had a trial yet, would also be confined to the cells. This was typical of the casual cruelty of the imbecile. It was not the result of some specific directive from the ministry but another example of his mind-set. He was a blustering drunkard, hated by the prisoners and commanding no re-spect from his officers. Every month or so he would disappear for a couple of weeks to dry out and then return pumped up with some scheme for more re-education through misery. He spent a lot of time and effort devising ways to increase the punishment and behind it all, like all Cuban state officials, he knew that if he commissioned some building work there would be materials which he could steal and use on his own house. A hatch was even being knocked through to the mess so that prisoners would not get to go outside and queue up for their food three times a day. Their lives would shrink to contact with just three other people and an hour of daylight and fresh air. It amazed me that the guards could cajole pris-oners to willingly build an environment that would increase their suffering a hundredfold. They had been told that they would be paid $10 a month for working a six-day week on an eight-hour shift. For some of the poorest prisoners who never received any money from the outside this meant they could buy some food and thus was understandable. I accept that my moral high ground is built on relative wealth.

But after the first months, when it came time to put the money in the prison shop, it was announced that prisoners receiving salary would have to pay for their uniforms and food and after deductions they got a mere $2 for a month's work. So after the first month there were some angry scenes and half the volunteers promptly un-volunteered. The rest were bribed with the promise that the re-education officer would guar-antee the discretionary two months' discount on the current year's sentence. (Sadly, as they were to find out, this was a lie as well.) And so the conversion of cellblock 2 proceeded at a snail's pace.

A tribe of cats had taken up residence and one young tom with itchy feet and a keen nose had realised there was food cooking in cellblock 1 and thus there was a possibility of some tasty scraps from Elroy. It stood perched on the shattered window void, tail flicking in anger at the thought of getting wet and cold, its eyes focused hard on the line of low plants that obscured the path that was its accustomed landing spot. It knew that there was a possibility that the path was underwater, hence the hesitation. From my side I could see that the path had totally disappeared beneath a three-inch stream of diarrhoea-yellow water that rushed through the open door of the mess and straight through the servery behind. The moronic assholes had built the mess and servery in the low spot between two buildings that channelled all the runoff from the prison yard. And this being a country that has at least 1.2 metres of rainfall a year, they had not bothered with any drains either. So every time it rains we prisoners have to troop through ankle-deep, foul water and sit with it sloshing around our feet while we eat our sodden meals. The cat jumped and virtually disappeared for a second, then it bounced like a hairy wet meteor and clambered hissing through my window, sparks of fury at the world flashing in its eyes.

Beside me, Bob collapsed in a fit of laughter. Tears poured down his face. Bob was a funny guy. Every time I walked past his bunk he would shout:

'What's a white boy doing coming down the ghetto? I know yer see. He come to buy some blow. Drugs is the only reason he come to the ghetto see. Hehehehe.'

We got on just fine. He was terminally bored and would go into a sort of trance for days or even weeks and then just snap out of it and be a fast-talking smart-ass. It was possibly something to do with the black market in meds that flowed from the pockets of a couple of the nurses.

A few gusts of chilling damp whistled through the metal slats, splatting mattresses, socks and mosquito nets. Salim came bouncing past and with one chirpy suggestion dispelled the mood.

'You like coffee? I like coffee, I prepare coffee. Very nice. Let's play hakimatti.'

He calls chess 'hakimatti'. It is his La Condesa word for chess, a sort of Algerian Spanglish mash-up typical of Salim. He has a huge book on chess in French which he studies with great eyebrow-wrangling intensity for hours and then challenges somebody to a serious thrashing as soon as he closes the cover. When I came here, a chess dullard like myself stood no chance and gleefully he used to pick off my pieces, prolonging the agony.

'Oooohhhh, strategy not good. I like my soldiers, give me one castle.'

But I slowly detected his weakness; he had an irrational love for his knights and whether defending or attacking would use them as the centrepiece of his game. Take one of his 'my horsey' and he would become very agitated as his defensive screen fell apart. Actually his real weakness was his book. I used to hide it and then challenge him to a game a few hours later. The entire cellblock used to enjoy watching him playing Gadhafi. Gadhafi, like his namesake, had suicidal tendencies and a volcanic temper. He was actually good at chess but used to play a rapid and violent game, usually losing a piece for a piece in a bloody war of attrition.

Losing, he would say through gritted and hideously blackened teeth: 'I not concentrate, I beat you next time no problem. You are a pussy. Come play.' And then if he lost again, the closing cry of 'hakimatti' would be followed by the board going up in the air, the pieces flying every which way and a stream of Arabic swearing. He would sulk for a week before repeating the entire performance. It must be exhausting being him. And so I play three games with Salim losing two to one, which is good enough for me.

The rains stops and after dinner I wander out to the back to see who is there and for a change of air before lights out. There are couple of Latinos out there, teeth chattering while they smoke as fast as they can. Being strangely vulnerable to the damp they suffer during the cold fronts. They wear spare blankets draped over their heads and some don't wash for weeks on end, so a cheesy fug follows them around. It's a kind of clammy cold in an English sort of way so it doesn't bother me much and the black drug runners are used to cold nights at sea so it doesn't bother them either. Bob and Shagga and Jay are out there sitting on buckets and perched on the sink. They are discussing the finer points of boatmanship for drug runners, retelling stories and adventures they have shared a million times over the years. There is a strange politeness here. People don't say: 'Hey, we've heard this a thousand times.' They may think it but they don't say it, I figure because after a while we all do it as our life experience telescopes into a fading dot.

'Well, you see, I chopped this boat and added an extra section. It was a good runner but I needed extra tanks plus I wanted to get it up to a ton see. So, I puts another section in, must have been 'bout six foot. Anyways. I was kind of heavy anyway as we put half-inch steel plate on the back of the seats see, as well as over the outboards. Sort of armour plating like. Them 'copters use machine guns see. Legally they can shoot the outboard out. Stops you dead in the water and then waits for theys boats to catch up. Never could catch us any other way. So you see when they start spraying thirty-calibre at the outboard an' the boats bucking every which ways people gets shot see. So plenty of steel plate which creates all sorts of problems with balance.'

Bob takes a ruminative puff, the audience all nodding along to the story.

'So we need to get from Bahamas to Florida in one run. Night-time. We like to dip in and out of Cuban waters 'cos the Americans can't catch us there and the Cubans can't catch shit with their dumb-ass cissy boats. By the time they get their helicopters up we be long gone.'

Another puff.

'Anyways, I had double dose of bad luck. Somebody told

them we was coming 'cos when we passed the Tortugas they was waiting. I should have cancelled see as the weather was real choppy. And I should have checked the new gas tanks. What happened was the weight on the back causes the hull to flex see and the new tanks opened up so we leaked a whole tank away. Lucky we didn't blow up to shit. Anyways, should have checked them see. We outrun them for about sixty miles, smoked 'em. But the helicopter kept following and then when I see we were cracked I had to shut off one engine and speed dropped right off. Then they started shooting and that's when I knew it was all over. So I thinks well they videoed a ton of dope, no point throwing it overside so we decide to stop and wait for them to come and get us. We actually in international waters but that don't fuss them none. They pitch up, handcuff us and hood us and put a tow on us see. Then when we close to Cuba they arrest us. Kidnapping I call it. Anyways, what pisses me off man is that I had a ton of dope on that boat. I ain't risking my ass for anything less than seven hundred kilograms. So when we gets to the trial I says to my lawyer don't do no Perry Mason on me boy. I guilty as hell. I plead guilty, you get me reduced time. What the fuck, they say I have three hundred kilograms on board and give me twenty years. They stole my dope. Shit.'

He shakes his head at the memory.

'Yea, them fucks steal our dope and then sell it themselves. Fucked up man.'

Another voice chimes in.

'What you care. They found a hundredth of a gram of coke on my boat and gave me fourteen years, all the same to them man. The judge said "Well I know you moving drugs you just on the way home that's all. Still guilty as hell nigger." No justice.'

'Listen, I is guilty no problem. Let me out, boom I do it again. What ain't right is that back home I get four years maximum. Maybe out in three. I gotta a family to support.

Shit, what is they supposed to do if I spend my whole life in this crazy place? Just ain't fair, that's all.'

'Man, I wish I had some cunny and smoke.'

'Oh yes.'

A guard pops his head over the parapet and shouts down through the cage. He's been up there listening. They sometimes do that to listen if anyone is saying anything counter-revolutionary. The joke is this one doesn't understand English.

'*Buenas noches.* Cómo estás?'

'*Buenas noches*, official batty man, yo wife is a ho that suck my dick and goodnight.'

And sniggering we all troop in to brush our teeth.

I lie still, eyes closed, thinking about these stories and trying to figure out what I think about these people. Sure, at one level they are bad men. They do things I don't agree with, like shoot people and deal drugs. But their motives are simple and it's not all about gold chains and loving that life. In fact they sound horribly familiar. I struggle to categorise few of them as actually evil. To start with they know full well that what they do is wrong. They are not even particularly proud of what they do. They have no reason to justify their actions to me, the sentence has been handed down, and they are surrounded by criminals. But what I find extraordinary is the pattern. They have another job, a low-paid, hard-work type of job that pulls in a few hundred bucks a month, and large families to support. They don't have the gangsta lifestyle of an MTV video, they do a run once or twice a year because they say they have no alternative way to earn that kind of money. I have no idea if that's true or not. Maybe they do have alternatives, the majority of people don't choose to take that path, but then I am an architect from London and kind of spoilt in so far as the only limits to my choices are in my head.

So they make up a load from a handful of dealers and then borrow money from some seriously bad guys to fund a stake themselves. Then they often take a few passengers, as there is a trade in moving bad guys in and out of the States which is almost as valuable as the drugs. A single run a year will see the household bills paid, healthcare, a car on the road, university fees and a little put away for a rainy day. They accept the risks of being caught are high and the coast guard often seem to know when and where they will be. So the question I find myself kicking around in my head, 'Are they bad men?', is a difficult one to answer. I guess you have to be Jesus to know the answer to that one but I am starting to think that a handful could probably be good men who have done a bad thing. But that leaves the other big question, which is what does happen to all the dope that gets taken and why is it only the little guys who get caught?

Sea of flames

One day after exercise I get called out beyond the wire. I am escorted in cuffs to the office of the shiny head. His adoring secretary is bashing away her frustrations at the typewriter, still attractive but a little plumper and with the badger stripe of a village dye job. Expecting a more interesting visitor she pauses mid-keystroke to glance up and then with disappointment confirmed she returns to work, tapping away at the rest of her life. Mr Shiny Head is busy with his papers and just points with his chin at a large plain-clothes guy lounging in a derelict armchair in the corner, humming to himself. The guy has the full State Security dirty Sanchez moustache and is amusing himself beating out a salsa rhythm on his knee with a manila folder.

'Get the handcuffs off him.'

Inwardly I smile. In Cuban Spanish the word for handcuff is '*esposa*', wife. There is a level of honesty in their jokes that seems to be missing from official life.

'Oi, sit.' He opens his folder and takes out some grey papers. He hands them over. 'Ivan wants you to sign them. Sign them.'

I read them carefully. They are various official documents already stamped, signed and sealed by MININT. They confirm the dates when I entered Villa Marista, that I know what I am being charged with, that the process of instruction has concluded, the date when I was moved to Condesa and the date when I first saw my lawyer. Some of them were replacements of documents I had already signed ages ago and some were new. What was interesting was that all the dates had been changed to show that everything had been done according to international or Cuban law. I also didn't like the wording of one in particular, which looked suspiciously like an acknowledgement that I knew I had broken the law.

'What if I don't sign them? He has changed all the dates.'

He smiles. 'Do you want a trial or not?'

'Tell Ivan I'm not signing them until my lawyer can advise me.'

He stood up and with hand on chin cracked his neck from side to side by way of a farewell.

On the way back through the wire I thought about what had just happened. It's coming to a close. They are cleaning house.

That afternoon my Slovak friend came back from his trial in Cienfuegos. His prosecutor's petition had asked for three years, but at the trial the judge worked himself up into a froth of self-righteousness and demanded five. Poor Slovak's case was a scandal. Yet another tale of paying the staff, years ago, but in this case they had fooled him into returning so as to arrest him. In the time of Fidel his company had been contracted to complete a mothballed Soviet oil refinery. It was paid for by Chávez and was considered a matter of urgent, strategic necessity. They were given one year to do it. This meant working seven days a week and to keep the staff motivated the foreign company gave the locals a small monthly cash stimulus. The refinery was completed on time and a very happy Fidel and Chávez came to push the starter button on the big day. Slovak left Cuba with handshakes and photos and went to work elsewhere. Then, out of the blue, five years later he was invited back to tender for an extension to the oil refinery. He was arrested after the meetings. Slovak is so angry at the unfairness and dishonour of his treatment that sometimes I think he will explode. He is convinced he is just part of a

Byzantine plan to get rid of the remaining Fidel-era senior officials in basic industry.

We sat around discussing his case, trying to cheer him up. But all we did was make ourselves depressed. The judiciary now seem to be competing with the prosecutors to see who has the most revolutionary zeal for punishment. This doesn't look good for any of us.

Later that evening after lights out the night sky starts turning a flickering orange and a faint smell of smoke on the breeze gets stronger. I sit up and stick my head out of my mosquito net, concentrating on whether it's getting brighter and smokier. I climb down. Other people are stirring and exchanging confused words. It's definitely a fire and it's certainly getting closer. I can hear it now. I go to the gate and look out. Like some Japanese comic book monster, a long roiling tongue of greenish smoke is pouring over the prison wall and coming towards us up across the exercise yard and a billion cinders fly through the air as the cane field self-incinerates. The abandoned watch towers are silhouetted by flames that look to be a hundred feet high. The whole prison camp is surrounded by a roaring wall of fire that licks over the wire. We have to shout to make ourselves heard. In a flash the flamboyant tree in the prison car park catches fire and burns to charcoal. The cell is now full of dense, burned-sugar smoke and the breeze has turned into a gale. Thank God everything is made of concrete. The guards are all running about like headless chickens and everyone is shouting. Some crazy prisoners find it funny, oblivious to the danger, but then as quickly as they flared the flames die down. The cane is burned out and we go back to our bunks. Everything now reeks of smoke and we eventually fall asleep to the sound of coughing.

In the morning we are greeted by an extraordinary sight. There is a dense black snow falling out of the sky. Big whispery black feathers of carbonised cane rain down. We stand in line waiting to troop off to breakfast, silenced by the post-apocalyptic scene. I catch some flakes in my hand and I can see the filigree trace lines of the individual cells, but they disintegrate to a sooty smudge in my damp palm. There was something about last night that made us all feel very alone. We have all got used to being abandoned, adrift in an ocean of green whispering cane tops. But last night the benign, soporific sea turned into a raging and unstoppable monster that wanted to consume us. And now it is raining Auschwitz ashes on to our prison camp.

The camp got more or less back to normal in a few days and before we knew it the great cane-field fire passed into the grey history of days that have been ticked off our sentence.

I am called out beyond the wire again one afternoon. It's back to the office of the shiny head. We stop outside and unusually the guard uncuffs me and tells me to go in. Ivan is there, in pressed uniform. Shiny Head and his girlfriend look busy, terrified in the presence of the teniente coronel but clearly straining to hear every word.

Ivan gives me a huge smile and shakes my hand vigorously. 'Purvis, how are you? You look a lot better. Lots of exercise?'

'Erm, yes, I'm fine thank you. How are you?' I reply, still surprised to see him in the flesh after so many months.

'I'm fine, thank you. How is your family? I hear your wife is a lot better. How is your mother? She's quite a lady. Hahhah. And Adam? Did he get into university?'

I am utterly taken aback. I don't know what to say.

'Sit down, sit down. Well Purvis, I have completed the instruction, the file is now open and you will get the petition very soon. Expect the trial within one month. Your lawyer has twenty-one days after the petition to prepare the defence. How is the old man?'

'I didn't sign the documents you sent. You changed everything.'

He laughed. 'It doesn't make any difference.'

Standing up, he takes my shoulder and moves me out of the

door. Out of earshot. We stand in the sun.

'Listen to me Purvis, it will soon be over. You will go home soon. Don't do anything crazy and it will be okay. Trust me.' And then he repeats a weird phrase I had last heard from my lawyer eight months ago. 'We thought you were a mountain, but you were a little mouse.'

'Really? Ivan, why did I have to spend eight months in Villa Marista?' Just saying the words makes my eyes go teary.

He pauses, scans the horizon and then looks me straight in the eye and says simply: 'I'm sorry.'

The moment passes in a millisecond but I could swear that there was some small, buried part of that hard, hard man that actually meant it. One tiny little scrap of human decency. He coughs himself back into uniform and orders the guard to cuff me and take me away.

I am excited because Adam my eldest son is coming. I haven't seen Adam for six months now and he has managed to get a few days off university to get here. He is accompanied by Giles, an old friend of mine from London, who is providing moral support and fatherly advice, plus of course beer and ciggies. Giles very kindly drove Adam to Newcastle for freshers week in the autumn, yet another family rite of passage that I have blown because of this bloody nightmare. The penal code actually states that prisoners have the right to a certain number of visits per month and does not limit visits to family-only. But it also says that the prison commander can change the code according to his wishes. So being a vindictive and scheming piece of work he has applied a family-only rule. But all the inmates are foreign, so this means that visits involve hugely expensive and complicated foreign travel for families. Most prisoners never have any visitors as a consequence. He does, however, make exceptions. If you agree to act as an informer or trusty then he will allow Cuban 'friends' to visit. This means the vegetable whores of Güines. So he gets a small army of rats and creeps and he and the staff make a tidy amount on the side business of selling 'access' to local pimps. My mate has a Cuban wife and even she is asked to pay twenty-five bucks a pop to the re-education officer for her right to see her husband. It's a sick state of affairs and I hope the bastard of a commandant rots in hell.

So my lawyer and the embassy have been writing letters and organising for Giles to get to see me at least once. MININT has assured everyone that it will not be a problem.

The day comes, and Adam arrives. I had last seen him as a sweating, mumbling adolescent. Now he is slim and self-confident. He's turned into a man. Incredible. He has brought a huge lunch prepared by Giles but no Giles. At the visitor entrance they said not today as they were waiting for some document from Havana. So having flown three thousand miles to see me poor old Giles sat in the car park dozing under a tree for three hours while Adam and I wolfed down salads and cheese and all sorts of forbidden delights. The hours flew by as we caught up on all the news and I heard all about his adventures in his first year.

The next day again it's Adam solo. He tells the pathetic story. This time, waving a copy of a letter from MININT to my lawyer, confirming the visit was approved, they asked to see the commandant. He came after twenty minutes, breathing rum fumes. Adam and Giles showed him that both their names were entered into the visitor register on the desk.

'Look, it says I am approved. Right here. Look, it's my name,' said Giles.

The commandant took a pen out of his pocket and drew a heavy line across the page. 'It isn't now,' he said, and with that he left the room.

Adam tells me Giles is very upset and has gone back to Havana. I beg them to try again tomorrow. The last chance. That afternoon I go and see the re-education officer and complain. I telephone the embassy and ask them to help. I call the lawyer.

But they all say the same thing. There is nothing anyone can do.

Tomorrow comes and before exercise I see the major returning from having his dental work attended to. As always he is in a blissful reverie. I accost him and beg for his assistance. He tells me that the commandant is away today but that he may be able to do something.

The hour comes and then instead of going to the visitors' room I am cuffed and led out beyond the wire. After a quick search in a guard hut I am shown into an empty office and there is Giles, his usual grubby self but in a jacket and inexplicably with a front tooth missing. We hug and fight back the tears. We have ten minutes apparently. Just enough time to joke and punch each other for no good reason. He thinks I look good in the prison blue. And then it's over till the next family visit, which won't be for at least two months.

Oh God, when will this end? Seeing my kids a few times a year is killing me.

Case open or closed

Salim's transfer comes through. He will go to Canada to serve out his sentence, which will probably mean that he will be out very soon as there is a hugely different sanction applied to his crime there. He is overjoyed. Our business class is very sad to see him go and we shall miss his mad strength and spirit, but we are very happy for him. At last his kids will be able to see him. On his last day he gets his clothes out of storage and puts on a suit he wore at his trial. With shiny shoes and tie he walks up and down the hut as if he were walking through a city street to the office.

'What the fuck are you doing?' shouts Cy, laughing. 'Have you gone nuts?'

'I'm practising being a normal man. Go to work.'

In the afternoon he divvies out his belongings. Food and toiletries to the poor. He hands over custody of the chess set with some final advice, 'remember to guard your horsie', but keeps his famous chess book. And then all of a sudden he is gone, exiting to clapping and cheers from his mates.

Next day and Cy's in trouble again. Every time Pupi turns the electricity off and the fans stop and the heat starts to build like a furnace, Cy manages to attract the attention of a passing trustie and begs them to go round the side and flip the isolator, with the promise of a few packets of Upmann later. It drives Pupi nuts. This time he's decided to make a fuss and so Cy is taken off on his regular visits to see Simiento to be disciplined. Overhearing the exchange is hilarious. Simiento is shouting about disobedience and Cy, not taking any notice, is shouting about human rights. We can hear Simiento say sternly: 'I will give you a notation in my book.'

'I don't care about your silly book.'

'What! It's the book. We have rules and we must save electricity.'

'I have human rights. We must have our fan. My God, what is this country? Are you trying to kill me! First you take away my chair and I have to sit on a bucket and now this.'

Now shouting, Simiento retorts: 'You don't have any rights. You have to obey the rules!'

'What? Are you stupid? Are you stupid like your stupid brother? Was your mother stupid? Are you trying to kill me or what?' Cy shouts back.

'Shut up and get out!'

'You are stupid. When I get out and I see you hitchhiking down the road because nobody will give a stupid man like you a job, I will slow down in my Mercedes C class, you will come running up and just as you touch the door I will go. Whoosh, the stones will fly in your face and you will know you are stupid.'

'Get out!' Simiento thunders.

And with a final cry of 'Stupid!' Cy is manhandled out of the tiny office. He chuckles when he gets let in through our gate: 'Well, that will get me another two years but what the fuck. He is very stupid. Isn't he stupid?'

'Sure, but I don't have the balls for that,' I replied. 'I couldn't face another week in this shithole.'

Later that night I ask him: 'Cy, are you sure getting all this extra time is a good idea?'

'It doesn't matter. They will either kill me in here or they will have to let me go before too long. Maybe I will get a hundred years.' He laughs. 'It doesn't matter. I am an embarrassment to them. But he is a very stupid man. Anyway, what is for supper? I have some aubergines. Can you cook them like my wife does them?'

Next morning there was a shout. 'Oi, *Británico* – you have a visitor! Get ready.' The official starts impatiently banging on the gate.

'Who is it?'

'Don't know.'

I grab my notebook and a pen and paper, just in case it's the lawyer. After all the rush I have to sit on the wall for thirty minutes while they get him through the various gates and the dog run. He walks like an elderly man with not too long to go and who really shouldn't be staggering about in the boiling sun. But despite his arthritic body he carries himself with a pre-revolutionary, courtly elegance and he is a tough customer. Panting, he mops his brow with a clean handkerchief and shakes my hand.

'Hello Arturo. Are you well? How is your wife?' I enquire.

'Well, you know wives. I spoke to Sarah and your mother yesterday. They were pleased with the news.'

I give him my arm to get him up the step into the interview rooms and turn to shout at some guys going to exercise to bring me some cold water for him. They will pass it through the window in a few minutes if I can wangle a room facing the exercise yard. He sits heavily, dumps his briefcase on the table and catches his breath.

'Before we start, Arturo, I did the painting you asked for.'

And with that I removed a watercolour hidden in my A4 pad. He had asked me to copy a mouldy print of an old painting of St Theresa. My copy was pretty useless really. The folds on her blue habit are good and the lectern and woodwork are okay, but her face looks sluttish and coy. Not saintly and virginal like the original. I've clearly been doing too many prisoners' wives.

'Thank you,' he beamed, and quickly slipped it into his briefcase.

'My friend, the case is no longer secret. I have read the

petition and been able to examine some of the statements. I am very positive.'

'Fantastic, that's good news. What's next?'

'Well, we have twenty-one days to prepare your defence. I have the petition here. It's in Spanish but Rebeca is translating and you should have it in English tomorrow or the day after.' And with shaking hands he gets the document from his briefcase and flips it across the old table.

'We have a lot of work to do. I shall come here every few days. Do you agree?'

'Of course. So finally, what am I charged with?' And I start scanning the pages. Curiously it seems to be about seven defendants, of whom I only know three.

'Illicit activities. It is in relation to the bills of exchange that your workers prepared. There is no mention of revelations of state secrets in your case. Nothing, not one word. They are asking for three years.'

'Well I guess that's good news. Better than fifteen. But three years. Can I see the evidence against me? And who are these other people? I've never heard of them.'

'No. The case is no longer secret but the evidence is. I can see it but I cannot take copies and you definitely cannot see it.'

'What! Arturo, how can I defend myself if they don't let me see the evidence? What if it's all made up? Jesus, this is ridiculous!' I bang the table in frustration.

'Please don't get upset. Trust me. I am your lawyer. I will plan your defence, but you have to tell me everything.'

I'm shouting now. 'But it's not right. I demand to see the evidence. This is a basic human right. Does the embassy know? For God's sake, Arturo!'

The guard pokes his head around the door. 'Hey English, stop shouting or I will kick you both out.'

Arturo is angry now. 'Don't think you can be a lawyer in my country. Don't tell me about the law. I am your lawyer. If you don't like it then I will resign, understand?'

Furious at how totally cornered I am by the system, I breathe a huge sigh and try to calm down. With perfect timing a mysterious hand passes a bottle of cold water and two cups through the slatted window.

'Now, can we work, please? So tell me once again, when did you first employ Pepe . . . ?'

An hour later we part company, friends again. As he shuffles off through the dog run I wonder what possible use he is going to be in all of this. Still, at least I know the worst, even if he does absolutely nothing. Three bloody years! Oh well, it can only get better.

The next day after football Santiago comes up and asks if I will help him with something. It's not a demand, it's almost like asking an uncle for a favour, but with menaces. Last time we spoke was after I had punched him in football. I'd been expecting a battering ever since so I was rather taken aback.

'Erm, maybe. What is it?'

'Shagga say you help wid his boat business. Well, my aunt she bought land in Quito and she wants me to run a sports club and bar. I need some ideas for plans and how to run it and you be a architect an' all.'

'Okay. Let's talk after inspection.'

So later that night he explained it all. I figured the aunty part of the story was crap. He must have bought the land with his ill-gotten gains as a low-level drug mule and enforcer. He had a half-baked business plan and some sketches. Behind the tough-guy face I could tell he was embarrassed about his handwriting. Over the next few days I showed him how to put together a simple revenue-forecast model, how to figure out how much cash he needed to raise and what he could afford to pay for finance and what it would roughly cost. It was interesting. In his barrio there was no gym, swimming pool or football court and he figured that people would pay for somewhere to do sport and relax. He wanted to help keep the kids off the street and wanted to have somewhere for families like his to do something nice. He had a little girl but had been in and out of prison in three countries for much of his adult life and had seen little of her. He worried what she thought of him and he was on the verge of admitting that he was sick of his life. We did some sketch plans. I enjoyed using my brain and he was fascinated. With no thanks it stopped as suddenly as it started and he sent all the papers back home and relapsed into his default mode, which was to ignore me completely and carry on being a loud-mouthed bully to his minions. A few days later, totally out of the blue, while I was passing him in the jungle gym, he shouted across with his steroid squeaky voice.

'Hey Steve, come here.'

Shit. I wandered over wondering what was coming. But he looked sheepishly at the ground while fiddling with his weightlifting fingerless gloves.

'Ummm. Thanks man. Guys like you don't have nothing to do with bad people like me. Nobody ever talked to me like that before, like I was the same an' all. Thanks.'

I was kind of embarrassed and so mumbled 'no problem', then walked off to try and phone home.

The twenty-one days pass very quickly. Arturo comes as promised and I hand over the handwritten copy of the statement I had painstakingly made the evening I was asked by Ivan to write my 'confession' in Villa Marista.

'Arturo. You said I can't see the evidence and that includes my statement. Well here is a true copy of my statement. Whatever they have in the file that they sent to the prosecution, if it doesn't match this one then they have faked it. I don't trust them at all. Ivan has been trying to get me to sign new documents that change what actually happened. I won't do it.'

He clears his throat. 'Harrumph, my friend I really don't think they would fake your statement,' he says, without any conviction whatsoever.

'So will I get a chance to read it out in court? In my own words?'

He doesn't answer but instead reads it through carefully. Then he looks at me with his wise old eyes, sighs and puts it in his briefcase.

'Oh well, it's late, I'd better be getting back to Havana. It's a long drive.'

A few visits more and then he asks for a couple of days off to prepare my written defence statement. Then a phone call, and he excitedly tells me that he has been able to discuss my case with the prosecutor, Duma. Oh my God, it's the imbecile that screwed JL.

He returns a few days later with his defence. I read it in disbelief, my elbows on the table, while he studies my face. A bluebottle, stupefied by the heat and so lacking its normal whizz, batters itself repeatedly at the window slats trying to escape. But it's too hot and too hopeless and above all too stupid. It will die in this room.

The one-page pleading is not something that would grace the Old Bailey.

I have a good character. I don't have a criminal record in any country in the world. I am sorry. And I cannot have committed a crime by allowing people to do something illegal if the people who actually did the act are giving evidence for the prosecution and are not being charged themselves.

That's it. I read it again and thought it through. On first reading I was about to go berserk at the childishness of it. Apparently the MININT file contained thousands of pages for the prosecution. And our defence was this? But then the sense of it dawned on me. Fighting them head-on was hopeless. The best we could do was to point out that they had made an unfortunate error in the legal fundamentals.

Arturo was hugely relieved when I smiled: 'That's great Arturo. Perfect. Send it in to the judge and give a copy to the embassy please.'

That evening there is a big fight. Ever since they banned personal music players the tension has risen. Some sadist now blasts out distorted music from the PA system at random intervals. It is always Venezuelan or reggaeton. The Caribbeans are slowly boiling and it's giving me a headache. It is so loud I cannot concentrate to read or do anything and there is no escape. It was actually off after inspection and there was a big crowd ranged in front of the TV shouting and acting like the serious criminals they were. All of a sudden fists start flying as two guys go at it hammer and tongs. Before the guards find their keys and get in, other prisoners have broken the brawlers apart. The guards haul them off for a couple of weeks of solitary and a captain stands hands on hips shouting at us all to behave or else. This is a regular event. Maybe it's my turn tomorrow.

I lie in bed wondering whether I can take three years. When I look at the guys who have been in some time, it seems three years is the point of no return. After three years your family and friends have sailed so far out of your life you can never swim hard enough to reach them. No matter what they say in letters or phone calls, you are gone. After three years your old life is lost and you slip into dependence on your fellow inmates. I guess that's one reason they have gangs and call them family.

Arturo calls me next day. The trial will be in ten days.

The trial

Seven days later I have a nasty surprise. The guard shouts my name and tells me to get ready. For what, I have no idea. I have a short interview with Simiento.

'You are going back to Villa Marista. You can take your wash things and underwear. Nothing else.'

'Erm, what for?'

'They want you to be relaxed before the trial,' he smiled.

'Can I take my notes?'

'No.'

'But I need them for the trial. Does my family know? Will I see my lawyer?'

He merely glares and returns to his forms, calling the guard to take me back.

After a hurried farewell to my friends and some sober good-luck pats on the back I am off in my dusty prison blues. Cy shouts some slightly illogical advice from the window.

'Tell them the instructor is stupid and to go fuck themselves and then you will be home soon.'

I am handcuffed at the dog run and shoved into the back of a Soviet-vintage paddy wagon. No barred windows this time so I sit with my feet pressed against the bench opposite while the wheezing old van sways about like a drunken sailor. In my mind's eye I can just about guess when we leave the country-side and enter the city, but it is very obvious when we get to Marista. I am unloaded in the covered dock and processed at the same desk I kissed goodbye all those months before. The same fat git gives me the once-over with rheumy eyes and signs a receipt. And then away down the gloomy passageways, keep to the left, hands behind and eyes down, all the way back to my old cell.

I remember every crack, blister and water stain. They have been burned into the backs of my eyes. The insects, mice and cellmates are all new but most of the guards were not and I am met with knowing nods and winks and one almost friendly: 'Ah, you. Two one seven, back again.'

A simple calculation using prisoner ID numbers shows that around 300 to 400 should pass through the meat grinder per year and from chatting to my new cellmates the attempted suicide rate has apparently stayed constant at about one a month. My fellow prisoners are interesting. One, a cheerful rogue, is obviously a police plant – all that is missing is a revolving blue light on his head – and the other camp, hysterical and on the edge of a nervous breakdown. His boss Pedro Alvarez had, for about eight years, been in charge at Alimport, responsible for all the food imports from the US, which have averaged about $700 million a year in cash sales. He had the job because he was a top party dog and totally trusted by Fidel. Last year Pedro fled on a late-night launch to the promised land and has set up in the real-estate business in Tampa. It has been entertaining to watch the Miami newspapers trying to figure out how he is financing his business. The gossip is that apparently Fidel is incandescent and will murder him if he can get his hands on him. He definitely knows too much to enjoy a long and peaceful retirement. The trembling wreck in my cell had the dreadful misfortune to have been the chief accountant for Alimport and will now get a good whipping for it.

After supper I was told to get ready. I was taken off down the passageways to a room and there sat Ivan and a plump, fastidious civilian in a suit and tie, with a pointy moustache and dyed hair. His manicured fingers drummed a manila file that must have been six inches thick.

'Hello Purvis, this is Duma the prosecutor. He has some questions for you.'

'Purvis. Your lawyer has presented your defence. What will you say at the trial?'

'Pardon?'

'What will you say? Are you going to surprise us? I don't like surprises. If you try and make us look foolish you will get more time.'

Ivan just smiles helpfully, as if to say: 'Nothing to do with me mate.'

'I will just say what I have said since the first day. I don't believe I have done anything against the law. If I have without realising it then I am sorry. But I have no idea what Arturo is going to say and I'm not sure I even know what he has written. It's all still a big secret so there is nothing more for me to say. So I won't create any drama.'

They sit there looking at me and the seconds tick by. Duma continues to drum his fingers. Ivan clears his throat.

'How do you like being back in Villa Marista? Your old cell is comfortable?'

'You know I hate it, it's inhuman. But I tell you one thing, at least the guys here are not thieves. The officials at Condesa steal everything, take bribes, use us as slaves to work on their houses and run whores. You should investigate them if you want to find criminals.'

Ivan laughs and calls for the guard. As I turn to stand and present my faded and tatty blue rear he says: 'One minute, what clothes do you have?'

Turning to face them again I reply: 'Just these.'

'Oh shit. Fuck your mother's cunt! Those idiots! You have to go back to Condesa tomorrow and get some clothes. What do you have? You can't go to trial looking like a prisoner.'

Duma and Ivan look at each other in minor panic. Their stage management had encountered a last-minute hitch. They clearly want people kept for years as prisoners in maximum security to appear as if it has all been just a brief but not too uncomfortable inconvenience.

'Just some old T-shirts, shorts and a pair of jeans. I also have some shoes and socks,' and adding helpfully, 'and some swimming trunks.'

Ignoring my attempt at a joke, Ivan continues: 'No shirt or jacket?'

'Well no. We don't generally dress for dinner.'

'Oh fuck. Has anyone in Havana got a shirt for you? Will Alberto be able to get one?'

'I guess he can get one from somewhere.'

'Those fucking cretins. I will see you at the trial. Get out.'

The next day was spent going all the way to and from La Condesa to rescue jeans, shoes, socks and pants from the locked store. A pleasant relief from the dungeon.

The day of the trial dawned. I am hauled off for a shave and a haircut, given ten minutes to dress and then off in a shiny Lada with no handcuffs but a cheerful guard who showed me his gun to dissuade me from considering a last-minute dash.

The courthouse, a rambling freshly painted domestic-looking structure, was in a large walled compound in a residential part of Havana. There was nothing to announce its presence except a lot of men in moustaches milling about outside, looking very cocky. The high metal gates with a razor-wire Afro opened as if by magic and we slid up the kerb and in.

In oversize, fusty jeans and a rather mouldy shirt that Alberto had spirited up from somewhere, but with a photo of my dad in my pocket to watch over me, I walked from the car to a simple ancillary outhouse and the Associated Press photographer snapped my picture from over the courthouse wall. The press, of course, are not allowed in or to speak to anyone involved, but they knew the trial was set for today and they lurked in the street outside. My image was relayed around the world within minutes, my ten minutes of fame.

There was nobody in the outhouse, which just contained an

empty Cuban protocol room with sparse furniture, obviously bugged to hell. Then in short succession my boss walked in, looking remarkably well, and also rather suspiciously X, who was not scheduled to be a defendant in the trial but who tried to get us to chat about old times, which of course we side-stepped. My boss and I had just had a few minutes to enquire about our respective families and each other's health for the benefit of the hidden cameras when the boss of bosses from Villa Marista, a rather sinister little Yoda-like creature with a monster bodyguard, walked in. X sidled out of the room and we were left with Yoda. He sat down, beckoned us to lean close and in a low unemotional voice gave us one final threat. He explained that various diplomats were in court and told us what would happen if we tried to make the Cuban state look like fools. I was tempted to say that they hardly needed our help with that, but bit my lip. And so it was five minutes to kick-off, and we were escorted across the yard by plain-clothed stewards who smiled as if we were unknown guests. Defendants' families, witnesses, diplomats, lawyers and Ivan were all milling about in the porch, chatting with each other as if it were a pre-theatre foyer. The three witnesses for the prosecution, all my staff, greeted me with kisses and hugs but couldn't look me in the eye.

Only family and a maximum of three Cuban friends were to be allowed in for each of the seven defendants, plus diplomatic staff. I had specifically told the family I did not want them to come in case it was too upsetting, and I had asked Arturo to request permission for Gilberto, Niara and Daniela to come. But Gilberto's blood pressure got the better of him at the courthouse gate and he had to go home to bed. From the embassy only the acting consul came, which I thought was a piss-poor statement of support from the current ambassador.

For a secret trial it had a surprisingly farcical atmosphere. The courtroom was a modern hall that could seat about fifty in rows of plastic chairs, with two rows of benches for lawyers,

defendants and witnesses. On a simple dais at the front was a
table for the three judges. There is no jury as there is no vot-
ing on the matter. The judges' role is simply to endorse what
the prosecutor asks for: he in turn has built his case on the file
and verdict of the secret police. To the left is a simple witness
stand. The entire place was formal yet low-key, decorated in
hacienda style with the doors left open to the courtyard and
people wandering in and out to the toilet or for a cigarette at
whim.

The proceedings start without much fanfare and it appears
that Arturo was right. There are seven accused involved in
three separate charges, only one of which applied to me: a
mixed catch in the fisherman's net. The first morning is taken
up with Ivan reading out a summary of each case. He starts
with the actual charges and then runs step by step through his
investigation, the evidence and the conclusions. It dawns on
me that their modus operandi is to start from a single point,
in this case it seemed to be the denunciation of my boss by a
business competitor, and from there radiate out like ripples
in a silent pool and follow everything and anything that is
suspicious in their eyes. Hence the unrelated radial arms of
the cases in the trial that was based on a phantom conspiracy. When it came to me I was relieved to hear that they had
indeed dropped revelations of state secrets and it was just a
charge of illicit activity, for which they requested a three-year
sentence. He also confirmed that I was not eligible for a reduction of sentence under clause 52(ch), as I hadn't ratted on
anyone.

The reason for the original spying nonsense became a little
clearer today. The old employee, a former coronel in Security,
to whom we had given a small monthly pension, was charged
with the idiotic crime of trying to get his son based in Florida
in order to publish his memoirs in the States. Big mistake
for him and for me as I had once researched investment into
the charter air business that operates under a handful of

tightly controlled licences and it transpires that this same son was an advisor to the Americans I had dealt with.

Sadly, it also became horribly clear to all that the reason I had spent all this time in prison was not just this revelation that some old fool had tried to sell his memoirs, or the widely known fact that some pathetic worm of a competitor of ours had denounced the company, but because I had been falsely denounced by a work colleague. He is definitely off my Christmas card list. It was also clear from what was not said that a series of officials had also been caught up in the net and would be dealt with elsewhere and by other means.

The afternoon was devoted to Ivan calling witnesses for the prosecution and when it came to my turn three staff were called to the stand. I had become increasingly disillusioned about Arturo during the run-up and as the trial progressed my heart began to sink to my boots. So far he had sat sprawled across the bench in a suit and a shiny nylon robe looking like a partially deflated Frankenstein. Immobile, he sat with his eyes shut while he slowly manoeuvred his dentures around his mouth. A vision to frighten children but not one to inspire confidence. At the sound of the first prosecution witness being called, he opened one eye to inspect the two weeping women and one very shamefaced man.

One after another they confirmed that they had worked for the company for simply ages, that I was a director and representative of the company and that they had processed bills of exchange. When it came to Arturo's chance to cross-examine, he asked each one in turn a simple question.

Creaking to his feet, he said: 'Throughout the many years you have been undertaking this task, during which the company has been audited each year by the ministries of foreign investment, finance and the central bank, did at any time any official explain to you that what you were doing was not permitted?'

'No.'

'That's all.'

And then he sat down and went back to dozing. The most remarkable aspect of the day was the brevity of the prosecution statements for cases where sentences of five to ten years were requested.

The day ended with the return trip to VM, and a miserable meal back in the cell. Surprisingly I slept well. I had waited so long for this trial but it was obvious that short of running amuck in the courtroom there was nothing I could do to influence events. It was all so carefully planned and scripted that it was clear I should just rest and not try to second-guess the second act and finale tomorrow.

The next morning passed with a succession of lawyers presenting the same defences they had submitted for dissection weeks ago, then defendants taking the stand and the subsequent cross-examinations. One judge appeared to sleep through the entire thing, the other doodled and the senior one did her best to look fierce but inscrutable.

When it came to my turn and Arturo was called to present the defence, he surprised the hell out of me by leaping into life as if someone had rammed the sword of justice up his arse and given it 3,000 volts for extra pizzazz. He was vigorous, incisive and merciless. His case had the benefit of simplicity.

'The prosecution states that my client is guilty of permitting workers to engage in activities that were not authorised by the state and are thus illegal and therefore he should be charged with illicit activities.'

This elicited suspicious nodding from Duma.

'The witnesses produced by the prosecution were these same workers, but strangely they have not been charged. A basic rule of law has to be that all are equal before the law; therefore, if my client is guilty then why are the Cuban workers not guilty? It is either not permitted or it is, it cannot be both.'

Duma and the judge look at each other and shrug as if to say: What is the old fool on about? But the three staff members start to look a little green about the gills.

'I would like to call an expert witness,' Arturo growls. And everyone swivels around to see what rabbit would be pulled out of the hat.

At which point a boffin from the central bank timidly sidled up to the stand and proceeded to confuse the hell out of everyone about the legality of endorsing bills of exchange. I think the gist of it was that they had been gaily accepting and processing these transactions for years because they provided an essential additional line of credit for the state when times were tight, and all relevant ministries were involved in this.

'So,' Arturo hurrumphs, 'I shall summarise the words of expert witness for those of you who had difficulty following. The central bank actively participated in the supposedly illegal activity and all the relevant ministries audited the company regularly and were involved in approving the transactions. So logically it should not be an illegal activity.'

Duma was pretending to look like he was thinking about it, Ivan was clearly bored and the judge continued to glare at everyone. And at the end, when it came time for him to sum up, Arturo became positively Shakespearean. He ladled on the pain and suffering caused to me and the family by my unfortunate detention and treatment and demanded I be set free immediately. I was really surprised and proud of him, it was a stellar performance. At which point I was called to the stand.

In a few minutes I repeated what I had said to Duma. I apologised for any confusion I might have caused or any laws I had inadvertently broken, and asked the court to look favourably on my case. Then it was Duma's turn to conclude matters. When it came to me he simply said that taking everything into consideration he would like to amend his recommendation and reduce the sentence he had called for from three years to two and a half.

The judge wrapped the court up very quickly, confirming

that judgement would be made within the statutory period, and that was that.

In our brief post-mortem while they tried to rustle up the transport, Arturo confirmed that he thought I would be given a sentence sufficient only to justify my period of detention.

The return to La Condesa after the trial passed in a blur, a sea of cane parting before our rumbling and rattling Lada. The driver and two guards cackle about other people's wives at the top of their voices and mercifully ignore me. They shout lewd suggestions at schoolgirls we pass on the road. Dangerous, big kids. The handcuffs dig into my wrists and I think about the few words and the sneaky hugs I could share with my friends at the end of the trial. But mainly I think about what Ivan said to them as they were leaving,

'Stephen isn't a crook but he is an idiot.'

At this stage I have to agree with him. And I think about that weird little prosecutor: his solemn little wave goodbye and creepy smile from an upstairs open window as I was leaving the courthouse. What was that all about? These people are so very odd.

*　　*　　*

I was happy to see the entrance to La Condesa again and looking forward to seeing my mates and discussing the trial. How bizarre that I felt a kind of comfort in the familiarity of the place. Clearly I have become conditioned to my pathetic existence.

The re-education officer looked up from his desk, cracked his knuckles and signed for me with a bored grunt. He accompanied me to the security entrance. His pace was the slow measured pace of a man used to calculating the seconds, minutes and hours of punishment and then multiplying them with random malice.

'What was the charge and how many years?' he smirked.

'Illegal activities and two and a half years. The prosecutor argued for a reduction.'

'Congratulations, that's nothing,' he grinned, 'you'll be home soon.'

'How soon?'

'Probably before the end of the year. It depends on your comportment. You know.'

I had already done the maths a thousand times since getting my petition. The official calculation is that each year of sentence is equivalent to ten months of physical completed after the first year. So assuming the judges ratify a two and a half year sentence it means thirty months sentence less five, which equals twenty-five months of actual prison time. Then, if you have been a good boy and everyone agrees, they will release you on a conditional basis, which for foreigners means expulsion from the country in chains after you have completed half of the time. So if all goes well then I should be expelled after fourteen months, which laughably is three months ago.

But in Cuba the rulebook is infinitely flexible. The reality is that unless your lawyer, and more importantly your embassy, is pushing, the prison ignores the date. And only when everyone makes enough of a stink about it do the prison officials start the process. The coronel, the major in charge of documents, the re-education captain, the captain of discipline and the counter-intelligence coronel all meet to decide if they will agree to giving you conditional liberty. They review your record to see if you have earned the two months off per year. If you haven't done sport, worked and attended lessons your goose is cooked. If you have discipline notes in your book you can expect extra time. If you have made an enemy of any of these people then it's all over. The odds are pretty heavily stacked against you. Once they all agree they write to the headquarters of prisons in calle 15 y K with a recommendation, who then review the entire file. They in turn write to the prosecutor's office and court with their own recommendation.

The prosecutor then does a review and sends it up to the ministry. The ministry decides and then sends the denial or confirmation back down the chain. From talking to prisoners I discovered that the fastest this has ever been done is three months, the average is six months and the longest is forever. So in a nutshell, even though the penal code says that you are free it can take around another six months of imprisonment before that becomes a reality, and your time to serve could be anything from half to all of the actual sentence. So my inscrutable re-education officer is right; once the judges confirm the sentence the process will start but it could drag on for ages. It all depends on the whims of my captors. I could be here for another year and a half if they feel like it. A person's time has no value in this country.

A nameless guard did a desultory pat-down, took me through the dog-run gates and removed the handcuffs. I had missed the evening meal so the yard was quiet, just the muffled blare of TV from the cellblocks and the far-off sound of mess trays being scraped and washed out at the back. The sun was losing heat as it started to dip behind the walls and dusk was claiming the corners. A dry wind blew dust devils and the bored watch officer called me over to let me back into the cellblock. While he fumbled with the padlock a sudden wave of exhaustion washed over me. The last five days had been stressful.

I sit down on the bottom bunk and my friends crowd round to hear the news. Thank God there haven't been any new inmates, so I still have the top and bottom to myself. I don't feel up to having to deal with a new person invading my personal space. My enemies look up from what they were doing and conversations falter to a halt as everyone wants to catch the latest gossip. I had seen the same many times. Prisoners gloat when an enemy gets bad news, snigger and chuckle in their little gangs. When it is a friend they are elated if things have gone anything less than disastrously. Nobody ever expects to be found innocent and nobody expects anything less than the time demanded by the prosecutor. Usually at a trial the judges all work themselves up into a revolutionary froth and throw an extra couple of years in for good measure. The years dished out seem to ebb and flow depending on how angry Raúl is about life.

I give my mates the bare facts, which they receive with a genuine joy inevitably tinged with a bit of jealousy. The news is picked up on enemy bunks and goes through the cellblock in a flurry of mutterings. Two and a half is considerably less than any of the other business cases and a lifetime shorter than all the others. Many of the bad guys are visibly angry. They throw me dark looks and start to dream up ways to derail my departure. I have seen this many times as well. There is a particular warped kind of man that wishes ill on the rest of humanity, and there are certainly more than one or two in here. Consumed with indignation and jealousy, they set all sorts of traps and plan all sorts of provocations: knives planted under mattresses, denunciations, fights and thefts, anything to delay a fellow human's release. I shall have to be extra careful now. I am a target for their frustrations.

Salim, God bless him, would have been very pleased. I wonder how he is doing. I bet the prison in Canada has better food. I wonder if he has seen his wife and kids yet. I could do with him to watch my back. Cy had kept some food for me and I eat it ravenously while they leave me to my thoughts.

I go out to the back, joining a few people smoking before lights out. The stars are twinkling bright, the night air is refreshing; cool with the faintest hint of the sea. The Bahamians are talking up their favourite fantasy. Escape by fast boat.

'Fuck, we be home by breakfast. Them pussy clart no catch us.'

They enjoy working out the details, knowing full well that it is just a dream. The bit that scares them is not breaking out of the prison or organising the boat and running the gauntlet of the coastguard machine guns and a helicopter. No, it's being on the run inside Cuba: that three- to four-hour period they need to get from prison to the moonlit beachhead. The reason that people don't escape prison is that the whole island is in effect a prison. There are so few private vehicles, so few vehicles of any kind in fact. Society, particularly in the countryside, is very immobile and outside the tourist areas strangers are noticed within seconds. That and the fact that the countryside is crawling with police, secret police and informers means that evasion is not a thing for amateurs. So the Bahamians dream of the perfect escape and resign themselves to do the time.

The next day is Cy's seventy-third birthday and I buy two eggs from a pretend diabetic and with the help of Elroy manage to rig up a primitive bain-marie and make a steamed cake. We celebrate after lunch. At afternoon exercise there was yet another face-down at the telephone. I am desperate to call home. They have heard nothing from me since the day before I was whisked off back to Villa Marista before the trial. The usual suspects are creating trouble in the telephone line. A guard has to break it up and send them both off to discipline. The rest of us in the queue watch in silence. It's too hot and too predictable to comment on. I raise an eyebrow to a friend in the other line and he nods slowly in agreement.

Glancing at my watch for the hundredth time, I shout: '*Tiempo!* Get the fuck out! You've had ten minutes.'

I get through to London. It's my wife.

'Hi darling, you're famous, there's a photo of you going into the trial and loads of press.'

'How the hell did they manage that?'

'I spoke to X and her husband took it from across the street. Nobody will say anything. How was it? Why were you smiling?'

'Well I was smiling 'cos I could see Niara and Daniela waving as they were waiting to go into the courtroom. There were also people from the office, witnesses. The first friendly faces I have seen in months. That's why I was smiling. Anyway I'm fine. It went okay I think.'

And I recount the whole story. I tell her that hopefully I will be home soon and not to worry but that we have to wait for the judge to ratify the court's decision, which could be weeks. I manage to have a few words with the girls and do the stiff-upper-lip schtick, even though my heart is bursting. I keep my misgivings to myself. My ten minutes is up in a flash and people are shouting at me to get out. I say goodbye, pick up my bottle and continue walking around and around the yard. Burning up my frustrations in exercise. The counter-intelligence officer is observing me from a chair in the shade. He doesn't say anything but just watches me, letting me know he is keeping an eye on me. It's all a mind fuck in here.

When I get back inside I write to the outside world with the news. This one I shall smuggle out via my hat. Someone I trust has a family visit tomorrow.

The tree frog

The day after that, on the breakfast news, the silly newsreader
has some jaw-dropping news in the business section. I have
become fascinated with this man and wonder what he really
thinks as he reads out the latest surreal rubbish. He usually
sports a badly fitting maroon sports jacket and has matching
bags under his soulful eyes. His gigantic and luxuriant moustache is a thing of wonder. Each day he rolls out his stock
repertoire: defiant triumphalism when talking about the latest glories of the revolution or anything to do with Venezuela,
wearied despair when recounting the horrors of western de-
mocracy and all who sail in her, and stern lecturing if the laser
beam of Cuban investigative journalism lands on some act of
deviancy. The opening five minutes are met with a barrage of
abuse from the bus-station seating. Our friend has the uphill
struggle of trying to persuade Cuba that the new president
of Venezuela is a modest genius who will rule with an iron
fist for eternity and never turn the oil off. After an absolutely
riveting piece about the dramatic increase in the production
of charcoal from the rampant thorn bushes that have rendered
half of all the productive land in the country depressingly
unproductive, there was a hilarious bit of reportage about the
agricultural reforms sweeping the country. These are raising
efficiency and productivity to the levels last seen in the late
Middle Ages. A cocky little reporter corn-holed some peasant
in a vast field where he appeared to be farming stones. The
peasant asked his buffalo to cease pulling the wooden plough,
a stripped-down design consisting of a large section of tree

trunk with a stake drilled through it. He stepped down from his 'vehicle', brushed the dust from his tattered shirt and politely answered the questions.

'Yes, the reforms are needed to improve productivity,' he says, his eyes wandering around his waterless desert. 'Yes, the collective will supply us with fertiliser and seeds and then collect the produce and take it to market where we shall be fairly paid for our labour.' The camera pans across a huge landscape with no sign of any other human activity. 'The planned investment will allow us to improve our equipment.' The buffalo stares at the camera thoughtfully.

Then we are back in the studio where the walrus delivers his stunning news. 'Yesterday, the minister of tourism signed an agreement with a Vietnamese group for the development of the golf and real-estate project Bellomonte in Playas del Este Havana.'

'That's my bloody project,' I blurt out. 'You fuckers!'

I had already had to endure the news of Beyoncé waving to her hordes of fans from the balcony of our hotel a few months earlier to an admiring press corps, but this was really unbelievable. Actually, it wasn't. Maybe it's not the reason that all this happened but it's an amazing coincidence that the day after the trial the project I have worked on for three years has been sold on with a big pink 'love you lots' ribbon round it to some mysterious government-backed outfit from Vietnam.

Last night we were all woken up by a piercing scream from the washroom. It sounded like somebody was being murdered but then it quickly subsided into hysterical laughter. Some half-asleep guy had tottered off to take a midnight dump. A tree frog had taken up residence in one of the toilet bowls and was minding his own business under the seat. The tree frog, having his sleep rudely interrupted, had apparently leapt on to the dangling tackle, thinking it was some kind of small branch. You can imagine the surprise of the guy, suddenly in the clammy grip of a large tree frog. Today, we've been laughing about it all morning and now the cellblock is divided between those who think it should be killed, those who want to leave it where it is and those who want to liberate a fellow amphibian prisoner and chuck it over the wall. But one of the Ecuadoreans just goes and kills it, leaving the body on the floor. It's a calculated part of a simmering argument between two rival groups and an act of provocation.

The Caribbeans and most other folk are appalled by the bathroom activities of a few of the more primitive South Americans. There are a few drug-gang guys who regularly shit in the showers when it is the turn to clean of somebody they dislike. The fact that one of the phantom shitters actually serves food in the mess adds to the bad feelings. These scumbags are also some of the worst snitches in the place and are irredeemably bad people. They need to be locked up for life. I just wish it wasn't with me. This bad feeling between them and the rest of us is never going to go away. We hate their guts and they hate the whole world.

A few days later during exercise there is a big sweep. We are all given an extra hour while the guards lock down the cellblock and check it from top to bottom for contraband and evidence of something to upset the coronel. What will it be this week? Too many pairs of socks per person? Photos on the inside of a locker door? Is this just to show who's the boss or is it to uncover the knives and pills that the snitches have spilled? A few trusties work with them. We are called back one by one to hand over our locker keys as they go through everything. Since the trial I have been extra-careful, keeping my locker locked all the time, emptying it once a day and checking everything before I put it all back, and checking under the mattress and in all the nooks and crannies every time I have to leave the area.

I'm pushing weights in the jungle gym when word comes round. 'Simiento wants to see you.' Shit.

I put my shirt back on and walk back. A group of five of

us have been assembled outside his office. There is a dripping pile of stuff from the freezer. This meat thing again. For the last few months I have been really careful with the meat. I only ever have the permitted 2lb of smoked pork in slices per month. That's it. The additional and forbidden stuff that comes in through a window is cooked there and then so there is no evidence unless we are caught in the act of cooking or eating it. The guy who holds the freezer key is just an occasional snitch; he only rats out when he has to and only targets people he has no business with. As I always regularly give him a meal or an offcut of something, plus, more importantly, I talk to him like a human being, I don't think he has tried to screw me. The captain is very disappointed to find that I have no forbidden products in the freezer. All he can do is say I have too much pork, which we both know is not true as he was the asshole that checked it when it came in.

He starts shouting at me. 'One more infraction and you will have a note! I have been informed that you eat meat every night. Where does it come from?'

'Captain, I have my allowance which I share with my friends. Nothing more.'

'You will get a note. Do you understand? Get out!'

Talking to the others caught up in the sweep we figure out who the rat is. This particular rat has a visit from a whore next week and he wants permission for her to bring an extra bag of food in, hence the snitching. So the pressure is on. One crazy guy actually had six lobster tails in the freezer and he is totally screwed. Six bucks will cost him two months.

Seventeen days after the trial a shout goes out for me. A fish-faced guard calls me out. I put on my uniform shirt and shoes. Major Redi is outside. He tells me: 'Get ready.'

I am confused. Does this mean transfer to *Minima* or freedom? Or extra time?

'Why?' I ask limply.

'The coronel will see you.'

We go through the whole rigmarole of handcuffs and gates and I am led into a room I have never been in before. It's the front office. There is a blank-faced plain-clothes State Security guy standing by the door with his hands clasped in front of him. Sat on a collapsed black vinyl sofa is a tremendously fat, sweaty woman in civvies who introduces herself as an official from the court and beside her is an incredibly thin woman with the skin and teeth of someone who has lived life in an ashtray and who says she is a translator. But her English is worse than my Spanish. I wonder how I will fit between them on the sofa. Behind the desk is the coronel looking like he is about to have a baby. He is spluttering with emotion. I look from one to another and wait to see what they have to say. The coronel blurts it out through grinding teeth.

'This woman is an official from the justice office. You are free.'

I look at her in wonder. 'You're joking. What kind of freedom? English freedom or Cuban freedom?'

She smiles and then after a deep breath starts a very serious two-minute sentence that begins, 'Under section X of the penal code of the Republic of Cuba' and ends 'sign here and you are free'.

With a heaving bosom and a huge intake of breath she handed me a pen and a weaselly little form, while the thin one did the entire thing again in mangled English. Although she nearly passes out halfway due to her nicotine-raddled chest I am not listening. I am staring at the piece of paper in disbelief. It is here in grey and yellow. As of today I am free.

The coronel waves the guard over to unlock my handcuffs and I am dismissed.

The major takes me back. He explains that a car will take me to Havana but they have to know where I am staying until I leave. This is amazing. I thought I would be taken in chains to the airport and expelled, which is the way they always do it. But although he hasn't said it, it looks like I am not being kicked out. I have a thousand things racing through my head. I need to call home but there is no time.

Taking me back to the cellblock, the guard tells me charmlessly: 'Get all your things. You have ten minutes. First collect everything from storage.'

My tennis pal Jay comes with me to help carry stuff. There is a nice officer there, one who has always turned a blind eye to food coming in during family visits and who let us have extra time to enjoy our hours together in peace. With a genuine smile he shakes my hand and wishes me luck. He says he is thinking of leaving and opening a pizza shop. I wish him luck.

Jay and I stagger back with two suitcases. One full of books, which I donate to the library. Back on my bunk, my friends crowd around. I give out my cooking stuff to the executive dining club. I give all the architecture class stuff to my best student. I give all my medicine, food and clothes to my poorer friends. I give everything away except a few civilian clothes, my flip-flops and my trainers. The guard is shouting to hurry. I tell him to wait.

'I've been waiting a fucking year and a half. You can wait five fucking minutes.'

I have one last cold shower to freshen up and change into clothes that hang off my spindly frame and then I give my mates a hug and a handshake goodbye. As I am let out I get the traditional round of applause and cheer from almost all the prisoners. Most of them are pleased to see somebody get out even if it's not them this time.

When I get outside the world is silent except for some birds tweeting. By rights there should really be my family waiting, a brass band playing, fireworks going off and champagne corks popping. But instead there is the State Security thug waiting. He takes my suitcase, puts it in the back of a brand-new car and asks me: 'Where would you like to go, Havana?'

I'm tempted to say Varadero but instead give him the directions to a friend's house. As we drive off he actually asks me: 'So what do you think of Cuban justice then?'

Momentarily at a loss for words, I bite my lip and respond tartly: 'Well it's definitely different from English justice.'

It seems we can agree on one thing at least. With one arm out of the window he chain-smokes and we chat about this and that like old chums on a road trip. As we near Havana he gives me some instructions.

'You have to go to Villa Marista tomorrow with a letter for Ivan, confirming where you are staying until you leave. You need to see your lawyer. He will arrange with the court to get you an exit visa. When you have the exit visa you can leave when you want.'

When we drew up outside my friend's house he carried my suitcase to the front door and rang the bell. The wife opened it and nearly fainted. My erstwhile driver confirmed their names with her on a piece of paper and then with a jolly handshake said: 'Well, I hope you have enjoyed your stay in Cuba. Goodbye.'

I replied in English: 'You are all totally fucking mad.'

He shrugged his shoulders and drove away.

Free fall out

After a quick and slightly hysterical call home to confirm the good news and a failed attempt at a celebratory whisky, I try a hot shower. The first in eighteen months. It is absolute agony as my skin is no longer desensitised to hot water. It was to be about three weeks before I could actually enjoy hot water and the same before wine tasted of anything but vinegar. I borrow a clean T-shirt and shorts while the maid takes my clothes away to wash away the stink of La Condesa's mouldy tin shed.

The Havana grapevine has been working overtime and by the time I am dressed many people have called up. I beg my old friend Monchi to tell his staff that I am out or asleep. He wants to know if he should invite people around to celebrate. But I don't want to talk to anyone. 'Please no, not yet, I can't deal with a lot of people and questions and emotions. I need peace and quiet I think.'

But I do want to see my three Villa Marista saviours. They know what happened and with them I don't need to explain anything. They were with me at the absolute rock bottom and helped me climb out.

Niara is out of the country so she can't come over, but Gilberto and Daniela can and they arrive just as the sun is setting. There is a ring at the gate and over the chorus of seven mad barking dogs I trot down the steps and throw open the high, sheet-metal gate. We look at each other for a brief composed second and then I grab them both in a messy bear hug. Arms entwined we go inside and sit on the terrace to share a beer.

We sit and chat quietly for an hour or so under the warm Havana stars.

This first night in freedom I lie awake for a long time. The door is freaking me out. I can't decide if I want it open or closed. This is very odd. I wake at 5.30 a.m. prison time and obsessively make the bed and tidy up my few belongings. I pace around uncertain what to wear and at 6.30 prison time on the dot I take my seat for breakfast at a wrought-iron and marble garden table shaded by a jasmine-shrouded trellis. The maid hasn't even started work yet. I get up and wander around. Finally at about 7.30 she arrives and with a smile quickly arranges things. Crisp, white linen together with a place setting in delicate china. An antique coffee set, water jug and glass and proper cutlery complete the table. I haven't seen anything so fine and delicate for a year and a half. I take the cup in my hand and turn it over and around to check the maker's mark. 'Hmm, Sèvres.'

She politely interrupts me and enquires what I would like for breakfast. Momentarily incapable of thinking of anything, I actually hear myself say: 'Ermm, bread and water.'

She nods sympathetically and asks if I am sure. 'No, how stupid. Eggs please, with toast and coffee and do you have any fruit? Thanks.'

I seem to have forgotten how to ask for things politely. In prison everything was a brutal statement, usually with a swear word in the middle and an insult like 'fish' or 'batty' or '*chivato*' thrown in.

After breakfast I have a mechanical need to comply with the exercise period, so I fart about in my friend's garden doing press-ups for thirty minutes then go for a half-hour jog down 5th Avenue. Another painful shower and then I have work to do.

I tap away in my friend's home office. It's the short letter confirming my temporary address that I have to deliver to Villa Marista today. I print a copy, sign it and fold it into an envelope. It's time to go. Monchi says goodbye to six hounds, one hops in the back and off we drive. It will take around half an hour and he is nervous, rabbiting on about all sorts of inconsequential things. I ask him if he would be really kind and take the letter in for me, as my courage seems to have deserted me and I have a paranoid feeling that they will take me in and start the whole thing all over again. He shakes his head.

'Please, I cannot do that. I don't want to go in there.'

The closer we get the more erratic his driving becomes. We get to the dreaded city block and drive past the front. Behind an old wrought-iron fence is a huge manicured lawn shaded by majestic trees. The old seminary building, freshly painted, looks more like an imposing colonial museum than the headquarters of State Security. There are signs up saying no stopping, so we pootle along and turn left. The flank walls of the entire block are high, razor-wire-topped cement walls, painted a lurid hospital green. There are guard posts every hundred metres. More signs. 'No cameras'. 'No stopping'. 'No walking on the pavement next to the complex'. I was expecting a new one saying no drunken dancers shouting after midnight. Monchi is leaning forward, sweat trickling down his temples with tension. We are crawling along trying to work out where to park and he is muttering to himself: 'Aye aye aye, no left, no right, no stop, oh dear God what to do?'

We manage to circumnavigate the entire block, arriving back at the front. Monchi is panicking now and his voice goes up an octave. 'My God, they are taking down the number plate. They will arrest me.'

He is right. Two sweating foreigners in a bright red jeep slowly circling Villa Marista is suspicious. We look like journalists. Putting his foot down, we move on a couple of blocks. Pulling the handbrake on, he turns to say earnestly: 'My friend, I love you but I am parking here. You have to walk. I will wait.'

'Okay. If I'm not back in a hour you can have my flip-flops

but ring the embassy,' I say with fake bravado.

Steeling myself for the unknown I walk fast to the entrance and push open the gate. There are no obvious guards in the front. It all looks so benign. I wander up to the open front door and enter the lobby. The intact monastic architecture is clean and freshly painted. Some rather flashy Italian chromed-steel public benches are provided for visitors. A few glum, frightened-looking family groups sit in hushed silence. There is a typical laminated chipboard counter plonked down with casual communist disregard for beauty or function. An attractive, young female officer is sat behind it, the only official presence in the cavernous hall. I approach in trepidation.

'I have a letter for Teniente Coronel Ivan.'

'Really? You?' She seems surprised. I guess it's pretty unusual for a foreigner to be on name terms with the chief interrogator.

'Wait please.'

I can't sit as I'm too nervous. In a few minutes a side door opens and a middle-aged woman in captain's uniform emerges. She walks briskly across.

'Good morning Stephen, how have you been? You look well.'

It suddenly dawns on me. This is the lady that controlled the visits. She was the stern one who usually escorted me to the visiting room. She runs an eye over the letter. 'That's fine. Just remember to go and arrange things with immigration and the justice office. Ivan sends his greetings. I hope you enjoy your stay. Goodbye.'

And with another shake of the hand I am free to go. I leave as fast as I can, not daring to pause for breath until I am safely behind the door of Monchi's cherry-red jeep.

'Shit, let's go, I need a drink.'

'Well tell me, tell me. What happened?'

'Jesus, this country man, they treated me like I was a

returning guest at a hotel. Like it was just a minor inconvenience and no harm done.'

Our good friend Jenny invites me to my first civilised lunch
for a long time. She finds a quiet, secluded table at a nice pizza
place under some vines. Out of the corner of my eye I see a
table of women, vaguely familiar from school. They are cran-
ing their necks to look at us and are whispering. I have prawn
salad as my appetite is small and a bottle of beer. She's a lovely, jolly person and tells me she thinks I probably don't want
to talk about things, so she keeps me distracted with tales of
disaster at her travel company. She has to get back to work,
but before she goes she promises to buy my ticket as soon as
I have an exit date sorted. I wander over the road to Arturo's
house where I have agreed to meet him in order to discuss final details. His charming, tiny wife answers the door and I sit
in their orderly front room with its calm paintings and books.
I see my little offering propped up on a desk. She serves coffee
and asks after the family as if I have been off travelling for a
week or so. After coffee Arturo gets down to business, something about having to go to the justice department for a piece
of paper to exit. But my head is swimming and my stomach
churning. I barely make it to the bathroom before I project-
ile vomit. I seem to be allergic to prawns now. Making my
excuses I leave and walk for thirty minutes back to Monchi's,
where I lie under the air conditioning and recover my senses.

That night a couple we've known for years and who emi-
grated to Miami come to visit. It's nice to sit and chat in
private and being Cuban they know not to ask about what
happened. They know people who have disappeared into Villa
Marista. But they insist we go to a new, trendy rooftop restaurant and there we bump into some raucous, boozy foreigners
who want to make a big song and dance, buy drinks and ask
stupid questions. We leave early as I can't stand it. In the
garden I sit under the stars for hours and wonder what's up
with me. I can't eat normally. I can't drink normally, I can't

sleep or shower like I should. I avoid people I used to like and if somebody touches me I flinch. I have to get a grip before I frighten the kids.

The next day I go to the justice office. Strangely it's the same building downtown where I went to court when those bandits stabbed me all those years ago. The chain-smoker is there and after waiting for a couple of hours she gives me a letter, fag in hand, for immigration. It says I have no charges pending against me and that I have been released from detention. As she hands it over she says through a cloud of smoke: 'Do not lose this, okay? It's important. Don't go to immigration without it.' And she waves me off with a smile.

On the way back I pass by Arturo's office. He has the letter from Ivan confirming that State Security say that I am free to stay in the country at liberty until immigration sort out an exit visa. Blimey, he has actually done what he said he would do at last. That's a first.

'But don't try and leave Havana, they are probably watching you,' Arturo warns, as he waves me off.

The next day Monchi invites me to his beach house. It's lovely and I'm excited to see how his vegetable plot is getting on. Oh, the dreams and conversations I've had about vegetables this past eighteen months. But his other guests are diplomats I don't know and they want to hear all about my troubles. I escape to the beach after picking at my lunch. However the sea here is shallow and muddy and not at all what I need. I need something big and clean to wash away all the shit. I decide I have to go to the proper beach but it will have to wait. Tomorrow I must go to immigration.

I go to the immigration office and ask to see the top guy. I had the letters from the Ministry of Justice confirming that I was a free man and could leave the country and the other from State Security stating that I was allowed to stay in Cuba without a visa until immigration issued an exit visa. It became immediately apparent that this was a bit of a first for them.

Normally it's straight from Condesa in the immigration van for a humiliating deportation. I passed a very sweaty couple of hours while they debated whether it was better just to lock me up until they got to the bottom of it. I told them to call the teniente coronel, but the thought of bothering a scary individual like that was too much for them. I called my lawyer and passed the phone over to the boss. He caved in and the mood changed. Inviting me into his office, he offered me a cup of coffee so strong you could repair roads with it.

'The visa will take a few days. You can collect it on the twenty-third and you should leave on the twenty-fourth. Can you organise a flight for that day?'

I texted Jenny. While we waited I asked about coming back. 'You wish to return?' He looked at me as if I were stark raving mad. 'Really? I don't think a business visa would be a good idea do you? But as a tourist, after one year you are free to return.'

'Good, I like Cuba,' I said brightly.

'Huurumphh, okay, but I suggest it would be a good idea to ask at the Cuban embassy in London before you got on the plane.'

The text came back affirmative and we were good to go. Now I had four days in Havana with nothing official to do, just hang out, see people and try and get as normal as I could before I flew home.

I don't want to go to the beach on my own so I call the gang. Gilberto doesn't do beaches, he says he gets sand in his prostate, and Niara is still away but Daniela agrees to take the day off work and we take a taxi to Playa del Este, which is outside Havana limits, but what can they do? Arrest me again? It's a weekday and it's everything I needed it to be. Miles of clean sandy beach, a beautiful blue sky, crystal water with a gentle swell pushing at heaps of broken shells and above all it's empty except for a guy selling coconuts and the pest renting umbrellas and sunbeds. We laugh about the visits and the trial and Gilberto's haemorrhoids and drink far too many coconuts for the long ride home. On the way back to Havana I tell myself everything is going to be alright. I can get over this but I need time.

After my morning exercise I decide to walk to the international school. It's closed for summer now so I called ahead to see if anyone was there. The secretary said that Ian the headmaster and some of the board were on site. I sauntered in and surprised them. They were warm and welcoming to the ghost that walked in and it was certainly good to see old, familiar faces. One of them was actually one of the people that Ivan wanted me to denounce, but I kept this to myself. I had heard that they had confiscated his passport for a few months and he had only recently stopped looking paranoid. So no point in freaking him out. When they started asking questions about what had happened I made my excuses and left. But on the way out I made a special point of thanking Ian. He had been wonderful with the kids during those first dark four months and especially supportive of Adam, who had to endure a graduation in the worst possible circumstances.

The remaining days flew by and before I knew it, the time had come to go to the airport. My faithful number two from the office came to make sure I finally got away and Ricardo our long-suffering driver took us. It was with great relief that we all shook hands for one last time as dusk started to fall.

It was dark as the plane taxied away. I was in tinker's class but the Virgin rep knew me, came on board and as a lovely surprise upgraded me and made sure the girls looked after me really well. As we climbed and circled out to sea, gaining height for the long flight home, I could see the distinctive pig's-head shape of Havana Bay glistening in the moonlight, while great swathes of the city were black from tonight's blackout. It was probably my last sight of a land and people I loved.

Bamboo

Sarah is waiting as I exit customs. It isn't Hollywood, it's better than that. No tears and hysterics, we kiss and embrace with an easy familiarity as if I had just been away for a month or so and it's just everything that's good and normal.

'Hi darling, thank God that's over. You look great. Did you drive? Where are the kids?'

'Yeah, I'm off the pills now and the doctor says it's okay. You look good too, but too skinny. The kids are all at school and Adam's coming down from uni today. I thought we'd go straight to see your mum.'

We walk slowly hand in hand and I tell her about the flight. I notice her movements are fluid again and there isn't that millisecond pause that the drugs induced. Then there is the inevitable quick hunt for change for the parking machine, followed by the much longer hunt for the car.

'Hmmm, I'm sure it was in this row. Or was that last time?'

I cannot but smile as we circle up and down the aisles, and think: 'Well, she's back to normal.'

Everything is so shockingly clean and orderly after Havana. The suburbs of London look just like I left them, smugly complacent with a large affluent bottom. Whizzing over Kingston Bridge I see a childhood snapshot. The water-boatman wake of a few sculls disturbs the mirrored Thames, and not a breath of wind stirs the chestnuts that frame the tow-path, their bright summer candlesticks pinpricks of whiteness against the deep sun-dappled green. Then bursting through the backside of Bentalls, a criminal elevation if ever there was one, we push on through the melee of shoppers and students pouring down the streets. We fly through the grotty one-way system and then plunge back into the brick-red suburbs for the last stretch to Mum's house.

The sound of the heavy old front door opening and the cool Edwardian breeze that carries the smells of home transports me back. My last visit before prison, leaving for Cuba eleven years before that and my dear dad's death. Further back than that, bringing babies round to their grandparents and our wedding reception, and stretching across the decades, leaving for university and adolescent indiscretions and adventures, back and back beyond. The old paintings and family photos in the hallway charting our course through the years, back to my safe anchorage.

We wander out to the back. Mum is gardening, poking at some recalcitrant weed with a determined gleam in her eye. She is probably thinking of Ivan or maybe of somebody at the Foreign Office.

After she'd wiped her hands on her jeans, we hug. 'Oh hello darling, welcome home. Would you like some tea or something stronger? Bugger it, I know it's only eleven but I think we all deserve a gin and tonic.'

Five months of recuperation in London. The family slowly heals itself as they hear my story, I hear theirs and we try and make it better again. Each of us keeps part of our experience private; there are certain things that are best left unsaid and there are some things too painful to talk about. Better just leave them under the pillow and let time heal whatever it can.

There are beaches and parties and booze and meals: Italian meals, French meals, Indian meals, Chinese meals, all the wonderful flavours that I have dreamed about. There are camping trips to the glorious, wind-blasted mountains and moors. There are sailing trips on my beloved soupy English sea and a hapless Italian boat trip where the engine caught fire miles from port. I potter around exhibitions with a child in tow and wander in and out of shops, fingering clothes and thumbing through books. I enjoy all those wild and bright things I planned from the bleak dungeon, and snuggle into all the fond familiarity I missed in the lunacy of La Condesa.

There has been a lot of laughter and a few surprises. There are sulks and silences, but not too many tears thank God. I think each of us has shed enough over the past two years. Certain little details come to light that make me hate our tormentors afresh. The kids really suffered in a thousand ways. Changing school was tough enough; no friends, everything unknown and then on top of that the worry about what's happening to their father and the fear, the shame.

* * *

I call La Condesa weekly. I miss it and I miss my friends there. Is that strange? I guess so. Perhaps it is because I became so dependent on the twenty-four-hours-a-day companionship. Putting it into context, on average I see my wife for an hour in the morning and three hours in the evening, whereas for months on end I was trapped with strangers for every second of the day. I find it impossible to talk, I mean really talk, to my friends in London about what happened. The only people who truly understand what I went through are my dear Cuban friends, the ones who stood by me through thick and thin. I call them as often as I can, I don't want to let go of them. Part of me is bored to tears with the subject but I can't let it just fade to grey.

There is good news: both Jesus and Matej are released. From our supper club only Cy remains, and he will continue to fester another year before his trial and release.

* * *

We go and visit Frans and Lotte in Holland, partly just for the hell of it and partly because they can fill in some of the gaps. It's damp, old and rather two-dimensional in Delft. How strange to see the pre-Christmas festival of SchwarzPieter. Just suggesting a public festival that obliges half the population to black up, don daft clothes and prance about playing St Nicholas's jolly imps while the other half laugh and clap their hands would get you stoned to death in England. But here it's okay, it's cultural heritage; a bit like the Japanese chasing whales to extinction and Cubans accepting the inevitability of the system. What does it take for people to stand back, look at themselves and say 'time we moved on'? I wonder what Shagga, Chino and Bob would say about it all. Probably not too much about the whales.

Frans and Lotte tell me about what really happened to my wife in those first, shocking months. It is horrible to hear some of the details and yet being essentially a Cuban tale it is riddled with surreal humour and paradox. Frans, who had years of professional dealings with MININT, had slowly developed a degree of understanding with Ivan; not a friendship, but recognition that they both knew the score. Frans stunned me with a revelation.

'After a couple of months Ivan let me know that he knew you were not guilty but he had to follow orders. I think he even liked you, but he had no choice.'

'Bollocks.'

'Listen, it was one professional to another. And I knew that when I looked into his eyes. He was honestly upset about what had happened to Sarah and grew to like your kids.'

'Fuck you, what is it with you guys with moustaches?'

I thought about it a lot. Ivan a human being? Maybe he was being genuine when he came to give me a hug a few weeks before the trial and told me not to worry. I will never know. The trouble is once you become a professional torturer you lose the right to be given the benefit of the doubt. Is he just another victim of the system? Some soft, social studies student might argue so but I couldn't give a shit. I do forgive him for what he did because life is too short to be bitter forever, but he did have a choice. If he really felt morally compromised by the misery he created he could just walk away. Become a gardener or something. But he won't. The system understands people like him, it gives them what they want. It understands human weakness. Power and prestige go with the three stars and there is the delicious frisson of smelling the fear from anyone that looks into his eyes, for he is a man who can condemn you and your family to a lifetime of misery on a *'conviction morale'*. He just has to say the words and it's all over. This is the power that corrupts.

And then one afternoon I am up a ladder putting the finishing touches to a timber structure at my mum's house, and getting scratched by old roses, when she calls for a tea break. It's cold but clear and so we sit outside in the sun, the first of the brittle copper-beech leaves whirling around our feet in the autumn wind. Through the tea steam she surprised me by returning to an old theme.

'You know, Ivan realised after a few months that you were totally innocent. He changed overnight. Every time after that when I arrived he would carry my plastic bag and take my arm. If it was raining, hold an umbrella. He agreed to bending his own rules about visitors. He loved Naomi coming as she reminded him of his own sister when she was a child. He never said it but I could tell in his eyes that it was a terrible mistake.'

'You've told me that before but I don't know. They are master manipulators. Maybe it was just you hoping it was true and they wanted to stop us causing any trouble in the press.'

And we leave it at that.

We move house. I guess I am about ready to find a job. I think I've just about finished everything that needed painting, mending, building or chopping down. The financial loss was the least important thing for me but I certainly need to find proper employment as we are quickly going broke.

Various kindly disposed shareholders from my company

had proposed me for developer or project director positions but none of them were for suburban London or indeed Britain. Over a Mayfair club breakfast I was offered a large infrastructure scheme in rural Angola, over drinks a posh real-estate development in Quito, Ecuador, and a prison in Jamaica made me laugh. All of them difficult jobs in very challenging places, most of which involved a high degree of personal risk. The idea of having to sleep with armed guards outside my door was a total turn-off. The chairman of my old company suggested Myanmar of all places, a country loathed by the *Guardian* and struggling to shake off a repellent dictatorship. But it was the safest and least insane of all the opportunities that came my way.

It was money of course, but there was something else. A lurking thing both nasty and shameful. It showed itself as a reflection in the concerned faces and words of my kids – 'Dad, don't be so aggressive, it's not his fault the train is late' – and the look askance as if I was overreacting to everything from dirty dishes to the Npower answering machine. Forgotten yet familiar dark patterns were stirring. In 1982 I returned from a civil-war-torn Uganda where during my gap-year wanderings I had been caught up in some horrendous things. I got back in one piece but with a hair-trigger temper and a brooding intolerance of antisocial behaviour that manifested itself in self-righteous anger. I started my Masters in that mood and it was not a fruitful experience socially. This dark menace was back, but a lot stronger. For obvious reasons my default reaction to any threat during my incarceration had grown in force. I sensed a frightening capacity for violence if provoked, something which both appalled and shamed me but I couldn't even begin to unpick the knots that bound me. And then there was the dread of having to explain all the endless, godawful details to acquaintances who saw me as some kind of interesting novelty. Banged up abroad by proxy, wheeled out at dinner parties. I looked in the mirror and saw a bitter, bruised and emotionally inarticulate version of myself. People think they see a big, burly guy with imperturbable calm solidity, but I still jump a mile when touched and inside there is a boiling cauldron of sour emotions.

So it wasn't just about the money, I realised I had to get away and sort myself out before I could finally come home as the person my family wanted. Go somewhere where nobody knew me and there was no social pressure to be anyone. Where I could heal but not hurt anyone, lose myself in beer-fuelled evenings with construction guys behind God's back.

* * *

I quickly found out that people are a bit sniffy about employing fifty-year-olds fresh from a spell in clink, however outlandish the reason, but I had a lucky break and was introduced to a wonderful man in Yangon who has given me a second chance.

'Something like that happened to me,' he said. 'Twice in fact.'

He agreed to give me a three-month try-out and shaking my hand said: 'To have survived that with all your marbles intact is a testament to your character. Let's see if you can do the job.' So I am officially inducted into a peculiar kind of survivors club.

And now I find myself in another country the Foreign Office says is appalling. But this one is different from Cuba. Here the dictatorship looked in the mirror a few years ago, listened to their people, realised the entire world thought they were assholes and came to the decision that they had no choice but to change. And the change is now an unstoppable force. It's messy, it's imperfect of course, but people are optimistic and insanely busy. I am here playing my own little part in that transformation. I have about two thousand workers on site, five tower cranes and a crazy development schedule. Professionally I am as happy as a kid on the beach making sandcastles but instead I am building homes and schools and useful things.

The contrast with Cuba is painful. This is an even poorer country, with an abysmal standard of education and health, and they have been screwed for the past two hundred years, but overcoming all that I see more positive change here in a month than I did in years in Havana. Roads and bridges are being built, not just patched up. I see schools and hospitals opening, not collapsing. I see people working in a free labour market for a living wage and paying minimum taxes, not being robbed by the state. I see the military relinquishing their absolute power, not consolidating their grip on the juicy bits of the economy. I see all manner of newspapers expressing all sorts of nutty opinions, rather than the same tired old rag repeating the same crap that nobody believes. I am inundated with job applications from repats returning to be part of rebuilding their country. Show me one Cuban who has gone back in the last ten years, one who has gone back because they feel there is something useful that can be done. There aren't any. The lifeblood of Cuba will continue to drip, drip away until those warped windbags are in their graves.

I live on site and work all the hours that God sends so I don't have time to mope about. I don't think about what happened or the total bloody unfairness of it all. In the lonely evenings I sit on my balcony in a half-finished block watching the lurid sun set over the teeming city. The lights come on in our rickety old batching plant that faithfully churns out concrete all day and night, and a few tiny figures tend their delivery trucks like peasants from a forgotten age cajoling reluctant water buffalo. It's the end of the dry season and the vast, swift river rumbles past, heavy with silt from the upstream ravages of miners and loggers. A gravel barge is tying up at our mud jetty, the tug struggling to control the stern which threatens to whip away in the current. A hundred women patiently sit on a gravel heap, waiting to unload the fifty tons by hand before they return to their camp and rest. The dying gold and orange reflects where the water heaves over the midstream mud banks. It's merely biding its time until the rains come and then, as it has done for centuries, it will decide on a whim whether to sweep all before it into oblivion. Nothing really matters in the end it seems, but I was brought up to at least give it your best shot. That, and never give up.

I miss my family every minute of the day and I have no interest in making new friends. There is no doubt a giddy social whirl out there but I have no appetite. I need to rest my heart for a while and concentrate on mending broken things rather than find new things to occupy the emotional void. I haven't been able to paint again, which is frustrating. This country is so extraordinary and, just like Cuba, there is a poetic intensity to the street. There is something graphic about the lovely, indomitable handsomeness of the people, contrasting with the shambolic faded dereliction of everything built in the last fifty years of insanity and then, pushing all before it, the dark, green slitherings of nature. I don't know why I can't paint, it's like something isn't quite ready yet. Maybe I will when I feel a bit better about myself. To keep me sane I make time to sneak off some weekends and explore the country.

* * *

The boatman cut the engine. It coughed a few times and the teak canoe glided the last ten yards to a crunching halt on the gritty bank. A cloud of blue diesel smoke whipped past us. Pushing myself up with aching hips I wobbled forward and hopped out before doing the decent thing and giving GiGi a hand out. The cold breeze caught the rim of her flowery bonnet, and with a practised podgy hand she caught it before it flew off to a watery end. She has the engaging smile of that ballet-dancing hippopotamus in *Fantasia* and is wearing a military padded jacket, a check lumberjack shirt and a floral wrap with flip-flops. The overall impression is of a tiny, shy schoolgirl who has been mysteriously inflated while trying on her parents' clothes. She has a rather fine moustache that reminds me of someone but I can't put a finger on who. I can't help but like GiGi. She has an infectious enthusiasm for life.

GiGi had previously explained that she had moved five times in her childhood. Fighting in the mountains during the endless tiny but vicious tribal wars had made fleeing a fact of life. But she had spent one happy year in a bamboo forest where her father managed to find work as a labourer, so she would be thrilled to visit one. So when we came round a bend and a vast, splintery green sea of bamboo flowed up the mountain I asked to stop.

We wandered off into the bamboo forest and with her curious whispering singsong voice she started to explain about the plants and creatures of the forest and the lives of the villagers. The local language is impenetrable to my ear. We had stopped earlier at a market where the hill tribes came to buy and sell. She had ordered wild rice fermented in pigs' blood for breakfast, which actually tasted like a fine Irish black pudding, and the process of ordering sounded a bit like a random exchange of machine-gun fire, with bursts of vowels, return volleys of consonants and random 'Mongs' thrown in. She had enjoyed a little schooling but had taken herself off at seventeen to learn English. From an Australian missionary she says. It must have been one with a cut-glass accent and a gift for teaching because GiGi could get a job with the World Service.

We quickly lose sight of the river and take a generally westerly uphill direction. A walk in a bamboo forest is an extraordinary thing. The stems grow in dense clumps from a common, untidily pubic rootstock. They seem unfeasibly tall. The stalks and leaves are an identical yellow-green and everything is swaying back and forth in the wind, creaking and groaning like an abandoned sailing ship, while the leaves flutter and flash like mirrors. The ground is carpeted in silver-grey debris and dappled sunlight dances about making the ground itself seem to ripple. The entire effect is like being lost underwater in a kelp bed with infinity stretching above and below. An occasional massive tree trunk rises to form a stable island of sanity for thousands of strange birds. Hesitant creatures flit across the forest floor. I can't work out if they are rodents or reptiles or imagined.

After a while we come upon a strange glade. A wizened old tamarind tree festooned with giant cobwebs stands guard over the entrance to a simple corral of blackened bamboo. We step over a crunchy mat of fallen husks as old as the tree and pass into the sunlight

'This is where the village spirit lives. The nat. It has been here ever since the tribe settled here. When it falls down they build another one and so on forever.'

In the middle of the small clearing was a miniature village hut, well built in hardwood, sat atop eight chest-high wooden piles. Cracked and split, the timber panels had been creosoted. Its silent, still blackness seemed to suck all colour from the fluttering silver world of the bamboo forest. There was a miniature door, shut but not locked, daring anyone to open it. An offering of rice had been left on the veranda. Hung from the eaves a weathered scarf, red on one side and white on the other, flapped in the breeze.

'The tribe had come very far. They left the Himalayas and travelled down the big rivers thousands of miles to the sea, searching for somewhere to live. But nobody would let them settle. So they started to head north again, following strange rivers though immense jungles and swamps. Eventually the king let them stay here.'

What do the red and white flags mean?

'The spirits suffered a lot when they were men. They were tortured and in great pain. It was the king's pleasure. So the red is for blood and suffering. The white is for healing and redemption. We believe this. When we drink water, we offer a little to the spirit because we know he is thirsty or because he suffered from burning. When we eat we offer some because he is hungry. If we do this he protects us. Also, when we do merit we offer some to him as well so he can eventually find peace in nirvana.'

She picked up a bamboo stick and walked to a smallish tree I hadn't noticed. Hoiking a branch down with a deft flick, she reached up and plucked a fruit. With her gap-toothed school-girl grin she handed me a green knobbly ball scribed with deep, violet cracks.

'This is a type of custard apple. Very nice.'

I took out my knife. 'I ate this twice before, a very long way from here and a long time ago. There they call it a chirimoya.'

We slurped up the overripe flesh and spat out the oily black pips in silence. I couldn't explain to her the random memories that flooded back. That happy first fruit one sunny Saturday, that in a way started me on this crazy path. That second fruit, an ambiguous gift from my tormentor, the last fresh fruit before he condemned me to the dungeon. Who can I explain it all to? Nobody but the trees will listen.

We continue on our way, her pink flip-flops skittering over the shifting leaves and me rather enjoying kicking showers of fluttering silver blades and pissed-off ants into the air.

We have been wandering aimlessly. There is nothing to aim for so we just wander generally uphill. Apparently it is all the same, stretching for miles and miles, just a creaking and rustling wilderness. But it isn't. Strange notches and some paint slashes indicate where one village concession starts and where mysterious forest workers have cut out the giant parasitical larvae to grill as a snack.

A haunting, three-note melody echoes across a valley. I ask GiGi what it is. I would like to track it down.

'Ah, that is the poo a wee,' she beams. Pausing her step, she continued.

'It gets its name from a story. There was once a beautiful girl, the daughter of the headman, who lived in a village at the edge of the bamboo forest. One day a merchant passed through the village, a rich man who travelled far and wide. He saw her and immediately fell in love. He asked her father if he could marry her. He agreed and because he was handsome and kind and rich she was very happy. She went to live with her husband's family and according to our custom she had to respect his mother as her mother. But this woman was very cruel. The beautiful girl was with child and the husband was away on a very long trip.'

Her voice became quieter and the pauses between sentences lengthened.

'The mother made her work all day and was very cruel to her. In the end she could stand it no longer and decided to walk back through the forest to her own village. She was very pregnant and tired. After walking for days she could walk no longer and she lay down and the baby was born that night. The next day, she realised she must get help. She wrapped the baby up and left it in the bamboo, and with the last of her strength she managed to walk to her village. She died almost immediately and the villagers went to the forest to try and find the baby but it had disappeared.'

Her voice dropped almost to a whisper.

'The forest spirits had taken pity on the baby and turned it into a bird so it would not die. The merchant came back to the village and went mad with grief to find his wife dead and his baby lost. He wandered through the forest trying to find his baby until the day he died. In my language *poo a wee* means "where is my daddy?" And that is why we call the bird this: "where is my daddy?"'

She wiped her eyes with her sleeve and I wiped my eyes on mine. We walked on in silence, each lost in our thoughts. There was something unbearably sad about this simple tale told by this eccentric lady. I guess she was weeping over the misty memories of her father from a time of innocence. I am not sure what I am upset about, everything I guess.

We came across a medium-sized tree with peculiar very long, thin brown salami-like seed pods and sparse, tinder-dry leaves.

'Ah, what is this one called?' I say, forcing myself to snap out of it.

Anticipating another poetic forest tale that would cause us to reflect upon the ups and downs of life, and mainly the downs, I was rather taken aback by the simplicity of the answer.

'Um. That is the dogshit tree. We call it that because it smells of dogshit.'

And with that we retraced our steps to the canoe. By the time we got there she had recovered the bounce in her flip-flops and decided that she would go and see her family next day and I decided that as soon as I got back to the office I would go and book a flight. Daddy's coming home.

Acknowledgements

Firstly, of course, my darling wife: this is just as much her story as it is mine. My dauntless mum filled in a lot of the gaps in the parallel world outside of Villa Marista and La Condesa. My entire family gave me endless encouragement, ideas and were merciless in their criticism. I guess it was cheaper than therapy and took a lot longer than expected, but in a strange way it was probably a necessary thing to do. I owe them so much more than just their help in writing a book. Grainne Perkins, my friend and agent, gave me great advice on some essential truths of writing for an audience, and found me a publisher. Over a friendship that lasted thirty-six years, Dundee and I developed a mutual obsession with genres, authors and topics and his spirit has guided me stylistically. So many people helped us in our difficulties that they are too numerous to mention, close friends, relatives, colleagues and virtual strangers all made the unbearable bearable in some measure. They know who they are and have our undying gratitude, in particular the many Cubans who stood by us in the face of obvious personal risk. Finally, I would like to thank the Cuban people. Despite the unhappy ending, we loved our time on the island. My personal, Kafkaesque story gave me a glimpse of the complexities of life that so many have to suffer with a smile.